THE INDIVIDUAL IN TWELFTH-CENTURY ROMANCE

THE INDIVIDUAL IN
TWELFTH-CENTURY ROMANCE

ROBERT W. HANNING

NEW HAVEN AND LONDON, YALE UNIVERSITY PRESS, 1977

Designed by Sally Sullivan
and set in Baskerville type.
Printed in the United States of America by
The Murray Printing Company, Westford, Mass.

Published in Great Britain, Europe, Africa, and
Asia (except Japan) by Yale University Press,
Ltd., London. Distributed in Latin America by
Kaiman & Polon, Inc., New York City; in
Australia and New Zealand by Book & Film
Services, Artarmon, N.S.W., Australia; and in
Japan by Harper & Row, Publishers, Tokyo
Office.

Library of Congress Cataloging in Publication Data

Hanning, Robert W
  The individual in twelfth-century romance.

  Includes index.
  1. Romances—History and criticism.
2. Individuality in literature. I. Title.
PN682.I5H3   1978   809.1'9'14   77-75378
ISBN 0-300-02101-1

For Barbara, Gina, and Robert

CONTENTS

ACKNOWLEDGMENTS

Before sending my reader off on a quest through the pages that follow, I should like to acknowledge some of the debts I have incurred during my own twelve-year adventure exploring the artful forest of the chivalric poets. As I consider the fruits of such a long labor, I am sometimes beset by memories of false starts, dead ends, obscure trails crossed, followed, lost, and found again; at those moments, recollections of the aid and comfort offered by a legion of friends and colleagues make the journey seem more than worthwhile. I beg the indulgence of any benefactor I may have inadvertently omitted from this list: in the course of more than a decade, obligations accumulate at a faster rate than memory can store them.

The impetus for a study of medieval romance came originally from Norman Cantor, with whom I had several highly profitable early conversations on the subject, and at whose request I put some very preliminary observations into the form of an essay, "Medieval Romance and the Critic's Quest" (*Colloquium* 6 [Fall 1966]: 1–9). Throughout my research and writing I have been inspired by his example as scholar and teacher. As my conclusions matured, I benefited from the interest and genius of my teacher, later colleague at Columbia, Andrew J. Chiappe. His untimely death in 1967 deprived the world of a brilliant study of romance on which he was at work.

Jonathan Tuck and P. Jeffrey Ford shared with me their perceptions about medieval and Renaissance romance, the former in a variety of New York and Oxford settings, the latter in an ongoing officemate dialogue that remains one of my happiest

Columbia memories. Howard Needler and Hope Weissman participated in many discussions about romance from which I emerged not only wiser but more dedicated. Linda Georgianna, George Santiciolli, Robert Stein, and John Thoms—partners in my most memorable learning experience, the fall 1970 doctoral seminar in medieval literature at Columbia—will always have a special place in my affection, not least because they taught me so much about the issues that now dominate my thinking about twelfth-century literature. Their insistence on clarifying those issues contributed greatly to my essay "The Social Significance of Twelfth-Century Chivalric Romance" (*Medievalia et Humanistica*, n.s. 3 [1972] : 3–29), which has been absorbed in good part into chapters 2 and 6 of this book. An invitation from Peter Haidu to contribute an essay to a collection of "Approaches to Medieval Romance" resulted in *"Engin* in Twelfth-Century Romance: An Examination of the *Roman d'Enéas* and Hue de Rotelande's *Ipomedon*" (*Yale French Studies* 51 [1974]), now expanded into chapter 3. To Professor Haidu I owe thanks for astute editorial guidance and for many stimulating conversations about romance.

In the closing stages of my work Saul Brody, George Economou, Joan Ferrante, Frederick Goldin, and Esther Quinn—fine medievalists all—offered invaluable moral support and constituted an enthusiastic but happily not uncritical audience for several portions of the manuscript that I prepared as lectures for the International Courtly Literature Society (Philadelphia, May 1974), the Columbia University Seminar in Medieval Studies (February 1974), and the American Historical Association (December 1974). To my colleague Joan Ferrante my gratitude is especially heartfelt; years of close collaboration with her have left their mark on many pages of this study, and I profited further from her reading of, and suggestions about, a complete draft of the manuscript. Professor Stephen Nichols's commentary on my penultimate draft led to many improvements of structure and style; I much appreciate his good ear and his generosity, as I do the professional expertise and personal concern shown by Ellen Graham and Lynn Walterick, my editors at the Yale Press.

Three summer grants from the Columbia University Council for Research in the Humanities, as well as a fellowship from the American Council of Learned Societies for the academic year 1966–67, enabled me to pursue my research and writing.

My parents have, as always, encouraged and applauded, helped and understood. To my children, who have had to compete with this book for my attention quite literally all their lives, and to my wife—the inspiration and object of all my best quests—the dedication of this book is a small token of an immense affection.

INTRODUCTION

The special interest of this literary study of twelfth-century chivalric romance is to relate the rise of the genre to the contemporaneous development of the concept of the individual in European culture. My strategy throughout has been to scrutinize a representative body of texts in order to show how the *theme* and *problem* of individuality emerge from the constant interplay between the chivalric hero's inner and outer (or private and public) worlds, each with its own standards and goals. But I have embedded this exegetical exercise within a larger examination of what might be called the grammar and syntax of chivalric romance, that is, the genre's structural, artistic, and mimetic techniques. I hope, by my double approach, to answer the basic question, How and to what extent does the sophisticated literary artistry of chivalric romance support a thematic treatment of the problem of individual fulfillment?

Recent research into various aspects of twelfth-century European culture convinces me that one of the central motivating forces of the twelfth-century Renaissance was a new desire on the part of literate men and women to understand themselves as single, unique persons—as what we would call *individuals*. This impulse to understand operated in three distinguishable but not totally distinct areas: the individual in relation to his own makeup and character; the individual in relation to his social and institutional environment; the individual in relation to his God. The necessary setting for such a treble quest was a Europe finally free of barbarian incursions, economically stable and prospering, and witnessing the growth of towns and cities in a manner unprecedented since the decline of the Roman Empire in the West.[1] In addition, one of post-classical Europe's periodic attempts to reconquer its classical heritage resulted in both a new grasp of Latin as a literary language capable of expressing personal reactions in all their complexity, and the impetus for a new, nonarchaic vernacular culture, greatly expanded in mimetic strategies, which creatively adapted classical works and themes. On these matrices, the churchmen, clerical intellectuals, and courtiers of the twelfth century erected new structures for their institutions, their ideas, their educational processes, their moral insights and spiritual yearnings.

That the efflorescence of the concept of the individual—and the problems of action and expression attendant upon it—underlay much that was unique and central to the twelfth century can be and has been shown by exploring the period from within various disciplines.[2] Indeed, there now exists an excellent summary of such investigations, incorporating additional supporting analysis, in Colin Morris's penetrating *The Discovery of the Individual, 1050-1200*. The centrality of the concept of individuality to twelfth-century European society can now be argued forcefully in such introductory texts on medieval history as Norman F. Cantor's *The Meaning of the Middle Ages*: "In the twelfth century there emerged a new consciousness of the self and recognition of the importance and distinctiveness of the individual, marking a significant departure from the group and typological thought of the early Middle Ages. Men began to develop a sense of individual reality and to appreciate the dignity and worth of individual human personality. With the new consciousness came new forms in art and literature."[3] The relationship between the emergence of individuality in European culture and developments in literary expression, here referred to by Cantor, has been noted by cultural historians for some years. R.W. Southern gave it classic expression in the chapter "From Epic to Romance," describing crucial changes in spiritual and social sensibilities during the twelfth century, in his *The Making of the Middle Ages*. Having called the romances of Chrétien de

Troyes "the secular counterpart to the piety of Citeaux" because "of both, love is the theme," Southern concludes his brief discussion of the romances by claiming that "the religious and romantic quests" were "the great alternatives opened out to the imagination in the mid-twelfth century."[4] Colin Morris, on the other hand, considers Chrétien's romances along with satiric writings under the rubric "the individual and society,"[5] while Norman Cantor borrows the literary term *romance* to apply it to the twelfth century as a "romantic century" in which a "liberation ethic—an emphasis on personal fulfillment irrespective of tradition or order or hierarchy" found its "chosen form of expression" in literature whose "key motif . . . is that of the perilous quest."[6]

Following the lead of these and other scholars, I believe that chivalric romance, as it emerged in twelfth-century courtly society, offered a literary form in which to work out the implications of individuality—implications which twelfth-century theology and philosophy were beginning to confront, but were not yet able, for lack of technical and conceptual vocabulary, fully to describe and categorize.

The form of chivalric romance made the quest of the single hero its organizing principle. Moving through time and space which he both organizes (for the audience) around his personal quest and experiences or perceives in a subjective and limited way, the romance hero deliberately opens himself to experience in all its variety and unexpectedness. This active acceptance of life as an adventure, rather than as a battle for endurance or an attempt to protect hard-won security in an enclosed place against threatening, unknown forces, leads the knight into situations which challenge his acceptance of social values and therefore offer an alternative to an identity defined by forces outside himself. The main form taken by that alternative is the experience of love, which produces within the romance hero a purely personal vision of happiness and fulfillment, tied to his obtaining the beloved permanently. Through the adventures by which the hero almost loses, then attempts to gain (or be reconciled with) his love-object, his inner awareness (and often that of the heroine as well) is progressively (or climactically) heightened; that is, he comes to see clearly that he has acted against his real happiness, in being led astray by false or received values, and consequently perceives the necessity of shaping his actions so as to attain his imagined self-perfection—the vision of himself made complete by fulfilled desire.

Just as the vision which comes to dominate the chivlaric hero is increasingly a private one, pivoting on inner awareness of where he is in life vis-à-vis where he must go (in other words, of present versus future identity), so his struggles to overcome the obstacles that impede his adventure quest are progressively shown by the chivalric poet to be metaphoric versions of his inner struggle to control impulses which would lead him away from self-fulfillment. In chivalric romance, the problematic impulse is the aggressive one, which, within the heroic conventions of chivalry, takes the form of armed prowess aimed at winning honor, that is, external approbation and an exalted social identity. The chivalry topos, evolved in twelfth-century narrative, ostensibly states that aggressive and sexual impulses, or impulses toward public and private fulfillment, can coexist and reinforce each other; love prompts prowess, prowess prompts love. In fact, the romances of the twelfth century all derive their plots from the exposure of problematic elements in this conventional formulation. By investigating, and representing, the tensions between love and prowess, and by focusing on the manner in which knights and ladies become conscious of these tensions, the chivalric romance makes of its adventure plot the story, nay the celebration, of the necessity of men (and women) to face the fact of their private destiny, and to attempt to attain that vision which, born within the recesses of the self, makes of life a process of dynamic self-realization. The great adventure of chivalric romance is the adventure of becoming what (and who) you think you can be, of transforming the *awareness* of an inner self into an *actuality* which impresses upon the external world the fact of personal, self-chosen destiny, and therefore of an inner-determined identity.

Thus the chivalric romance urges the centrality of inner awareness on its audience as the key to happiness, and in the process effectively defines man as the product of inner vision shaping external experience. Since each person's inner experience will be different and unique, subjective, and marked by crises and turning points valid for him alone; and since in the romance plot there is no larger social or providential system giving meaning—the same meaning—to all human lives operating within it; it follows that these courtly narratives are making a strong and persuasive statement for the centrality of individual experience in our understanding of life and its meaning.

Given this basic orientation, the chivalric poets felt free to treat the fact of individual destiny, and the necessity of seeking it by sacrificing the stability of an externally imposed order for the adventure of self-definition, from widely different points of view. Adapting and manipulating the conventions of chivalry, they placed their heroes in divergent, contradictory situations, not simply for the joy of showing mastery of a chosen form, but to explore and expose the *risks* of individuality. In some of the romances the dangers and agonies of self-alienation figure centrally; the gap between imagined self-fulfillment (seconded by memories of a time when it seemed close at hand, or at least possible) and a state of present loss or denial caused by self-damaging *folie* leads to self-loathing, madness, attempted suicide. In others, an unresolvable contradiction between private desire and the public situation of hero and heroine makes individuality a socially disruptive force, or one which can only seek fulfillment in deceit and illusion. The "pure" chivalry topos is also criticized, adulterated, or repaired (if human limitations prevent its functioning) by the ambiguous human gifts of intellectual analysis and manipulation which issue in artful, as opposed to heroic or passionate, behavior. There is no one attitude toward, or canonic form of, the individual chivalric career. Only its existence and centrality are universally accepted.

The subjectivity of motive and perception which are inevitable corollaries of an individual-centered view of reality are presented and exploited by chivalric poets in a variety of novel ways, such as the inclusion of multiple perspectives on an event within a romance, and the mimesis of individual experience in the instant-by-instant presentation of inner and outer actions at moments of crisis. The subjective *kairos*—the time within or before which actions must be performed, and awareness sharpened, in circumstances and with effects crucial only to one or a few individuals—results from the hero's confronting of adventure, or from the chance meeting of characters who bring to the moment unique personal histories and outlooks. And all the varied action of the romance takes place within a world of time and space often described or represented in ways that stress the characters' personal experience of these media, and thus impart to them a new validity. (During the early medieval centuries, by contrast, the culturally dominant, Platonized Christian notion of human life as a pilgrimage through the distractions of this world toward the true homeland of heaven resulted in a view of earthly, sensorily perceived experience as an incomplete reality—at best irrelevant, at worst dangerous to the Christian *peregrinus.*)

Truly, then, chivalric romance is in many respects a new world of art, self-conscious in its artfulness and variety, inviting its audience both to involvement and detachment as it contemplates the perilous quest for the heaven-on-earth of self-fulfillment. The works of Chrétien de Troyes and his contemporaries are a jewel in the crown of twelfth-century culture, linked by their interest in the individual to other lapidary achievements of that age. It would logically follow, and I believe it to be the case, that the particular, defining achievement of twelfth-century chivalric romance does not survive its cultural moment. In the thirteenth century, romance and chivalry evolve in several directions—the great Arthurian prose cycles, Grail romances, the dream-vision quest of the *Roman de la rose*—the formal innovations of which reflect their new thematic interests. In the process, the particular balance of moral and mimetic forces that created the individual focus in the twelfth-century, court-culture-based romances was modified or destroyed.

The approach to, and appreciation of, chivalric romance just outlined results from the confluence of two streams of scholarly activity to which the present study owes great debts. The first, which I have already mentioned, is the work of cultural historians who have created, from the enormous mass of available evidence, an overall portrait of the "Renaissance of the twelfth-century" and established it as one of the most exciting and seminal periods in the history of Europe. (Charles Homer Haskins must always be given pride of place in this company, which has also included gifted synthesizers like Marc Bloch, Friederich Heer, Southern, Cantor, and many others.) The other determining force in my criticism of romance has been the literary-philological analysis of medieval texts performed so brilliantly by Erich Auerbach (whose *Mimesis* stands as the greatest monument to this analysis), and practiced as well by English, American, and French scholars intent on discovering the meaning of medieval literature by paying close attention to its language, narrative patterns, and paradigmatic situations. Close textual analysis of twelfth-century romances has dealt a mortal blow to earlier, patronizing criticism of these texts as an escapist falling-off from the bleaker but nobler vision of medieval epic; it has also provided a viable and happy alternative to an earlier dominant mode of romance criticism that attempted to reconstruct the network of lost Celtic sources (or the stages of evolution between a twelfth-century French text and a much earlier Irish or Welsh putative source), the reconstruction of which would explain the real meaning of episodes (or whole romances) perpetuated without understanding, and often in corrupt forms, by chivalric poets.

Despite the widespread acceptance of twelfth-century Renaissance historiography and close textual analysis of chivalric poetry, I believe there is still a need for a full-length study of a body of twelfth-century romances using the tools of the latter approach and organized around a central discovery of the former, in order to document more fully than has hitherto been attempted the emergence of the concept of individuality in the romances—not as a theme applied, as it were, from without to a body of adventure stories, but as a concern embodied in the total mimetic strategy of each text, reflecting a major interest of the society for which it was created. My conviction is a response to, and respectful dissent from, two other overviews of the achievement of chivalric romance that tend to dominate criticism of the genre today: the Augustinian or patristic approach (owing its ascendancy to the zeal, scholarly activity, and brilliant pedagogy of D.W. Robertson), and what I prefer to call the aesthetic approach, which uses formalist, structuralist, and other techniques of analysis to argue the autonomy of the literary text vis-à-vis social or historical "reality," and the consequent necessity to interpret romances as closed systems of literary and linguistic signs having their only relevant referents in other texts, not in cultural evolution or the history of ideas. In absolute contrast to the aesthetic critics, patristic critics insist that the only valid meaning to be derived from any medieval literature is its embodiment, at a literal or allegorical level, of Christian norms—specifically, the opposition between good and bad love, *caritas* and *cupiditas.* Significance, in this view, lies outside the imagined world of a romance (or epic, or dream vision) in a body of doctrine, conscientiously applied by the author for the instruction and edification of his readers. If the aesthetic critics deny the relevance of the kind of criticism I am attempting here because it seeks to read literature too directly as a metaphor of social experience, the patristic critics cannot subscribe to it because it relies on the evolution of that experience from one part of the Middle Ages to another, so that (in my opinion) patristic formulations—or doctrinal formulations of any kind—cannot be mechanically applied to texts expressing the preoccupations and crises (perhaps wholly secular) of the particular century or decade from which they spring.

I do not propose in this study to refute the patristic or aesthetic critics of romance directly; my task here is exploratory and pedagogical, not polemical.[7] Besides, such attacks would obscure my admiration for, and indebtedness to, many fine contributions of critics from both "schools" to the study of twelfth-century chivalric romance. My frequent insistence on reading characters, actions, or situations in romances metaphorically owes its technique (if not always its conclusions) to Robertsonian symbolic analysis (and to the analogous but unrelated symbolic analysis of R.R. Bezzola, specifically his *Le sens de l'aventure et de l'amour*), while my interest in the self-conscious manipulation of plots, characters, and symbols by chivalric poets, often at the expense of seriousness, and with the effect of heightening the audience's awareness of the poet's mastery over his fictional universe, has profited greatly from the aesthetically oriented criticism of Peter Haidu, Eugène Vinaver, and many others. My aim, then, will be to offer another *kind* of reading of twelfth-century chivalric romance—not the only one possible, by any means, but one that I hope leads to a richer understanding of, and encounter with, this body of literature that can still move, amuse, and educate us today.

The structure and strategies of this study require some preliminary comment. First, as to its primary materials, these include a group of twelfth-century texts, primarily chivalric romances: the well-known *Erec and Enide, Cligès, Lancelot,* and *Yvain* of Chrétien de Troyes, the anonymous *Partonopeu de Blois,* Hue de Rotelande's *Ipomedon,* Renaut de Beaujeu's *Le Bel inconnu.* For purposes of comparison and clarification, I also refer frequently to other twelfth-century courtly narratives that do not qualify generically as chivalric romances, since they are not organized around the basic situation or topos of chivalry, but manifest many of the same concerns and techniques. These include the *Roman d'Enéas,* the *Roman de Thèbes,* and Gautier d'Arras's *Eracle.* I could have worked with still other texts (for example the *Roman de Troie,* Gautier's *Ille et Galeron,* Hue's *Protheselaus*), but that would have made an already lengthy book somewhat unwieldy.

I have organized the study according to a plan that I will shortly explain. In opting for this plan, I have had to abandon another, to which I was originally (and in many ways still am) much attracted, namely, a series of chapters each devoted to the comprehensive analysis of a single romance. My decision reflects a desire to explore certain techniques and topics that contribute directly and massively to the emergence of the individual in chivalric romance, showing their existence and use by the juxtaposition of passages from different works, even at the cost of treating some important romances in less detail than others. I would hope in future work to return to the texts I have scanted, to offer full and integrated analyses of complete romances; meanwhile, I must beg the reader's indulgence for omissions made in the interest of clarity and brevity. (The same may be said with respect to the immense secondary literature on the romances I have treated. There is much I have not read, but much that I have and have not acknowledged, because of space limitations, if it did not contribute directly to a reading or interpretation.)

It seemed appropriate to begin my discussion by establishing a context for twelfth-century chivalric romance, without, however, duplicating the work of historians and literary scholars who have established the profile of the twelfth-century Renaissance and its literature, differentiating them in the process from characteristic texts and institutions of the early medieval period, up to about the mid-eleventh century. My procedure has been to offer evidence of a new tension between private and public, or personal and social, worlds—and new ways of representing the tension—in two twelfth-century Latin narratives, products of the age's thriving clerical culture and inheritors of generic conventions of personal history (my collective name for texts recounting a single career, whether in the form of autobiography, hagiography, or biography) developed in the early medieval centuries, specifically the conventions of the saint's life. The two works—Peter Abelard's (or pseudo-Abelard's) consolatory letter to a friend, the so-called *Historia calamitatum,* and the anonymous *Life of Christina of Markyate*—lay full stress on the conflict and harassment a gifted, highly motivated protagonist can expect to encounter while pursuing his or her personal goal. From the record of the confrontation between hero and environment emerge sharply etched portraits of Abelard and Christina that emphasize their uniqueness and the intensity of their private desires, and thus individualize them for us. My analysis of the stories of Abelard and Christina occupies the bulk of chapter 1.

Having established the representation of individuality as a concern of twelfth-century personal historians, I begin in chapter 2 to differentiate and assess the unique place of chivalric romance among contemporaneous narrative types, both as a literary form with its own conventions and as a metaphoric representation of the fact and problem of individuality as it was perceived within a specifically courtly social milieu. The first section of chapter 2 constitutes a brief survey of the evolution of the chivalry topos (the statement of idealized interaction between impulses toward love and aggression in courtly men and women) within some courtly narratives that, like the stories of Abelard and Christina, have their roots in earlier literature—in this case, the martial literature of classical antiquity's national and mythological epics. There is an inherent conflict of aim in these *romans antiques* between a chivalric subplot, focused on issues of personal happiness, and a historical or pseudo-historical narrative action that transcends personal careers. The conflict disappears in the new chivalric romance form as the chivalric plot attains full autonomy and becomes the metaphor of the protagonist's quest for individual fulfillment.

The remaining, major part of chapter 2 demonstrates the actual functioning of the chivalric plot by means of a close analysis of its basic component, the adventure episode. My intent is to immerse the reader in the themes and techniques of chivalric romance, using as my exemplars one episode each from *Erec* and *Partonopeu de Blois.* From this procedure emerges, I hope, a quite precise idea of why and how the romances can be read as imaginative records of individual experience. Of course, there must be criteria we can use to confirm or deny the presence in a literary text of the concept of the individual, in something like our current sense of the term. Three such criteria, which I find already functioning in the stories of Abelard and Christina, are developed and documented in my discussion of the two romance episodes. They are: (1) an interest in showing how characters use their personal wit and ingenuity to shape their encounters with the world outside themselves to their own benefit, self-consciously and in ways that are often morally problematic; (2) a mimetic rendering of the external environment and of the perception of reality from a personal perspective; (3) emphasis on the characters' inner life.

As a map of the romance terrain, with the loci of individuality presented in a high relief, chapter 2 is arguably the key part of the study. The succeeding chapters, like the episodes of a romance, are additive rather than progressive in nature, aiming to create an increasingly rich and articulated sense of both the literary form and the cultural theme under observation. The organizing principle of these chapters is provided by the criteria of individuality just enumerated. Chapter 3 explores the fascinating romance characteristic of ingenuity (the Old French word is *engin*)—the ready wit and cleverness with which a character solves problems that do not respond to the virtues of strong right arm or faithful heart. Ingenuity personalizes a hero or heroine by drawing our attention to the conscious use of a personal virtue. In addition, ingenious manipulation of people in events frequently carries with it amoral or antisocial implications, and stimulates in its observer a mixed response of admiration and condemnation. (The whole range of positive and negative meanings of *engin* and of its Latin avatar, *ingenium*, listed in chapter 1, testifies to the climate of ambivalence surrounding the concept, and the behavior embodying it, in twelfth-century culture.) Accordingly, we are often forced to take careful account of particular motivations and situations in judging the witty hero—that is, we are made to consider him (or her) even further as a particular person, an individual. *Engin* is also the characteristic that most clearly links witty characters and witty poets of chivalric romance; its exercise deflects our attention from the fictional world to the poet-creator of that world and back again. The consequent alternation on our part between involvement in and detachment from the romance world heightens our consciousness of participating personally in a literary experience. (Heightened awareness, we shall see, lies at the core of the inner experience of the romance protagonist, whose career we therefore not only follow but reenact in our reading of, or listening to, a romance.) Chapter 3 follows these many threads of *engin* as they run through the *Roman d'Enéas, Ipomedon,* and Chrétien's works.

Chapters 4 and 5 concern the mimetic representation of the environment. This second criterion of individuality is best divided into two subcategories: broad and narrow mimeis. *Broad mimesis* involves the articulation or elaboration of the social, institutional, or professional world in which the protagonist functions. The circumstantial rendering of the hero's larger cultural environment serves to define the external world as that which is outside of or opposed to him *and* possesses a sufficiently objective existence (established by description and analysis) to be recognized as the "other" which helps to define the "self"; the individual enhances his awareness of his identity by trying to establish a precise place for himself within (or outside of) a fully developed system of social norms, activities, and relationships. Lacking such articulation, the environment can be presented as simply an extension of the self, or of God, especially in symbolic or ideological narratives like saints' lives. (Broad mimesis is used with special effectiveness in Abelard's *Historia calamitatum* and *The Life of Christina,* where institutions and their representatives are fully, often mordantly, depicted in order to establish a context or foil for the protagonist's activities.)

Narrow mimesis is the precise representation of the hero's placement within the experience of the physical environment, especially as this involves small units of time and space. That is, the author offers an acute observation of the immediate, fleeting, sensory perceptions and intellectual apprehensions of a specific person, and an especially acute awareness of the single body's limited spatial extension and repertory of gestures. The moment-by-moment passage of time, the importance of a small portion of space, or the significance of a touch thereby become central to the task of representing reality. As a result, the audience vicariously experiences the outside world, the temporal and spatial environment, as it appears to the highly aware protagonist. Narrow mimesis, in other words, is an *affective* device prompting an appreciation on our part of the experience, and thus the fact, of individuality in sensory terms.[8] Chapter 4, which deals with the treatment of time and space in romances and other courtly texts, is primarily a contribution to the study of narrow mimesis.

One characteristic and innovative form of mimetic technique by which twelfth-century chivalric and courtly poets establish individuality as a human fact will receive special attention in chapter 5. Frequently, several characters in a romance respond subjectively and in sharply differentiated ways to a given narrative situation; in other cases we are shown, through inner dialogue or psychological analysis, how a character's reaction to an external event is conditioned by his unique perceptions, needs, and goals. Both types of incident illustrate the artistic strategy I call the representation of *limited perspective;* its effect is to suggest that each person experiences and understands reality from within perceptual limits perculiar to him and imposed on him by his position in space or time, his previous history, attitudes, expectations, or relationships to others. The sum total of these limited perspectives—what I call the *multiple perspective on reality*—is the basic frame within which the chivalric poet works, emphasizing now this, now that individual viewpoint. When a plot ceases to be an exemplary action consistently embodying a set of specific, absolute values (as was usually the case in early medieval narratives, whether epics, histories, or saints' lives) and becomes a human situation uniting participants who variously, incompletely, even incorrectly perceive what is happening to them, the audience is forcibly made aware of the limited perspective as a norm for rendering reality. In accepting this norm in a narrative, we accept, *a fortiori,* the normative status of the individual—the character whose perspective on reality does not coincide precisely with that of any other character. Of course, in accepting limited and multiple perspective, we may be made aware of the ironies and problems implicit in a situation where fragmented, self-interested viewpoints replace objective moral criteria as the grounds for human action. Here again, aesthetic distance becomes a factor, as we adopt with the poet an attitude of detachment toward the action, stepping back, as it were, to see things whole and to smile at those within the story who cannot do the same. Yet in such a case (for example the middle section of Gautier d'Arras's courtly but non-chivalric *Eracle*) the ambiguities complicate but do not destroy our heightened awareness of the concept of the individual.

The third criterion of individuality, depiction of the inner life, reflects a concern with that area of experience—the protagonist's emotions, will, motivation, spiritual longings—which is quintessentially private and subjective, and which can betray the crucial personal differences among members of a group whose behavior is outwardly uniform. In Abelard's *Ethics,* for example, where the emphasis is placed on intent—on inner consent to temptation—as the determinant of sin rather than on the external act that contravenes divine or ecclesiastical law, it becomes clear that only the sinner and God can know if sin has been committed. This hidden knowledge makes each person an autonomous moral unit, an individual in the sight of God.[9] Analogously, Abelard's touchstone of repentance is no longer the public performance of prescribed penitential deeds, as codified by the Church, but the inner contrition of the sinner, a purely subjective opening of oneself to God's healing love.[10] Inner repentance can come at a different time to each person, when he or she is ready and willing; the critical moment, the *kairos,* will depend on a combination of biographical and emotional factors unique to the person, and the *kairos* will thus be his alone, as opposed to an objective *kairos* like the Last Judgment in the Christian tradition, which operates with equally normative force for all men. Objective *kairoi,* like codes of public penance binding on all, treat human experience corporately, whereas inner, subjective *kairoi* individualize it.

The episodes dealt with in chapter 2 constitute subjective *kairoi* in the lives of the protagonists of the two romances under discussion. Returning to the subject of inner experience in chapter 6, I consider the structure and generic conventions of the romance plot, to show how, in the hands of a sophisticated poet, they become a metaphoric framework for and representation of a crisis of inner awareness that determines the goals and actions of the protagonist. In this reading, the external features of romance function as emblems of the inner landscape across which each chivalric hero must plot his lonely and perilous quest for self-control as he moves toward the inner vision of self-fulfillment he has personally created and must now personally attain. Using *Yvain, Partonopeu de Blois,* and *Le Bel inconnu* as my central texts, I conclude the body of my study of chivalric romance in this chapter by arguing for its interpretation, qua plot, as a strong (but also problematic) statement about the birth, testing, and confirmation of individuality as a direct result of the interaction between inner and outer experience. The chivalric poets' conviction that this interaction must be freely chosen and personally motivated also gives metaphoric force to incidents involving the protagonist's being forcibly restrained from freely pursuing his adventure quest; accordingly, I close the chapter with an examination of the dominant theme of imprisonment or constraint in two of Chrétien's romances.

The brief afterword justifies the chronological limits of my study by suggesting some of the changes wrought in chivalric romance and its cultural context in the late twelfth and early thirteenth centuries—changes that resulted in the fading of the theme and problem of individuality from the center of literary concern in chivalric narratives.

1: INDIVIDUALITY IN TWO TWELFTH-CENTURY PERSONAL HISTORIES

Where did chivalric romance come from? Many answers have been proposed to that question, based on the examination of real and hypothetical sources of romance in Latin and Celtic literatures. This study is less concerned with the literary than the cultural origins of twelfth-century chivalric romance, and argues that the romances of Chrétien de Troyes and his contemporaries took the shape they did, when they did, within the new courtly society of northwestern Europe because that society shared with its age a novel interest in the individual. Along with other texts of the twelfth-century Renaissance, the romances manifest a desire to portray human experience from an individual as well as (or instead of) a corporate or an ideologically exemplary point of view. It is the purpose of this chapter to provide a context and, as it were, a control for the romances as documents of emergent individuality in Western medieval culture by scrutinizing two of these "other texts" whose interests and techniques coincide to a certain extent with chivalric narratives, and whose divergences from the romances in literary genre and social milieu will allow us more accurately to characterize the unique achivement of the romances in the analyses contained in subsequent chapters.

Peter Abelard's *Letter to a Friend,* usually called (though apparently not by him) the *Historia calamitatum,* and the anonymous *Life of Christina of Markyate* antedate the establishment of the chivalric romance form in the last third of the twelfth century—the former by approximately thirty-five years, the latter, probably only fifteen to twenty. They represent an earlier stage in the evolution of literary individuality not simply because of chronological precedence but because, as products of the clerical, Latin-language culture of medieval Europe, they depend more than the romances do on forms and themes inherited from the early medieval phase of that culture. This literary legacy of an age not interested in the fact or representation of individuality sometimes hinders or obscures the more "modern" preoccupations of the *Historia* and the *Life* and complicates attempts at interpretation.[1] Nonetheless, despite these difficulties, and although the two works differ from each other in conception, in form, in use of literary traditions, and in overt intention, they still share an interest, new to high medieval culture, in modes of experience that define their subjects as individual human beings, conscious of a personal, indeed unique destiny, and betraying their consciousness by means of perceptions and behavior that often isolate them from their social world, thus reinforcing our sense of their uniqueness and individuality.

There is, of course, no way of knowing, in the case of Abelard, whether he is recording what he really thought and did or is molding his career retroactively into its shape in the *Historia*; nor can we be sure how conscious he was of presenting himself to the world (as well as to the real or hypothetical friend to whom the letter is addressed) in ways which go beyond the declared exemplary function of the letter (much stressed recently by Robertson and Southern) and etch him sharply as an embattled individual, standing out against the background of the varied, combative world of early twelfth-century intellectual life. (Indeed, in the light of present research we cannot be sure who wrote the *Historia calamitatum* and when, though I accept the ascription to Abelard on the thoroughly circular basis of what seems to me the work's profoundly twelfth-century cultural interests.[2]) The same problems apply, *mutatis mutandis,* to the *Life of Christina.* I will try to explain why and to what extent I believe the delineation of an individual, in our sense of the term, to be part of the thematic intent and literary strategy of each of these works, using the texts themselves for corroboration. That authorial consciousness of such intent and strategies exists in both cases can, I think, be demonstrated. But that it took the form, in either work, of an articulated program or manifesto, such as, "Now I will create a work in which, more than in previous works in this genre, my hero (or heroine) emerges as an individual," is much harder to document and, at best, a doubtful assumption.

In an interesting essay on Abelard's *Logica ingredientibus* Francis Wade argued that the philosopher's handling of the question of genus and species, or collective and individual identity, fails because, while Abelard's experience and observation convinced him of the *fact* of individuality, he could not adequately express this metaphysical *concept* within his logical methodology and system.[3] Inconsistencies in Abelard's *Ethics* between his theory of sin (in which the intent, not the deed done, is the touchstone) and his insistence on the necessity of absolute punishments by the Church for deeds that break its laws seem to stem from the same difficulty of perceived but not fully conceptualized individuality.[4] Indeed, similar judgments about incomplete and evolving formulations concerning individuality apply to Abelard's great rival, Bernard of Clairvaux. If we compare Bernard's comments in *On the Love of God* on the fate of the self when it unites with God with similar ideas in the somewhat later sermons on the Song of Songs, we see, as Colin Morris points out, a change from the conviction that individual personhood is annihilated by the union to a view which confirms "the continued identity of the soul in its encounter with God."[5] Bernard's refusal or inability to illustrate the stages of the soul's ascent to "seek himself in himself" in *The Steps of Humility,* while it challenges the reader to perform the task himself, may also reflect the fact that Bernard could experience his spiritual individuality but not express it effectively with the verbal and conceptual tools at his disposal.[6]

Having issued these caveats, I would still argue (or, more pre-

cisely, subscribe to the arguments of others) that the Latin culture of the twelfth century provides significant evidence of a
spiritual, institutional, and intellectual climate conducive to the
growth of awareness of personal uniqueness among at least
some advanced members of that culture, like Abelard and Christina (or, at least, her biographer). In the cultural patterns of
the age we are struck by the simultaneous dominance of two
analogous but opposite impulses: one toward the intense experience of inner awareness, the other toward the articulation of
structures governing institutional and intellectual activity.[7] The
former impulse unites such diverse manifestations as Abelard's
intentionalist analysis of ethics, Bernard's tracing of the soul's
ascent to God, the new theology of the Atonement, which
stressed Christ's suffering and our personal response to it, and
the literature of spiritual friendship, heavily influenced by
Cicero and finding an early exponent in Anselm of Bec.[8] Increased attention to the inner realm of experience could also
prompt feelings of isolation and vulnerability in the face of the
overwhelming, potentially hostile world outside the self. Accordingly, the twelfth century also gave new cultural centrality
to manifestations of pathos, the intimate sentiment combining
the empathic attraction to helplessness in others—especially the
infant or crucified Jesus—and self-pity that derives from the
recognition of the same helplessness (and potential for victimization) in ourselves. Pathos, we might say, lies at the opposite
extreme of inner experience from the spiritual exaltation of the
mystic, rising above himself to be united with God.[9]

Balancing the new subjectivism was the strong, "objective"
impulse to systematize, articulate, and clarify, which could be
applied to a body of doctrine, a problem like the reality of
abstractions, or the structures of ecclesiastical and secular
government. The activities of the first scholastic (that is, dia-
lectical or logical) thinkers at the cathedral schools of northern
France, of canon lawyers, of reforming popes and of clerics who
argued against papal encroachments on secular power all betray
in various ways this passion for ordering the world of ideas and

institutions beyond anything attempted in the early Middle Ages.[10]

Inevitably, these two impulses collided within twelfth-century culture. Tensions between private freedoms or desires and the structures on which a complex society depends for its functioning can be called endemic to Western society from this period right down to our own day. Less frequently noted, perhaps, but equally important for our purposes, is the double function that the intellect was called upon to play in the evolution of novel patterns of life within twelfth-century intellectual culture. On the one hand, the intellect—not heroic fortitude or unshakeable piety, the highest values of early medieval society—was the virtue by which the intensities of inner experience were recorded and comprehended, and by which order was imposed on divergent doctrinal traditions or on procedures that ruled the lives of men. On the other hand, in its manifestations of ingenuity, quick thinking, and shrewdness, intellect gave its possessors tools (sometimes, to be sure, tools of doubtful legality or morality) for manipulating existent structures in the cause of personal advantage or survival. In other words, what the mind created or systematized, the mind could also subvert.[11]

The new primacy of intellectual activity within learned, clerical culture in the twelfth century—especially in educational centers like Paris—prompted widely varying responses, from the professional pride of Abelard's defense of *intellectus quaerens fidem* to the counterattacks of Bernard and William of Saint Thierry, who stigmatized Abelard's new discipline of theology (*theologia*) as the study of folly (*stultilogia*) because they perceived a grave danger to Christian doctrine in unrestrained intellection.[12] Between these extremes lay a middle ground of ambivalence, in which admiration for ingenuity mingled with worry at the amorality of this human faculty and even with cynical conviction that men will inevitably use their wits for mere self-aggrandizement, whatever their pious protestations to the contrary.[13] The Latin term for the intellectual capacity here under discussion is *ingenium,* and we shall shortly find it occu-

pying a crucial place in the story of Abelard's calamitous relationship with his world, helping to define him for us as an
individual in a very special manner. In the very different circumstances of her life, Christina of Markyate demonstrates gifts of
wit and ingenuity analogous to the more professionally oriented
genius of the Breton philosopher. For both Abelard and Christina, the intellectual virtues of quick-wittedness and analytic
skill, however differently applied, become important weapons
with which to fight, in defense not only of Christian truth but
of one's personal vision, developed through inner awareness,
and often sorely tested in combat with representatives of social
or religious institutions sufficiently inflexible (and therefore
hostile) to be, for the first time in medieval history, the equivalent of our pejoratively termed "Establishment." These three
factors—articulated personal awareness, equally articulated and
sometimes adversary environment, and the use of *ingenium* in
some form in the struggle to confirm personal autonomy or attain personal fulfillment—determine the dynamic of the careers
of Abelard and Christina of Markyate. We shall see the same
dynamic at work in the very different, stylized, and conven-
tionalized world of chivalric romance, where love brings knights
and ladies to an agonized awareness of conflict between their
social roles and personal desires, and witty problem-solving,
often of an outrageously deceptive or morally ambiguous kind,
helps save the day.

No twelfth-century portrait is more famous than that of Abelard in the so-called *Historia calamitatum.* Recent scholarship
has once again called into question Abelard's authorship of the
ostensibly consolatory letter that sets forth the triumphs and
disasters of his career from its beginning to what we know in
retrospect to have been its nadir: his abbacy of the monastery
of Saint Gildas de Rhuys in Brittany (1125–35; the *Historia*
seems to have been composed about 1132). My analysis is in no
way dependent upon the authenticity of the *Historia.* Even if
the letter should prove not to be by Abelard, it is surely a

twelfth-century document by an author knowledgeable about his subject and anxious to make Abelard's personal awareness a defining factor in his experience.[14]

Whatever intention or intentions lie behind the *Historia calamitatum,* its undeniable effect is that of a work organized around the experiences of a single person in such a way that we can abstract from the account an analysis of the protagonist's *personality,* as opposed to an example or paradigm of God's power, as would be the case in an early medieval saint's life. Abelard is the first literary figure since antiquity susceptible of such analysis; beside the *Historia* the earlier twelfth-century "memoirs" of Guibert of Nogent, for all their psychological suggestiveness, offer a woefully truncated record of personal history.[15] But the impact of Abelard—the misunderstood, maligned, mutilated genius—on our modern sensibilities should not blind us to the fact that, as a literary document, the *Historia calamitatum* makes abundant use of traditions and conventions that do not aim at establishing the protagonist's individuality, and in fact militate against any such hypothetical program. A brief survey of some of these inherited features will comprise a catalogue of the impediments to an individual portrait in the *Historia* and heighten our appreciation of how the author surmounted them in making Abelard live for us as a particular person instead of a moral type.

First there is the form of the work. The *Historia* describes itself as a consolatory letter written by Abelard to an unnamed friend. R.W. Southern, treating the correspondence of Abelard and Heloise as "works of learning which follow the rules of contemporary letter writing," reminds us that the *Historia calamitatum* "was a letter of a well defined rhetorical type known as *consolatoria,*" the standard message of which is, "Take comfort; my troubles have been much worse than yours." Abelard's calamities conform to the accepted strategies of the *consolatoria,* whose theme provides, according to Southern, the "sole justification" of the work. Southern admits that Abelard's letter does in fact become an autobiographical statement, shaped on the anvil of his bitter recollections; still "the [rhetorical] form determined the scope and value of his autobiography."[16]

Another part of the *Historia calamitatum* that Southern singles out as occasion for a warning against a personal, autobiographical interpretation of the work is Abelard's famous account of his affair with Heloise, whom he coolly decides to seduce, using the avarice of her foolish uncle, the canon Fulbert (with whom she lives), as his means of gaining access to Heloise as a live-in tutor. The lovers' mutual passion, its discovery by Fulbert, their secret marriage, and finally Abelard's castration by ruffians hired by the uncle are events that have gained an unassailable place in the sentimental and poetic history of Europe—but, as Southern points out, they follow a moral pattern of vice exposed and punished Abelard could have found in dozens of historical and hagiographical narratives from the early Middle Ages or his own day. "Abelard portrays himself throughout [the affair] as half-beast, half-monk, sinking through sensuality into the filth of carnal sexuality, but rising through philosophy and bodily mutilation to the stature of a spiritual man." The rhetorical and moral themes governing the relationship and its unfortunate end are, according to Southern: (1) "These things were a judgment upon sin," and (2) "They have proved a blessing in disguise."[17]

In addition to these two instances of the *Historia's* dependence on formal and thematic traditions that tend to make of Abelard a type rather than an individual within the work, scholars have frequently noted Abelard's device of drawing parallels between himself and (in the words of Mary McLaughlin, perhaps the keenest student of Abelard yet to appear) "those Christian predecessors in whom he saw his closest companions in misery": Saint Jerome, Saint Paul, Origen, even the earthly career of Jesus.[18] Such parallels serve to present the beleaguered Abelard as one more example of the Christian witness martyred by the forces of evil, and while we may have reservations about this analysis of Abelard's virtue—especially in the light of his very different exemplary role in his relationship with Heloise!—we cannot deny that they militate against a reading of the *Historia calamitatum* as a record of personal experience organized by the hero's highly individuated sense of himself.

I will attempt to put these traditional facets of Abelard's career in the context of the *Historia's* total literary achievement later in this discussion. To provide a transition to an examination of the nontraditional strategies used by the author to give that career an individual, nonexemplary dimension, I will note one other model borrowed, albeit in profoundly modified form, from early medieval personal historiography. It has not been frequently observed that, within the frame of the consolatory epistle, the *Historia* organizes Abelard's calamities according to the adapted form of the hagiographic narrative that recounts an ascetic hero's isolation of himself from the world, and the temptations and assaults he must consequently endure at the hands of demons, who attack him in many guises. The work that established the model for this type of saint's life was the vastly influential *Life of Saint Anthony* by Athanasius, written in Greek in the fourth century and disseminated throughout the West in the Latin translation of Evagrius.[19] (The *Historia's* knowledge of the *Life of Saint Anthony* is confirmed by Abelard's reference to it at a climactic moment of his life, his condemnation at Soissons; the passage is quoted below.) As the *Historia* recasts this pattern, Abelard, now the warrior of the mind instead of the athlete of God, leaves his home in Brittany, not for the desert and diabolical temptation, but for the schools of Paris, where he will endure earthly and professional calamities thanks to the efforts of nasty, wicked, but all too human contemporaries.[20]

The effect of this secularization of the hagiographical plot is that instead of demonstrating the glory of God, operating through the saint to overcome temptation, the events now become a record of the persecutions whereby inferior men bring suffering and unhappiness to a hero unprotected by the Deity. The isolation (and therefore individuation) of the protagonist is heightened by the fact that his travail takes place not in the

desert, or some other essentially timeless, symbolic world that
serves primarily as a spatial representation of the battle between
good and evil in the Christian soul,[21] but within the ecclesiastical and intellectual milieu Abelard and his contemporaries
actually knew, the world of Paris and its environs. The realization of this world is one of the artistic triumphs of the *Historia
calamitatum;* it constitutes an excellent example of what I call
broad mimesis in the depiction of a protagonist's social (and in
this case professional) environment. The author has a keen eye
(and pen) for the weaknesses and shortcomings of educational
and ecclesiastical institutions, and of the people who inhabit
them. When Abelard tells us, for example, that Anselm of
Laon's students aroused the old *magister* against him for not
coming to lectures (p. 22),[22] or that William of Champeaux
became a regular canon "for the purpose, it was said, of being
considered pious and thereby of gaining promotion to the rank
of a major prelacy" (pp. 15-16), he thrusts us into a world of
petty jealousies, politics, and gossip as familiar to an inhabitant
of the academic world today as it would have been to a twelfth-
century reader of the *Historia* in Paris or at another center of
learning. Such a nonexemplary, fully articulated representation
of a society does not exist in early medieval literature; it prompts
us to relate to its denizens, good and bad, as people, like ourselves, at once part of and separate from their environment.
Similarly, the behind-the-scenes machinations at the Council of
Soissons leading up to Abelard's first public condemnation are
immediately recognizable as endemic to secular and ecclesiastical
politics even now. Whether or not he realizes it, the author of
the *Historia* creates through this broad mimesis a background
against which Abelard must stand out as a less mythical, more
personal figure than a Saint Anthony or Saint Martin of Tours
(the hero of another of the most influential early medieval
saints' lives).

The interaction between the circumstantially depicted, flawed
institutional environment and the intensely personal responses
of the beleaguered and isolated hero, while grounded in an

earlier, hagiographic model of confrontation, in fact propels the *Historia calamitatum* into a new category of personal history, at the most impressive moments of which we behold Abelard come alive for us as an individual. At Soissons, after the atmosphere of intrigue and human frailty has been carefully established, and after Abelard has been forced to throw his condemned treatise on the Trinity into the fire prepared for it, he prepares, at the invitation of the archbishop of Reims, to defend and explain his orthodoxy in his own words, presumably by means of a logical exposition. His enemies, however, successfully insist that he must instead recite the Creed from a copy they place before him. "I read it," says Abelard, "as best I could among my sighs, sobs, and tears" (p. 51). The shock of public humiliation fills him with despair, which he expresses in words borrowed from Athanasius's *Life of Saint Anthony*: "O God, who judges equity, with what bitterness of soul and anguish of mind I, in my madness, reproached You and in anger accused You often repeating the complaint of Blessed Anthony: 'Good Jesus, where were You?'" (p. 52). His grief, born of shame, exceeds that caused by his castration: "I considered my former betrayal of little moment when compared to this injustice and I bemoaned the damage to my reputation far more than that to my body; the latter was the result of some sin while a sincere intention and love of our faith which compelled me to write had brought this open violence upon me" (p. 52).

Central to Abelard's crisis at Soissons is the confrontation between his attempt to defend his treatise on the Trinity rationally, by expressing and defending the opinions he has personally arrived at through exercise of logic, and the objective, more typically early medieval approach of his opponents, who reply that they are interested only in his authorities (*verba auctoritatis*), not in his particular intellectual skill (*ratio humana*) and its products (p. 45). These opponents finally define Christianity solely in terms of adherence to the universally accepted Creed. Abelard sees Christianity as a matrix for individual expression, an environment to be ordered and clarified by the intellect; his opponents force him instead into a public posture that denies his personal, logical expression of orthodoxy, and thus, in a real sense, denies his individual identity.

Thus constrained, Abelard can only reestablish his individuality by another kind of self-expression, this one private: grief, shame, despair,[23] which offers the peculiar self-awareness that accompanies isolation and melancholy introspection.[24] Even when he is among friends after his castration, Abelard's shame heightens his sense of being alone, separated from men by his new mutilation. "The clerics and especially my students by their excessive lamentation and wailing pained me so that I endured more from their expressions of sympathy than from the suffering caused by the mutilation. I felt the embarrassment more than the wound and the shame was harder to bear than the pain. . . . How could I face the public to be pointed at by all with a finger of scorn, to be insulted by every tongue and to become a monstrosity and a spectacle to all the world?" (pp. 38–39). But this intensely felt psychic isolation in turn heightens our response to Abelard as an individual,[25] for it confirms the social isolation so evident in scenes showing Abelard seeking his personal destiny in the circumstantially rendered, hostile environments of Paris and Soissons.

An important episode in the *Historia calamitatum* illustrates the intellectual basis of Abelard's sense of being different from his contemporaries, and suggests as well the precise terms in which Abelard saw the conflict resulting from that difference. The insight provided by this episode allows us to comprehend more clearly both the way in which Abelard embodied a newly developing twelfth-century awareness of the individual and the function served by the *Historia* in its author's quest for personal fulfillment.

Having announced, after attending Anselm of Laon's lectures on the scriptures and the standard commentaries, that he did not see the need for such extensive training in how to read either text or commentary, Abelard accepts a challenge from some of Anselm's students to lecture on an obscure biblical passage and its gloss, despite his lack of the formal training regarded as essential for such public exposition. When his challengers urge him to take a while to prepare and practice, he replies, "non esse mee consuetudinis per *usum* proficere sed per *ingenium*" (Monfrin, p. 69; italics mine). The opposition of *usus* and *ingenium* takes on a general as well as a specific significance if we see Abelard referring, as I think we must, not only to the suggested practice sessions, but to the entire system of training used by Anselm (under the term *usus*) and to his own impluse to control the system through the power of the mind, rather than be controlled by it (under the heading *ingenium*).[26]

This incident has been frequently noticed by scholars, who usually consider it an instance of Abelard's precocity, aggressiveness, and high estimate of his own worth. To my knowledge, only Klibansky has recognized its necessary value as an embodiment of Abelard's sense of himself, and therefore, in its content and terminology, as a key to his career. "In the *Historia calamitatum* he portrays himself as a man with singular powers, able to rely on his genius (*ingenium*) where others depend on laboriously acquired learning [*usus*]. In each field of knowledge he can, trusting in his own powers, penetrate more deeply than others who, not daring to challenge accepted doctrines, have become mere slaves to tradition."[27]

My sense of the importance Abelard attached to the opposition between *usus* and *ingenium* derives support from their other paired appearances in the letter. At the beginning of the section on Anselm of Laon, foremost interpreter of scripture in his day, Abelard says, patronizingly, "And so I enrolled under this old man whose great name rested on long practice [*longevus usus*] rather than on ability or learning [*ingenium vel memoria*]"[28] (p. 21; Monfrin, p. 68). Further, Abelard confesses about his love affair with Heloise that his lovemaking interfered with his energy for and interest in his teaching. "I became negligent and indifferent in my lectures so that nothing I said stemmed from my talent [*ex ingenio*] but I repeated everything by rote [*ex usu*]" (pp. 28-29; Monfrin, p. 73).

Returning to the climax of the trial at Soissons, we may now

say that Abelard is ready to dispute—to use his *ingenium* in
public debate—in order to defend the earlier expression of
ingenium in his writings. Instead his opponents enmesh him in
usus at a ridiculous level—recitation of the Creed from a supplied copy—and thus deny him that method which, if my
reading is correct, constitutes the expression, and thus the confirmation, of his sense of himself as a unique, gifted individual.
In other words, Abelard's persecutors have struck not only at
his orthodoxy or reputation but at his very identity as he experiences it privately and publicly.

Abelard's exaltation of *ingenium* puts him firmly in touch
with that main current of twelfth-century culture that stressed
the manipulation of institutions and situations to impose a
favorable order on them. (Interestingly enough, Abelard uses
trickery, *engin* as it occurs in French fabliaux and romances, to
insinuate himself into Fulbert's household and woo Heloise.
The young cleric who fools an older man, usually a husband,
in order to sleep with the latter's young wife is a staple feature
of the fabliau.[29]) Because *ingenium,* within the context of
twelfth-century educational practice, involved both the formulation of ideas and their successful public presentation and defense
in debates, it provides an important link between self-awareness,
based on the use of mental powers, and the outer confrontation
of the intellectual environment.[30] In Abelard's case, his profound commitment to *ingenium* as a principle of self-definition
was the cause of his miseries and isolation, for it inspired his
confrontatory view of reality and suppressed any desire to com-
promise or use diplomacy to avoid disastrous reversals. His
adherence to his self-defining principles created the career
which prompts the comment of modern critics that he had a
genius for getting himself into trouble. He could not abandon
the life of intellectual challenge without denying who he was.
This was true even in small matters. His insistence, while a
monk of Saint Denis, that the monastery's famous patron was
not Dionysius the Areopagite infuriated the rest of the monastery and earned him the abbot's hatred. The incident seems to

us at once petty and suicidal on Abelard's part, but it does involve a conflict between the monastery's centuries-old tradition, or *usus,* and Abelard's new, independent deduction from a reading of a commentary by Bede. Envious of Abelard's superior moral stature, the abbot seizes on this conflict to persecute him, and Abelard begins to feel "that the whole world was conspiring against me" (p. 55).

The *Historia calamitatum* is organized around incidents like this one, which pit Abelard, champion of his own personal *ingenium,* against a hostile intellectual and institutional environment. From this adversary configuration, from the sense of intellectual uniqueness implicit in Abelard's characteristic behavior, and from the explicit renderings of inner reactions of shame and despair which accompany the frustration of *ingenium*—from these three sources spring our sense of Abelard the individual. But if this is true for us, could it not also have been true for Abelard? Lacking a living, analytic tradition of the individual enabling him to corroborate the apprehension of individuality that evolved from his professional career and its crises, Abelard may have written the *Historia* in part to illustrate and confirm this apprehension.

My conclusion may be supported by Abelard's letter to his disciples, written to ask their support in a later crisis in 1139. Its editor, R. Klibansky, quite rightly describes this letter as "a manifesto succinctly stating the same view of [Abelard's] own situation and the attitudes of his adversaries toward himself as that which pervades [his] autobiographical account." Abelard's long-time conviction, outlined by Klibansky, that he was the object of envy by lesser men, the conversion of whose envy into hostility was the cause of his suffering, springs precisely from, and confirms, his inner consciousness of his *ingenium* as the property which defines him and sets him apart.[31] As Abelard puts it in the *Historia calamitatum,* speaking of his rivalry with William of Champeaux on the question of universals, "From then on my teaching gained such strength and prestige that those who formerly had somewhat vigorously championed the

position of our master [William] and had most forcefully
attacked mine now flocked to my school. . . . Within a few days
after my taking over the chair of dialectics, envy began to eat the
heart of my master and anguish to seize him to a degree I can
hardly express. His seething soul did not long endure the misery
which had taken hold of him before he cunningly attempted to
depose me. . . . And the more openly he attacked me in his
jealousy, the more prestige he gave me, as the poet says: 'What
is highest is envy's mark: winds sweep the summits'"[32] (pp.
18-19).

The paradigm implicit in these remarks is simple: *ingenium*
breeds envy, which validates by its existence the superiority
and uniqueness of its object; envy then breeds hostile deeds
which cause shame and thereby confirm the persecuted one's
sense of alienation and singularity. Paranoid as this scheme
was—and we recall his paranoid utterances at the time of the
Saint Denis conflict[33]—it encouraged Abelard to act fearlessly,
uncompromisingly, even recklessly, since any resulting slights
and reverses, however painful, only confirmed his estimate of
his intellectual worth and therefore his identity. By recording
both the external pattern and Abelard's internal responses to it,
the *Historia calamitatum* becomes not merely a personal history
and an apologia but (if it was actually written by Abelard) a
profoundly innovative exercise in self-definition, as well. The
possibility that the reiterated pattern of Abelard's career
recorded in the *Historia* may contain a component, large or
small, of what we would call fiction in no way curtails its value
as a major document of twelfth-century sensitivity to the well-
springs, and costs, of individuality.

In the light of the overall, innovative effect of the *Historia
calamitatum,* the work's use of the inherited techniques and
conventions outlined earlier in this chapter can now be seen in
its necessary context. For example, the fact that Abelard used
as a literary model the consolatory letter—or, for that matter, the
desert saint's life—does not necessitate Southern's conclusion
that the accepted theme of such a letter offers the "sole justi-

fication" of the *Historia*. Acceptance of literary models need not rule out originality in a medieval author, as any student of Chaucer well knows.[34] The fact that Abelard used the same principle—the adversary relationship between himself and his envious detractors—to explain his calamities in his autobiographical letter and in the letter of 1139 not only argues in favor of the genuineness of the *Historia* but also makes it likely that he chose the established consolatory form, with its catalogue of disasters, because it accorded well with his sense of himself. (Similar reasoning would apply even if the author were not Abelard, but one who knew him and his assessment of his career.)

As for the purely moralistic and exemplary interpretation of Abelard's love affair, the passage on which Southern and others primarily base this interpretation comes at the very beginning of the section recounting the affair, at a moment when Abelard has already attained considerable philosophical fame and profit in Paris. It reads, "But success always puffs up fools and worldly repose weakens the strength of one's mind and readily loosens its fiber through carnal allurement. At a time when I considered that I was the one philosopher in the world and had nothing to fear from others, I, who up to that time had lived most chastely, began to relax the reins on my passions. And the more success I had in philosophy and sacred science, the more I withdrew from philosophers and divines through an unclean life. For it is well known that philosophers, not to speak of divines—I mean men attentive to the lessons of sacred scripture—were especially adorned with the virtue of chastity. And while I was laboring under my pride and lechery, God's grace provided a cure for each, though I willed it not, first for my lechery by depriving me of the organs by which I practiced it, then for my pride which my scholarship especially nursed in me in accordance with the saying of St. Paul: *Knowledge puffs up.* This was accomplished by humiliating me through the burning of the book which was my special glory" (p. 25).

There can be no doubt that Abelard is here relying on an

objective Christian formula quite common in early medieval hagiography and historiography. Yet his judgment on himself is also psychologically complex. Inner, intellectual pride, he says, leads to external, lecherous behavior; lechery's punishment by the destruction of the key part of Abelard's sexual makeup then becomes a prefiguration of the destruction of the book which is an equally crucial part of his intellectual makeup. The pain and shame of castration prepare him for the greater pain and shame of the negation of his prized *ingenium*—the destruction of his philosophical potency, as it were—when he is forced to recite the Creed at Soissons. We can go further, however. Abelard says in this passage that, flushed with success, he ceased to see himself in an embattled, adversary relationship with his intellectual environment and thus fell into false security: "I considered that I was the one philosopher in the world and had nothing to fear from others." I interpret this as Abelard's implicit confession that he temporarily lost his view of life as *agon*—the view which, we have seen, confirmed his sense of himself.[35] Pride in a way stands for loss of the identity so central to his individualism. Even as he saw himself as the unique philosopher, he had paradoxically ceased to be one at all, and the manifestation of this was his refusal to live any longer as philosophers were wont to do, that is, chastely. Abelard's relationship with Heloise therefore involved a willed loss of self or identity, which both castration and the humiliation at Soissons confirmed and manifested externally. Thus even traditional, objective moralizing is made, probably unconsciously, to serve the impulse toward self-confirmation that organizes and shapes the *Historia calamitatum*.

Abelard lived, one might say, at the cutting edge of twelfth-century clerical culture, expanding the frontiers of knowledge and using his intellectual faculties in ways that excited or outraged his contemporaries. He was certainly one of the best-known and most controversial figures of his day. By contrast, Christina of Markyate must be said to have been an altogether more peripheral figure—an Englishwoman who lived her life as

a recluse, then as the leader of a small religious community of
women like herself, within the shadow of the great Benedictine
monastery of Saint Alban's. Nonetheless, her story, as preserved
in the *Life of Christina of Markyate,*[36] is of real importance to
any account of the emergence of individuality in the twelfth
century. The tensions created by the age's new forms and insights of religious life gave rise to new styles of behavior and
new conflicts between personal imperatives of conscience and
the priorities of ecclesiastical institutions. Out of these conflicts
came novel kinds of heroism, and nowhere is this heroism, in its
inner and outer dimensions, presented more perceptively, or set
in a more circumstantial physical and social environment, than
in this example of what we may call individualized hagiography.

That the *Life of Christina,* like the *Historia calamitatum,* has
strong roots in antecedent literary traditions cannot be denied.
The author makes free use of exemplary material and methodology inherited from early medieval saints' lives. But by
dramatizing Christina's intense, inner spiritual life, by representing her environment through new mimetic techniques unknown to earlier hagiography, and by stressing the gifts of
ingenuity and resourcefulness that allow her to outwit her
enemies, he also infuses the *Life* with a spirit of individual, not
exemplary, achievement, portraying Christina as a unique
person of strong character whose quest for her private destiny
puts her at odds with the established forces—both lay and ecclesiastical authorities—of her world.

Christina was born in the closing years of the eleventh century,
the daughter of well-to-do parents of noble Anglo-Saxon stock.
Her story—or rather the extant portion of it, as the manuscript
is incomplete—as recorded by a monk of Saint Alban's who
knew his subject personally,[37] falls into three sections. In the
first, Christina's early decision to dedicate herself to God as a
virgin eventually brings her into conflict with her parents, who
wish her to marry a young nobleman originally chosen for her
out of spite by Ralph Flambard, bishop of Durham, after
Christina has rebuffed his advances. Her resolve unshaken by
various trials and ordeals, Christina finds that of her parents

equally firm, and finally leaves home secretly, having decided to become a recluse. The second section of the *Life* describes Christina's existence over a period of years as a guest in the cells of two hermits—one male, one female—where she has taken refuge from her parents, her husband, and their powerful allies, including the bishop of Lincoln, who has been bribed to favor the parents' claim on Christina. In the third section, Christina is finally allowed to lead her own eremitical and later conventual life without subterfuge or constraint. Her holiness and resulting clairvoyance make her a friend and respected counsellor among ecclesiastical circles around Saint Alban's; she is the friend of Archbishop Thurston of York, and forms a close relationship with Geoffrey, abbot of Saint Alban's (ca. 1147); her concern for the abbot's well-being, and his dependence on her aid in his busy and not always blameless life as an ecclesiastical luminary, form the core of this section. After further accounts of her characteristic activities and her encounters with a mysterious pilgrim who appears several times at her priory, the text breaks off.

This summary conveys some of the variety and adventurousness of Christina's career, but little of the interest and excitement generated by the author's narrative techniques, thanks to which Christina emerges as an individual within a structure of hagiographical episodes. The miracles which attend her life, even before and just after her birth (p. 35), and her resolve, formed in childhood, to remain a virgin out of devotion to Christ (p. 41) are recognizably traditional,[38] as is her overcoming of obstacles placed in her way by enemies of herself and God. Christina's early dedication to virginity and the consequences of it belong to a hagiographical subgenre in which a young woman preserves her virginity against odds and becomes a holy religious or martyr; its most famous example is the life of Saint Cecilia, the illustrious Roman virgin martyr of the early Church.[39] Indeed, at one point the author has Christina, in the course of a lecture to her would-be husband on the virtues of virginity, compare their situation to that of Cecilia and *her* would-be husband Valerian (p. 51). This self-conscious assimilation of his subject to a hagiographic exemplar of course testifies to the normative importance attached by the author to such exemplars. But balanced with this objective approach are details, not borrowed from other saints' lives, which create for Christina's sanctity a psychological and cultural context more complex than that of earlier medieval hagiography.

Perhaps the most striking example of the exploration of controlling motives in human conduct in the *Life of Christina* is the passage characterizing Christina's parents, Autti and Beatrix, who have been shown to be so intent upon their daughter's breaking her vow of chastity to marry her noble suitor, Burthred (to whom they have already forcibly betrothed her), that they have repeatedly subjected her to mental and physical harassment. Instead of stigmatizing their behavior as the work of the devil, the author declares, "there were two reasons for this which it may be worthwhile to give here. For when they are understood, there can be no hesitation in believing that parents can behave in this way against their own flesh and blood." He goes on to enumerate the reasons: first, "this family's characteristic of pursuing to the bitter end anything it had begun, whether it was good or bad, except where success was impossible," and second, Christina's conspicuous virtues which, besides winning her universal admiration, rendered her so capable "that if she had given her mind to worldly pursuits she could have enriched and ennobled not only herself and her family but also her relatives." Since her parents also wanted her to have children who would inherit her abilities, "they begrudged her a life of virginity. For if she remained chaste for the love of Christ, they feared that they would lose her and all that they could hope to gain through her" (pp. 67–69). From this complex of motives it emerges that Christina's battle with her parents is both a battle of wills, and of strong wills at that—but not evil ones—and what we may call the normal desire of well-off, well-placed, yet anxious parents that their daughter not squander her considerable talents on a scheme which, whatever its theoretical merits, in practice meant damage to her own interests (as her parents conceived them) and those of her family.[40] From what we are told elsewhere in the *Life,* we know that Christina's parents had already begun to entrust her with important responsibilities, such as holding the keys to Autti's treasury (p. 73). Of several children she was clearly the most promising and had been the most favored, and so they could not bear to see her ruin their plans for her future.

The author gives other indications of the embarrassment and even threat to their position which Christina's parents perceive in her refusal to conform to these plans. In a conference with Fredebert, prior of Saint Mary's Augustinian priory, to whom Autti has brought Christina so that she might be convinced by the prior and canons of the house to obey her parents, Autti says revealingly, and even with a well-rendered touch of pathos, "I know, my fathers, I know, and I admit to my daughter, that I and her mother have forced her against her will into this marriage and that against her better judgment she has received this sacrament [the forced betrothal to Burthred]. Yet, no matter how she was led into it, if she resists our authority and rejects it, we shall be the laughing stock of our neighbors. . . . Therefore, I beseech you, plead with her to have pity on us: let her 'marry in the Lord' [1 Cor. 7:39] and take away our reproach. Why must she depart from tradition? Why should she bring this dishonor on her father? Her life of poverty will bring the whole of the nobility into disrepute.[41] Let her do now what we wish and she can have all that we possess" (p. 59). The idea underlying this passage, that one must act in accord with tradition and in obedience to authority rather than seek a private way to satisfaction, is simply another version of *usus* marshalling its arguments against potentially subversive *ingenium.* To her parents, anxious to preserve the remaining respectability of the Anglo-Saxon nobility, which had fallen on hard times since the Norman Conquest some fifty years before, Christina's refusal to put her talents at the service of family and class, in return for all her parent's wealth, understandably seemed a disaster, and their obstinacy of character prevented them from being reconciled to her decision.[42] Instead, they attempted to control her by more and more draconian measures: "The more her parents became aware of her persistence in this frame of mind, the more they tried to break down her resistance, first by flattery, then by reproaches, sometimes by presents and grand promises, and even by threats and punishment" (p. 47).

On the other hand, the description of "this family's characteristic of pursuing to the bitter end anything it had begun, whether it was good or bad . . ." clearly applies to Christina as well. Her insistence matches that of her parents, except that she has chosen the "good," they the "bad." What we see at the center of the story, then, is less God and the devil locked in eternal conflict for the soul of the saint than a generational struggle between equally wilful parents and child, the former of whom represent an established order and its norms, the latter an individual and uncompromising response to God and Christ which ultimately pits her, in her quest for fulfillment, against those who have protected and honored her, and who in return expect adherence to accepted values—an adherence she cannot give without compromising her personal imperative.[43] The parallel with Abelard is obvious.

The established social order—Anglo-Saxon, mercantile, and materialistic—represented by her parents is not the only one against which Christina must strive in order to fulfill her chosen personal destiny. There is also the ecclesiastical establishment, with which she has a highly ambiguous relationship throughout most of her career, and which the author presents with a vividness and broad-mimetic realism parallel to Abelard's re-creation of his Parisian milieu. Ralph Flambard, one of the most powerful men of his day, both justiciar of England and bishop of Durham, was also a friend of Christina's parents.[44] Struck by her beauty on one of his apparently frequent visits to her home, he propositions her, only to be frustrated in his design by her quick wit. (She pretends to give in, then locks him in the bedroom and escapes; pp. 41–43.) Furious at being crossed (he is "first a slave to lust, and afterward to malice," p. 43), Ralph responds by inciting another, Burthred, to attempt to achieve what he could not—an act of frustrated wilfulness later repeated in more shocking circumstances when Beatrix, incensed at her daughter's refusal to consummate the match with Burthred, tries to arrange with the aid of assorted unsavory sorceresses to have Christina deflowered by anyone at all, the principle of non-virginity apparently being all that matters (p. 75). (Here we see Christina's intensity matched by that of her parents. Like Abelard, Christina defines herself by polarizing situations.) Later, another member of the institutional hierarchy of the Church, Robert, bishop of Lincoln, is bribed by Autti to declare against Christina's vow and in favor of her husband's and parents' claim that she must marry. When the unsuspecting girl appears with her husband before the bishop—who has already, unbribed, ruled once in her favor—she is callously betrayed in a scene which nicely catches the cruel abruptness of the revelation that bishops are corruptible (p. 71).

Beyond these flagrant examples of the shortcomings of the established order, which might simply be seen as examples of twelfth-century muckraking,[45] there is the more subtle and interesting encounter between Christina and Fredebert, prior of Saint Mary's, Autti's contribution to which has already been mentioned. After her father leaves the room, Fredebert urges Christina to accede to her parents' wishes in a speech that is largely a cento of biblical quotations on the sanctity and inviolability of marriage and an appeal to follow "the commandment given to children: obey your parents and show them respect." Christina, he says, is "doubly at fault" in flouting her parents' authority and in going against the Church's authority as well, in refusing to consummate a legal, though coerced, betrothal. He ends by remarking that one can be saved without being a virgin, while many virgins are indeed damned. "And since this is so, nothing remains but that you accept our advice and teaching and submit yourself to the lawful embraces of the man to whom you have been legally joined in marriage" (p. 61). Fredebert joins the attack on Christina's chosen destiny not out of evil, but out of a benignly myopic and authoritarian view of the necessity for the individual to bow to the claims of suitable authorities; parental, spousal, ecclesiastical. His is yet another statement of the claims of *usus*.[46]

Christina's reply to Fredebert opposes to his neat listing of scriptural texts a more impassioned argument against the coercion of anyone who has, as it were, chosen God by himself, and acts from inner compulsion: "Know that from my infancy I have chosen chastity and have vowed to Christ that I would remain a virgin. This I did before witnesses, *but even if they were not present God would be witness to my conscience continually.* . . . If I do all in my power to fulfill the vow I made to Christ, I shall not be disobedient to my parents. What I do, I do on the invitation of Him whose voice, as you say, is heard in the Gospel: Everyone who leaves house or brothers or sisters or father or mother or wife or children or possessions for My name's sake shall receive a hundredfold and possess eternal life."[47]

The argument on which Christina bases her defense is that of the primacy of the direct relationship between man and God, forged in the conscience, over that involving intermediary authorities and laws. This view is, of course, supportive of individuality and subversive of the articulated hierarchy of authority which increasingly characterized the institutional Church throughout the twelfth century.[48] Christina's personalist view finally carries the day with an unbribed ecclesiastic, however: the archbishop of Canterbury, impressed by her holiness, is also swayed by her argument that she should not be forced to fulfill the objectively lawful but subjectively oppressive obligations of marriage (p. 85).

Nonetheless, Christina's relationship with the official Church remains problematic, as the interests of its representatives serve more as a threat than a protection to her on her private quest. The first section of the *Life,* comprising Christina's various confrontations with established authorities, reaches its climax with her decision to escape from the stifling existence fostered by these unresolvable conflicts by becoming a recluse. The way in which this decision is forced upon, rather than freely chosen by, Christina runs counter to the traditional free choice of the monastic or eremitical vocation by hagiographic protagonists. The point is clear: Christina's inner, individual imperative toward a self-defining, self-chosen relationship with Christ does not in itself *require* isolation from her external environment, as Anthony's, for example, seems to; only the attempts of others to manipulate the structures of Christian society to threaten her private vocation and thus her individual identity drive her into isolation. Christina's situation is the reverse of Abelard's: the articulated environment, rather than the protagonist, creates the adversary relationship. But the effect is ultimately the same: a polarized situation which, by isolating the heroine, heightens our awareness of her individuality.

The theme of what we might call the acquired necessity to escape from society's enveloping constraints in order to find the freedom to perfect the self underlies a series of incidents in the first part of the *Life,* incidents in which clothing or other coverings and escape from someone's grasp are closely linked.[49] Actually, the text reveals a complex of symbols relating the ideas of civilization as constraint and constraining, self-chosen anchoritic enclosure as an aid to freedom, thus stating the paradox at the heart of an important type of twelfth-century religious and personal impulse which was to receive its greatest monument, and most perspicuous analysis, in the *Ancrene Wisse.*[50] The first relevant scene is that in which Christina hides in her bedroom to prevent her forcible delivery to Burthred by his friends for deflowering. She takes refuge behind a heavy curtain by the bed and hangs from the wall by a hook as the mob searches for her. One of them actually seizes her foot through the curtain, but the intervening layers of cloth prevent him from recognizing what it is, and he lets it go (p. 53). The motif of Christina wrapped or covered in such a way as to elude capture returns when she disguises herself in man's clothing as part of her strategem to escape from her parents, and then hides the masculine garb under a cloak until the proper moment (p. 91). But in other episodes clothes function as a hindrance, or as an artifact aiding the coercer, and must be discarded if liberty is to be gained. On one occasion, after the bishop of Lincoln's false judgment against her, when Burthred tries to detain her by grabbing her mantle, Christina escapes her husband by loosening the garment so that it comes off in his hand when she moves away (p. 73). A bit later, in a dream vision, Christina relives a version of this episode. She sees herself in a church with Christ and Mary, and as she moves to join the latter she must pass by Burthred, who is prostrate on the church floor. He grabs for her mantle but misses it, and, in rage and frustration, bangs his head on the pavement (p. 79). Finally, on the day of her escape, while awaiting the servant of the hermit Eadwin who has undertaken to harbor her from her parents, Christina meets the reeve of the town. "And he took her by the mantle and entreated her to tell him whether she intended to run away. And she smiled and said, 'Yes.' . . . So when he let her go, she entered the church" (p. 89), there to await her accomplice in the escape. Here the image of clothing as a means of confinement is recalled one last time and linked to the motion of entering the liberating confinement of a church, thereby anticipating the next part of Christina's life, in which she will hide from her persecutors for some years in the enclosed dwellings of holy men and women. The author verbalizes the force of all these images at the moment when Christina "put on the religious habit, and she who had been accustomed to wearing silk dresses and luxurious furs in her father's house was now covered with a rough garment" (p. 93). The change, outwardly for the worse, in fact marks the beginning of Christina's liberty from the unwanted life of the society in which she grew up.

What seems implied by all these incidents is that while Christina can, by the exercise of her considerable talents, and with the compulsion of her personal quest, use the constraining artifacts of society, including those symbolically related to her specific marital predicament (bedcurtains, male clothing) to remain free in society, she must eventually throw off the manner of living by which her natal world maintains, or attempts to maintain, a hold on her, and move to the real freedom of apparent destitution and harsher constraints, symbolized by the rough cloth of her habit. Thus, just before her escape, when

Christina, already in her male clothes and cloak, encounters her sister Matilda, the latter notices a sleeve hanging out from beneath the cloak and asks about it. Christina quickly takes off a veil and, pretending that this is the garment her sister has noticed, gives it to her "with an innocent look: 'Sister dear, take it with you when you go back to the house, for it is getting in my way'" (p. 91). Here, while giving another example of Christina's quick wit, the author has his heroine point, as it were, to the envelope of constraints within which she must operate, while prefiguring by her gesture the action she will soon take to remove from herself the burden imposed by this environment.[51]

The relationship between the saint and her world—how she establishes her separateness from it and remakes the meaning of its forces and images by her consciousness of herself in her inner relationship to God—is one of the main foci of the author's interest in presenting the life of his subject; but the other focus is of course the delineation of Christina herself as a person. In his portrait of Christina the author reveals his age's new awareness of the complexity of individual experience by offering a far greater variety of perspectives on her character than is the case in early medieval hagiography. We have already noted his interest in Christina's indomitable will, which he recognizes as a family characteristic and uses to account psychologically (rather than theologically) for the confrontation between Christina and her parents over her vow of chastity. Furthermore, in dealing with the problems posed for her by her choice of vocation, and by the schemes and desires of those who would thwart it, Christina gives impressive evidence that she possesses abundant wit, or *ingenium*. Several instances have already been given: when Ralph Flambard attempts to seduce her, she outwits him by locking him in a bedroom; when Burthred's cronies are searching for her, she hits on the idea of hanging from a hook behind the bedcurtains to elude them. It is, above all, Christina's *ingenium* that guides her out of her "frightful troubles" as her parents exert more and more pressure on her to force her to marry. Christina decides suddenly that she must escape from home when a servant of one of her supporters, the recluse

Eadwin, expresses a wish to carry her off with him and thus save her from her ordeal. At once she commands him, "Go and tell your master to prepare two horses, one for me and one for you, at a precise time. . . . When dawn is breaking, wait for me with the horses in that field over there . . . and when the horse is ready you will recognize me by this sign. I will place my right hand to my forehead with only the forefinger raised. When you see this, rein in the horses immediately. And if I do not come at once, take it that I am waiting for the right moment. For on that day my father and mother will go as usual to speak with Guido" (pp. 87–89).

The impression given by this passage is one of absolute self-control, clarity of mind, quickness to take advantage of an offered opportunity, and attention to detail. The moment is notably lacking in meekness, or in pious reliance on God's will (which, to be sure, Christina manifests in abundance elsewhere in the text). When the day of escape comes, Christina's disguise and her exchange with a suspicious sister, whom, as I have mentioned, she succeeds in throwing off the trail, complete the picture of a woman of remarkable *sangfroid,* well able to think and care for herself in tight spots.[52]

It would be quite wrong, however, to suppose that purely human virtue without spiritual reference dominates the delineation of the heroine and the progress of the story. Equally important and new to the twelfth century is Christina's sense of personal, intimate spirituality. Even before Christina's birth, the emotional tone characteristic of this spirituality is established in the prenatal sign (familiar in hagiography) given to her mother to indicate that the child she is carrying will be of exceptional merit. A dove flies to Beatrix from the priory of Saint Mary, taking shelter in the sleeve of her tunic on a Saturday, "a day specially set aside by the faithful for the devotion to the mother of God . . . between the feasts of the Assumption and the Nativity of our Lady." To this (for the genre) quite normal occurrence the following is added: "Furthermore . . . the dove stayed quietly with her for seven whole days, allowing itself to be stroked with her hands . . . and nesting comfortably and with evident pleasure first in her lap and then in her bosom" (p. 35). The tenderness of the passage resides in the relationship between the dove (evoked as a tame, flesh-and-blood creature, not a mere symbol) and the young woman, while its sensuality, real though controlled, resides in the specific evocation of the sense of touch and physical contact; the dove's arrival represents God's endowing Beatrix with insight into her unborn daughter's sanctity—but the insight is presented as having an undeniable component of sensuality. Moreover, as the whole passage clearly rests on the iconography of the Annunciation, its attempt to present the activity of the Holy Spirit in such a physical way testifies to a new appreciation of the sensory basis of individual interaction with the environment, even within a patently symbolic and exemplary narrative incident.

Throughout the *Life,* sharply visualized and circumstantially described physical contact figures in Christina's intimate experiences of Mary and Christ, often taking the form of caresses which translate divine favor into the vocabulary of intimate human affection. Such a representation of the comfort offered to the individual soul by its inner reaching for heavenly consolation is especially effective when the protagonist undergoes great trials. When, for example, Christina's parents have reached such a point of desperation over Christina's celibacy that her mother "wasted a great deal of money on old crones who tried with their love potions and charms to drive her out of her mind with impure desires" (p. 75), and the situation looks darkest for the determined virgin, "Christ, wishing to comfort His spouse,[53] gave her consolation through his holy mother" in a dream (p.71). Christina seems to be in a church in which a priest celebrating mass (presumably Christ) offers her "a branch of most beautiful leaves and flowers" and tells her to bring it to "a lady like an empress" sitting nearby. Christina obeys, and the lady returns to her a twig from the branch, saying, "take care of it for me." This dialogue follows: "'How is it with you?' . . . 'Ill, my lady: they all hold me up to ridicule [cf. Jer. 20:7] and straiten me from all sides [cf. Luke 19:43]. Among those that suffer there is none like me. Hence I cannot stop crying and sobbing from morning till night.'" The lady comforts her and walks away, taking the branch with her. There follows the incident of the prostrate Burthred seeking without success to clutch her garment. Then Christina sees the lady again in an upper chamber, and is invited by her to climb the steps, "steep and difficult for anyone wishing to climb," to join her. "And as she sat there enjoying the beauty of the place, behold, the aforesaid queen came and laid her head in her lap as if she wished to rest," first with her face away and then toward Christina, as a token of the day when "I shall bring you . . . into my chamber, [and] you can gaze to your full content" (p. 73).

Aside from the obvious allegory of virginity and the hard road to salvation, this passage is again notable for the striking physical act of intimacy when Mary rests her head in Christina's lap, as if in repayment for the trials suffered by her faithful servant. (Note that the gesture of facing first away from and then toward Christina is also symbolic of the heroine's alternating trials and inner satisfaction, with the iconography again realized in a manner stressing intimate physical contact.) In this scene, also, we see the heroine from a pathetic perspective as a lonely soul who suffers the terrible price of isolation and grief because of her vocation—that is, as one whose unique, great need explains the intimacy and tenderness of her consolation, while both need and consolation confirm our sense of Christina's individuality.

Later, in the second part of the *Life,* when Christina's trials are inner temptations to lust and other wickedness, "The Son of the Virgin looked kindly down upon the low estate of his handmaid [a paraphrase of words spoken in Luke's gospel (1:48) by Mary herself] and granted her the consolation of an unheard-of grace. For in the guise of a small child He came to the arms of his sorely tried spouse and remained with her a whole day, not only being felt but also seen. So the maiden took Him in her hands, gave thanks, and pressed Him to her bosom. And with immeasurable delight she held Him at one moment to her virginal breast, at another she felt His presence within her even through the barrier of the flesh. . . . From that moment the fire of lust was so completely extinguished that never afterwards could it be revived" (p. 119). Here both the intimacy of the vision and its function are more explicit. At a moment when desire for earthly pleasure is particularly troubling Christina (a problem one must consider endemic to young people who undertook the rigors and complete sexual denial of the anchoritic life at this time), the consolation and protection offered by her intimate contact with the divine is represented as a physical encounter with Christ, redolent with suggestions of purely personal erotic pleasure. Christina, to be sure, is presented here as an antitype of Mary, but what matters is that the religious imagination of the author (and possibly of Christina herself) should conceive of the relationship between God and man so differently from that of early medieval spirituality, linking the deepest, most private spiritual impulses to equally private images of bodily contact and satisfaction.[54]

The manner in which the author of *The Life of Christina* reproduces Christina's personal sensory responses to her environment through what I have called narrow mimesis—that is, his circumstantial representation of specific moments, gestures, and the disposition of bodies in a limited space—constitutes a last element of his individualized portrait of his heroine. We have already seen examples of this: the moment when Burthred's accomplice clutches Christina's foot through the thick curtain behind which she hangs from a hook, and then lets it go; Christina's momentary hesitation in embarrassment before leaping man-style onto her escape horse and giving it the spur; Burthred reaching for Christina in her dream and, failing to grasp her, banging his head on the pavement. A further incident holds particular importance for the story as a whole. After Christina has run away from her parents and taken refuge with a female recluse, Alfwen, she desires to stay with the holy hermit Roger, who, however, has been unwilling to assist her because of her continuing difficulties with her parents, husband, and their

ecclesiastical supporters, notably the bishop of Lincoln. A
marvellous occurrence makes Roger change his mind, and he
has Christina's cell brought near him, although he still will not
speak to or even look at her, "in order that there might be no
excuse for Alfwen to accuse him before the bishop of being a
cause of dissension. Nevertheless they saw each other the same
day. . . . [Christina] lay prostrate in [Roger's] chapel, with her
face turned to the ground. The man of God stepped over her
with his face averted in order not to see her. But as he passed by
he looked over his shoulder [to watch her pray]. Yet she, at
the same instant, glanced upward to appraise the beauty and de-
portment of the old man. . . . And so they saw each other, not
by design and yet not by chance, but . . . by the divine will"
(p. 101). As a direct result of this glance, the author says,
they decided to dwell together. "The fire . . . which had been
kindled by the spirit of God and burned in each one of them
cast its sparks into their hearts by the grace of that mutual
glance: and so made one in heart and soul [cf. Acts 4:35], in
chastity and charity in Christ, they were not afraid to dwell
together under the same roof" (p. 101). Putting before us two
slightly contorted figures in a narrow space (the chapel must
have been quite small, and the work's first readers would know
that), joined *momentarily* by the exchange of the glances that
they have sought to avoid, this independent moment of the
narrative is highly suggestive, and brings not only the characters
but also their position in space into vivid focus. The individual
experience and perceptions underlying the symbolic import of
the scene are thus drawn in purely spatial and temporal terms.
The use of such an "iconographic" approach (the exchanged
glance in a narrow place) to the revelation of a scene's larger
significance reminds one of sculptures of Giselbertus at Saint
Lazarus, Autun, where meaning is also communicated by means
of minimal contact between people: the angel touching the
finger of the sleeping *magus* to warn him of Herod's treachery,
and above all the Eve for the lintel over the north doorway.[55]
Eve is Giselbertus's daring attempt to reimagine the Fall not

simply as the first objective fact of salvation history, but as a subjective moment in time in which a specific woman, deceiving both herself and her lover (as suggested by the apparently casual way in which she reaches behind her to pluck the apple), exerts the seductive force of her body and her voice (she is whispering) to communicate with her lover as individual to individual, over-coming the barrier between discrete selves (concretely repre-sented by the vine between the figures) by the passionate intensity of her presence. Eve's sensuality, as Giselbertus represents it, is clearly part of her personhood to Adam—not just a symbol of her objective role as agent of mankind's fall. Analogously, by their first glance, Christina and Roger become persons to each other in the description by the Saint Alban's monk.

For its use of such vividly mimetic moments and for its por-trayal of the inner life—indeed, for all the innovations I have cited—the *Life of Christina of Markyate* deserves recognition as perhaps the twelfth century's most effective and revealing personal history of a woman. Its portrait of an individual, not simply a type of feminine holiness, claims a place beside Abe-lard's equally personal depiction of himself in the *Historia calamitatum* as an impressive witness to the twelfth century's discovery of the individual, and therefore a link between Latin culture and the perilous quest of the chivalric romance hero for self-fulfillment and private destiny.

In the analyses that have occupied the bulk of this chapter, my intention to delineate a literary context outside courtly, vernacular culture for the chivalric romances' concern with in-dividual experience has dictated the stress I have laid on the innovative features of two Latin personal histories. The Latin literature of the twelfth-century—including lryic poetry, satire, and historiography as well as saints' lives and other forms—was one of the glories of the age, in which technical and thematic richness derived from a mixture of recaptured and rethought anterior material. From the particular point of view of this study, the continuing hold of earlier forms and conventions on twelfth-century Latin writers placed a limit on the extent to which the age's nascent sense of the importance of the individual and subjective realms of experience could be fully embodied in their works. There are, for example, abundant clues to the emergence of the individual in the emphasis on character traits and idiosyncracies that one finds in the verbal portraits of kings in Anglo-Norman historiography. The pseudo-historical *Historia regum Britanniae* of Geoffrey of Monmouth, and even more so the same writer's *Vita Merlini* (apparently written about the same time as the *Life of Christina,* just after mid-century) intermittently betray a keen interest in exploring the often disastrous conflict between personal will or vision and political realities. But Geoffrey's explorations, like those of his contemporaries in historiography, remain tentative and even inconsistent, in good part because of the strength in their works of early medieval moral schemes and classical rhetorical topoi that govern the way they write about the past and the place of men and women in national or world history.[56]

In seeking the segment of twelfth-century culture within which new cultural concepts such as that of the individual had the greatest possibility for expression and examination in all their complexity, we must look to the age's new literary culture, that of the great courts, where, first in the south of France, then in northern France and England, a self-conscious elite society took shape and presided over the creation of a literature of entertainment and edification designed to fit its needs and mirror its aspirations.[57] Of course, courtly literature owed an immense debt to Latin culture; much of it was written by clerics trained fully in the learned and classical traditions, and many of its earlier texts were translations or adaptations of Latin works.[58] But within the new milieu of the courts there also appeared forms and techniques which courtly poets used to speak directly to their audience about its ideals and self-image, now celebrating, now parodying or subverting the life of *courtoisie* by elegantly manipulating the conventions of a new literature of *courtoisie*. One set of such conventions, concerning the private and public lives of brave knights and beautiful, refined ladies in an imagined world of love and adventure, provided a strong, flexible framework, called *chivalry,* for the exploration of the trials and triumphs of individuality. To the rise of chivalry as a literary topic, and eventually a literary plot, we must therefore turn our attention.

2: CRITICAL MOMENTS: INDIVIDUALITY IN CHIVALRIC ROMANCE

The circumstances—political, social, economic—that gave birth to twelfth-century courtly culture and presided over its efflorescence at English and French courts cannot appositely be studied here. Research into patterns of patronage and the backgrounds of individual writers continues to expand our knowledge and clear up earlier misconceptions.[1] Similarly, one of the greatest literary contributions of courtly society to its own and succeeding ages, the conventions of *fin amors* as developed in lyric and narrative, has been studied with great zeal—if not always great judgment—by modern scholars, and I have neither space nor desire to contribute to the tide of controversy that swirls around the question of "courtly love" today, even as it did nearly one hundred years ago.[2] Still, the centrality of love and its literary depiction to a study of the individual in chivalric romances cannot be denied, for love in its very nature is the private relationship par excellence between two human beings whose lives take on a unique configuration, and move toward the purely personal goal of union with the beloved, because of their love for each other. The lover, by his or her passion for someone singled out from among all other persons in the world, experiences and emblazons the fact of radical individuality in acknowledging love's dominance. In the chivalric romances, love must function in a world whose main social virtues are valor and excellence in martial prowess, through the exercise of which knights win honor, the approbation bestowed by society on those of its members who best conform to its norms. The creation of a system in courtly narrative literature that linked the public pursuit of honor through prowess and the private quest for fulfillment through passionate love made possible the exploration of individuality that animates the romances. The growth of the literary system of chivalry will briefly detain us in the first part of this chapter before we move into a detailed analysis of the individual-centered world of two fully formed chivalric romance texts.

In its most emblematic, least problematic form, the chivalry topos, as I call it, aims to reconcile the two contrary forces of love and prowess, or, in more psychological terms, the sexual and aggressive impulses, by making each one inspire the other: love of a woman (and indeed the very sight of her) inspires a knight to brave deeds, in order to win her favor, while the sight of a knight doing brave deeds (especially in her honor) inspires love in the lady who beholds them. The idea is as old as Plato at least.[3] Behind its artificial symmetry lies the profound conviction that a refined society can reconcile, and thus domesticate, two universal human drives potentially disruptive of all social harmony and progress. The process by which this paradigm of social aspirations became a mechanism for exploring individuality in all its complexity coincides with the evolution of the chivalry topos within twelfth-century courtly narrative toward autonomy as a plot. Once that autonomy was achieved, the chivalric romance was born, for the plot of the romances (which will be studied further in chapter 6) involves the working out, through a series of adventures, of a more or less sophisticated version of the relationship, and conflict, between martial behavior (usually aimed at winning honor) and the demands of love in the career of a hero and a heroine.

The stages of evolution from chivalry topos to chivalric plot are not hard to trace, though the exercise must proceed in the knowledge that many of the "pre-romance" courtly narratives cannot be absolutely or even relatively dated. One cannot, therefore, always argue securely that the chivalric element in a given work, though more rudimentary or less autonomous than analogous elements in other texts, has chronological priority.

Within a short period—in this case, about thiry years (1140–70)—innovations within a burgeoning literary form often overlap owing to the different talents and interests of the authors who use it. Therefore, even if subsequent research were to establish an order for the texts I am examining that differed from mine, it would not materially affect my point about the function and limits of the chivalric topos-become-subplot in these narratives.

The first extant instance of the chivalry topos comes in the ninth book of Geoffrey of Monmouth's *Historia regum Brittanniae*. Describing the festivities that accompany Arthur's solemn celebration of Pentecost, Geoffrey says that Arthur's court attracted all the elite of European knighthood, who came seeking the honor of serving the king, conforming to refined standards of dress and conduct, and proving themselves, through deeds of prowess, worthy of the favors of the ladies at court. The relationship of knights and ladies makes the former bolder, the latter more chaste and virtuous; each strives to be worthy of the other.[4] Geoffrey then describes a tournament during which knights joust while ladies watch them from atop the walls of Caerleon and spur them on by flirtatious behavior (ix. 14). The world of chivalry here evoked betrays Geoffrey's awareness of how sexual and aggressive impulses can be harmonized within the frame of a precise yet stylized iconography to create a moment at once symbolic and self-consciously elegant. However emblematic, the passage is also a diversion, ultimately irrelevant to the real concerns of the *Historia* at this point: national self-preservation and imperial conquest. Shortly after the chivalric display, a Roman embassy arrives to challenge Arthur's powers; a war council is called, and there Cador, duke of Cornwall, denounces the years of peace (during which, we recall, chivalry and refinement have flourished) as a period of laziness and decline (ix. 16). No one contradicts this opinion, and in the climactic campaign of Britain versus Rome which soon ensues there is no hint that chivalric considerations inspire any of the warriors. So the topos of knights and ladies functions only as an isolated, attractive decoration on a plot whose main themes have nothing to do with chivalry.

Subsequent appearances of the chivalry topos in vernacular, courtly literature attest to its attraction for court poets and their audiences, even though it is not yet the stuff of a plot. Wace's *Roman de Brut* (1155) and the *Roman de Thèbes* (1150-55?) offer the next examples.

Wace's translation of Geoffrey's *Historia* does not substantially alter Geoffrey's plot, but places it within a rich context of courtly comment and material, by turns refined and down-to-earth, serious and comic.[5] Wace's repeated use of the term *cortoise* in the passage (10,493-516) translating Geoffrey's references to chivalric activity and motivation among Arthur's knights and ladies confirms that to Wace and his audience this is an emblematically courtly moment, encapsulating the *maniera* of a refined, self-conscious aristocracy in an effective tableau.[6] And when Cador later charges, as in the *Historia,* that peace has made the Britons soft, Wace invents a reply by Gawain (often a spokesman in later romances for conventional courtly values) defending peace and concluding with a couplet defining chivalry (the first such statement by a character in a courtly work): "Par amistiez et par amies/Font chevalier chevaleries" (10,771-72). In the Roman war which follows, however, Wace refrains from having Gawain or anyone else act on chivalric principles; the dichotomy between peacetime topos and martial plot remains unresolved.

In the *Roman de Thèbes* chivalry begins to find a place in actual warfare, as part of the anonymous poet's adaptation of epic material from classical antiquity to the tastes of a courtly audience. The structure of *Thèbes* is quasi-episodic within the limits of its inherited plot, a single, grand, and fatal action—the legendary war between Oedipus's sons for the kingship at Thebes—deeply significant to an earlier (Roman) audience. The episodes added or modified by the poet draw attention away from the main action without actually supplanting it, and within this looser, ultimately unsatisfactory structure the chivalry topos is given fairly free rein. Besides being stated as a factor motivating heroic activity in war on several occasions, the topos is shown becoming a subplot.[7] In Statius's *Thebaid,* the source

for the plot of *Thèbes,* Ismene, princess of Thebes, loves Atys, a
young Theban warrior, though we do not hear of their love
until Atys has died in battle, whereupon the bereaved Ismene
voices a pathetic lament. Starting here, the French poet expands
the love of Ysmaine and Athes and creates a new, complementary love btween Antigone, Ysmaine's sister, and Parthonopeus,
a noble young warrior of the army besieging Thebes. Developing
these relationships permits the introduction of new kinds of
scenes into courtly narrative, for example, the first meeting of
Antigone and Parthonopeus, while the princess is on a mission
of peace from the besieged city to the surrounding army.[8] As
the love relationships flower amidst the battle for Thebes, what
was in Geoffrey's *Historia* a stylized iconography of knights
jousting while women watch them from above becomes an individualized human situation in which Ysmaine, watching from
the city walls, can exclaim, "Ce est Athes que je la voi,/veez com
broche a cel tornoi [the battle for the city]!/Sor toute rien
amer le doi,/car tout ice fet il por moi."[9] Later, we see the two
sisters at their observation post engaging in friendly yet intense
debate about the respective merits of their lovers' *prouesce,*
during which Antigone complains that she cannot physically
enjoy the pleasures of love as easily as can Ysmaine, since
Parthonopeus is on the opposing side in the war (5867–97).
At precisely this point, the individual-centered form of the
chivalry topos collides with the demands of the inherited plot.
The news of Athes' death in battle reaches Ysmaine as she tells
her sister of a foreboding dream she has had. A bit later in the
story, Parthonopeus is killed during a foray, as the plot moves
relentlessly toward general catastrophe and the final, fratricidal
duel of the story's "real" protagonists, Polynices and Eteocles.
Chivalry, no longer an ornament irrelevant to the larger narrative
in which it appears, has become symbolic of aspirations for
happiness which are frustrated by the larger imperatives of fate
in history. The juxtaposition of Antigone's complaint about
postponed sexual gratification and Athes' death marks chivalry
as an ironic topos within the imagined world of the *Roman de
Thèbes.*[10]

In assessing the *Roman d'Enéas.* (1165-70?), one must keep
in mind that this *roman antique,* whose direct influence on the
romances of Chrétien de Troyes and others has been fully
documented,[11] integrates the outer dynamic of chivalry, as
developed in the *Roman de Thèbes,* and an inner dynamic of
love developed, in all likelihood, within courtly Ovidian *contes*
like *Piramus et Tisbé* and *Narcisus.*[12] The short, nonheroic *conte*
laid great emphasis on the inner dialogue, in which the young
protagonist, experiencing the disorienting pangs of passion for
the first time, questions him- or herself about the significance
of the new feeling, and by the process of painful self-confron-
tation arrives at a new level of awareness concerning the conflict
between the private demands of love and opposing familial or
social obligations.[13] Similarly, the long additions to Vergil in
which the *Enéas* poet creates the love affair of Enéas and Lavine
(7857-9274, 9313-42, 9839-10,090) reveal a consuming
interest—at once clinical and sentimental, ironic and sympathetic—in the agonies of falling in love. Both protagonists
must come to grips with their desire, recognize its nature and
object, and confront the obstacles to its fulfillment. This Ovidian
tour de force is grafted onto the epic plot by means both of
Lavine's mother, Amata (who in Vergil hates Aeneas and prefers
Turnus as a husband for Lavinia), and the single combat between
Aeneas and Turnus to decide the fate of the Trojans in Latium
with which the *Aeneid* concludes. In the *Enéas* the queen's
hostility to Enéas neatly becomes an external obstacle which
sharpens Lavine's awareness of what she desires (Enéas, whom
she has seen from her window in a tower—a combination of
Ovidian sources and chivalric iconography) and how she must
behave (rebelliously and dishonorably) to get him.[14] Her desperate decision to reveal her love to Enéas (via a note wrapped
around an arrow, shot from her tower)[15] initiates love in him as
well and inspires him to defeat Turnus in order to win her (see
8982-96, 9046-66; the latter passage is a litany of love's effect
on prowess, while Lavine states the chivalry topos succinctly,
9340-42).

The *Roman d'Enéas* converts its epic hero's victory into an exemplum of chivalry heightened in significance by being linked to the idea of self-discovery through love. But the conversion is far from complete; the actual impression on the reader of the Lavine episode is that love conversations—internal and external dialogues of varying degrees of earnestness—have been massively intruded into an epic action to divert the audience's attention from the plot, or at most to modernize the plot without resolving the contradictions between Vergil's concern with the harsh demands of destiny on the *pius* hero and the more optimistic assumptions of the chivalry topos.[16]

Unresolved contradictions, in fact, mark every instance of the chivalry topos mentioned thus far. The inhospitality of large, preexistent plots to the intrusion of a topos imaginatively expressing courtly desires for an ethic of individuality which reconciles private and public needs (love and honor) restricted a full exploration of the possibilities for such an ethic; only with the rise of chivalric romance did this occur. Historical plots, such as those of Geoffrey and Wace, which traced the ebb and flow of national fortunes demonstrated in the process that, if heroes made history, history could also unmake heroes. Claims for the autonomy of chivalric heroism inspired by love could hardly be made in such a context of large and impersonal forces.

Similarly, the stories of Thebes, Troy, and Rome that provided the plots of *romans antiques* inhibited the dramatic possibilities inherent in the chivalry topos. Chivalry suggests that a personal relationship can trigger public action, but also that the ultimate purpose or effect of the relationship remains personal; as Geoffrey puts it, knights become braver, ladies more chaste and honorable. In a chivalric plot, our final concern should be how well the knights and ladies live up to the supposed norms binding them together and thus achieve private self-fulfillment; an epic or historical narrative, however, focuses on a portion of the body of legend or tradition shared by its audience and gains thereby a controlling context within which to define or judge personal deeds or interpersonal relationships. The manifest movement of history toward the fall of Troy or the founding of Rome suggests how we should evaluate the deeds of Hector or Achilles, the affair of Dido and Aeneas. In such a context, the more successfully a poet articulates the chivalry topos in action, the more ironic (as in *Thèbes*) or disruptive (as in *Enéas*) its relationship with the inherited "overplot" becomes.

The rise of chivalric romance after the middle of the twelfth century created a narrative form within which the chivalry topos could thrive, and within which, therefore, the ideals of courtly society could be fully and self-consciously explored as a metaphor for the individual's quest to become what he wishes within himself to be. The romance plot lacks any context larger than the lives of its protagonists; it permits the simultaneous presentation of external, heroic adventures and of an inner world in which the self-awareness born of love permits the control of martial impulses. The hero's discovery of his identity and his destiny (they are two aspects of the same phenomenon) is an act of individual realization; his shaping of his powers to control external reality and thus attain the perceived goals is self-realization of a longer and more arduous kind. In chivalric romances the chivalry topos expands to become the setting for the interaction of these two types of realization. The result, however, is not the monotonous repetition of the same chivalric story in romance after romance. The imagined world of chivalric romance probes the condition and needs of its protagonists and their quest for full individuality with conviction *and* irony, hope *and* cynicism, earnestness *and* comedy.

It is, of course, possible to seek other reasons than its suitability for exploring individuality to explain the adoption of the adventure romance form by courtly poets. Another major factor may have been the existence of the *juvenes,* the class of young adult knights who, having no inherited title or ecclesiastic profession, led peripatetic lives of adventure as mercenaries as they sought both social recognition and the security of an advantageous marriage.[17] The *juvenes* constituted a mobile, independent, socially unsettled, and potentially disruptive element of aristocratic society, and it is possible that their experiences are reflected, with a suitable degree of idealization, in the careers of adventure- and fulfillment-seeking romance protagonists.[18] Be that as it may, the romances offer a reflected image—now heightened in celebration, now subverted by parody—of the courtly milieu and a compelling record of its aspirations toward self-awareness and self-conquest, the necessary prerequisites to the successful imposition on experience of an order helpful to self-fulfillment.

The structure of the chivalric romance is biographical rather than familial, tribal, or national in its focus: a story of the adventures of one or two knights and their ladies is presented as a series of juxtaposed episodes, each one a complete, miniature action. The relation between each episode and the ones before and after it is not always progressive, or even evident, as there is no larger, overarching historic or epic action that unifies and frames all separate deeds (such as would be the case in epic). It follows that the episode is the main creative unit of the romance and should therefore be the focus of critical attention in any attempt to discover the thematic intentions of the chivalric poet or to evaluate his technique of presenting and developing themes. My consciousness of the episodic nature of chivalric romance has determined my strategy of alloting the remainder of this chapter to a close consideration of two episodes, in order to derive from them, by close literary analysis, a sense of the centrality of the problems of individuality to the poet's enterprise.

The two episodes I have chosen are from Chrétien de Troyes's *Erec and Enide* (ca. 1170?) and the anonymous *Partonopeu de Blois* (1180s).[19] Both episodes take shape around a subjective critical moment, a coming together of characters which is important only to them and derives its meaning from their individual histories, desires, and qualities. This is a true *kairos,* a limited moment in which the alternatives of action and inaction each carry farreaching consequences for the participants. The characters are themselves aware of, and communicate to the audience, this sense of urgency; they make us experience time as they do, from within a single consciousness and perspective.

Linked to the presentation of the critical moment in both episodes is a desire to get inside a character, in order to explore the relationship between perception or awareness and individual history in determining action in the face of a serious challenge. Both episodes show characters ingeniously manipulating facts and people in order to control a situation, or, more specifically, to "create" an artificial reality favorable to self-fulfillment. That is, these episodes illustrate *engin* in action. Both portray the external environment in ways that stress personal perception of, and placement in, time and space. Finally, both episodes explore the brief, critical period of the characters' existence— the *kairos*—from a number of different points of view, not only from within characters but also by means of the poet's own *engin*, his conscious manipulation of the audience and its feelings. These techniques make us aware of the limited perspective on reality which we too, as individuals, bring to our encounter with the world.

The episode from *Erec and Enide* has a thematic interest bearing directly on chivalry. It considers how a prowess too absolute, too unreflective, too undiscriminating can be tamed, socialized, made moral and discriminating, and thus placed in the service of specific individuals. The theme unfolds through three clearly defined phases, functioning somewhat like thesis, antithesis, and synthesis. First comes an outer, emblematic view of prowess, presented in the person of the knight, Guivret *le petit;* then a crisis of inner awareness, embodied in Enide, who sees Guivret coming to challenge and fight her husband, Erec; and finally, an armed combat between Guivret and Erec. The outer world of prowess affects and is affected by the inner world of love and awareness. The result not only socializes Guivret's prowess but also reaffirms Enide's assumption of responsibility for Erec and Erec's dependence upon and need for Enide. The amoral, chivalric challenge of the stranger knight, in Chrétien's hands, becomes a means of anatomizing a moral, reciprocal chivalric relationship between two aware individuals.

The *Partonopeu* episode approaches prowess thematically from the opposite extreme: here a knight has completely abdicated his aggressive impulse, to the point of no longer even wishing to survive. The action then shows the rebirth of Partonopeu's desire to live through his reestablishing an effective relationship with another person. The episode is in two parts (or perhaps I should speak of two linked episodes): in the first, the poet presents the hero's decline to a nadir of isolation, self-hatred, and abandonment of civilization for the waste forest in which he hopes to be eaten by beasts; in the second, we are caught up in a movement toward the recognition of Partonopeu by Urraque, sister of his lost beloved, who discovers him accidentally, reverses his attitude about himself, and helps restore him to love-inspired chivalric combat once again. The recognition scene invites treatment from four separate critical perspectives, which are also implicit in the Guivret episode of *Erec* but which the *Partonopeu* poet's more complex purposes in this episode render more evident to the reader. The relationship between the two protagonists who share the *kairos* of recognition is developed with considerable attention to Urraque's virtues and the stages of her rescue of Partonopeu; these stages are dramatized through the techniques of narrow mimesis and limited perspective.

At a certain point (3653 f.) in the course of their postmarital adventures, Erec and Enide, having just escaped from the clutches of the vain and treacherous Count Galoain, ride past a fortified tower, from which the lord of the district espies them. Summoning his squires, the lord, a small but hardy knight, arms himself for battle and issues forth to head off the stranger passing through his domain. He does so; the two knights fight, and Erec, with difficulty, conquers his challenger, who identifies himself as Guivret *le petit* and promises to be Erec's friend and to aid him if ever he hears that the son of Lac is in distress. Thanking his new ally, and refusing an invitation to stay at Guivret's castle so that his wounds can be treated, Erec, with Enide, continues on his way.

Recapitulated in this fashion, the episode seems a typical adventure from the corpus of chivalric romance. But we should not confuse typicality and simplemindedness, and a closer look at this episode will reveal some quite interesting strategies and assumptions on Chrétien's part.

Perhaps the most striking moment in the episode is the description of Guivret racing out from his tower to overtake Erec and do battle with him. Guivret

> . . . sist sor un molt fier cheval,
> qui si grant esfroi demenoit
> que il desoz ses piez fraignoit
> les chailloz plus delivremant
> que mole ne quasse fromant,
> et si li volent de toz sanz,
> estanceles cleres ardanz,
> car des catre piez est a vis
> que tuit fussent de feu espris.
>   [3692–700]

The description is actually that of the horse, or, more accurately, of the horse's headlong motion and its visual effect. Using an unexpectedly agrarian simile, Chrétien endows the image of the horse's hooves grinding down the gravel and bathing themselves in sparks with a hyperbolic and even symbolic quality. This is an evocation of speed, of relentless energy— but also the description of an illusion ("est a vis / que tuit fussent de feu espris"). Between the object described and the audience is the subjective reaction of the narrator (the simile) and the equally subjective reaction of an implied, hypothetical spectator to whom it would seem that the horse's hooves were on fire. The brave little man (". . . il estoit molt de cors petiz, / mes de grant cuer estoit hardiz," 3665–66) astride the horse is, in a way, subsumed here into the horse's energetic action; differently put, the horse and his fiery progress enlarge and externalize the spirit of the lord of the tower who, having seen a strange knight pass near his fortress, decides instantaneously to fight the passerby and as instantaneously puts his resolve into speedy action.[20]

At first sight, then, the mounted knight functions as an emblem of intense, simple, unreflective prowess. We comprehend its impact easily at this level: it is a thrilling but dangerous phenomenon—a pleasure to behold, a peril to experience. Yet, as Chrétien presents the image, it is not as straightforward as first sight suggests, either in impact or meaning. By using the hyperbolic image of the sparks and the mill, and by evoking the responses of a hypothetical spectator, the picture of the charging Guivret calls attention to itself precisely as a picture, a spectacle requiring the audience's imaginative participation. We are discreetly but undeniably made aware of Chrétien's artfulness in creating and presenting his emblem.

Furthermore, as an emblem horse and rider are ambiguous. The little man dwarfed by the big horse ("un grant destrier sor," 3669) suggests that in fact the latter, not the former, is in charge, or, in other words, that Guivret's prowess is running away with him. This impression is supported by the fact that the horse bursts forth into the plain from within the tight enclosure of Guivret's tower ("une haute tor/qui close estoit de mur an tor/et de fossé lé et parfont," 3657-59), offering an image of torrential release and of loss—or at least precariousness— of control over a great force of energy intent on liberating itself. Finally, the simile of the mill grinding corn, by its inapposite evocation of a noncourtly world, may well have added a comic element to the image for its first, courtly audience.

Chrétien is therefore able, with considerable skill, to present "unrefined" prowess in a guise at once strikingly simple and subtly complex. Consequently, we are emotionally involved in the image and at the same time rationally distanced from it by our awareness of its ambiguities. Moreover, the image does not exist frozen in an atemporal vacuum. It is a momentary phase in an unfolding, tautly structured series of events which has no absolute meaning in itself but will achieve its significance at the end of the temporal sequence, when Guivret reaches his goal and tests himself against Erec. We see, in rapid succession, Guivret's *perception* of the strangers (3662-63), the *actions* of arming (3667-75), his *intention* to beat the stranger or be beaten by him (3676-80), the *release* of his galloping departure from the tower (3681-88); but all of this is (in narrative as opposed to emblematic terms) less prowess than the *potential*

of prowess: energy moving toward its actualization in an encounter with an unknown knight. Only when that encounter
results in victory or defeat or some other outcome, such as discovery that the opponent is actually a friend or kinsman—as
happens, for example, in *Ipomedon,* a romance discussed in
chapter 3—can we judge the success or extent of prowess like
Guivret's and thus, in retrospect, establish whether the picture
of the mounted knight kicking up sparks is accurate or ironic.
In other words, Chrétien's emblem of chivalric heroism is not
objective or self-defining;[21] it will acquire its true significance as
the result of a *kairos*—the critical moment of meeting between
Guivret and Erec that will, moreover, be critical only for them
(and, as we shall see, for Enide), and that depends on each being
at a specific place (the head of a bridge, 3758) at a specific
moment.

Even before we see it in action, Chrétien has contrived to
suggest that prowess is not an absolute phenomenon or value.
It exists potentially within the continuum of personal experience
and comes into being when the unfolding careers of single
knights intersect in time and space. In such a heroic encounter
the protagonists give meaning, as well as blows, to each other.

Although Chrétien's subtle creation of multiple contexts for
his prowess-emblem undercuts its autonomy as a symbol and
encourages us to respond to it ambivalently, the fact remains
that Guivret's appearance expresses with great force his openness to and embrace of heroic experience, his absolute orientation toward the goal of armed encounter, while leaving
untouched all questions of character and motive. The next major
part of the episode, the reaction of Enide to the unexpected
and singular advent of the little warrior, concentrates instead on
precisely these last two issues. Enide, who sees Guivret coming
before Erec does because she is riding, as ordered, ahead of her
husband, offers a new perspective on Guivret's headlong motion,
from her position near its goal. Her response, as I have suggested,
establishes the other pole in the dialectic of this scene and, indeed, of twelfth-century chivalric romance as a whole; to the
sequence of Guivret's precisely observed but unexamined actions

stretching out through time and space, Enide opposes a hidden, inner world of analysis, anguish, and crucial decisionmaking. Perceiving alternatives that result from her unique experiences to date, and of necessity working them out in the isolation of her mind and emotions, she arrives at an important personal *choice* which reflects and reveals the character and motive of the chooser (and of noone else), and thus establishes for the reader her undeniable individuality.

Enide perceives Guivret's approach as he had Erec's. But her response is not galvanic action; rather it is shock, leading to simultaneous outer paralysis and an inner turmoil of mental activity. Enide's reflective, self-conscious, "feminine" inner world balances and contrasts with Guivret's "masculine" world of orders crisply given and quickly obeyed (see, for example, 3681-85), decisiveness, and lack of introspection. The two "scenes" operate like the opposed themes of a sonata movement. Within Enide's response, as within Guivret's, there are discernible sections linked in time in an inexorable sequence. After hearing the noise of the approaching horse (3701), she nearly faints; the blood rushes from her veins, and her face becomes as pale as if she were dead (3707). This is one extreme of her reaction: a passivity, induced by fear in the face of danger, leading to a quasi-death, the loss of all power to react.[22]

But Enide's physical response is only part of her total response. As soon as the narrator concludes his description of her outer reaction to the new element of masculine threat which has intruded into her environment, he turns to characterizing her inner state. This also is dominated by a masculine imposition: Erec's command that she not speak to him unless he speaks first. (The origin of this command is the personal crisis to which the marriage of Erec and Enide has come after he abandons the life of prowess to spend all his time with her, and she does not warn him of his resulting loss of honor, for fear of displeasing him. Awakening to a realization of his state, Erec takes Enide off on adventure with him and insists that she ride ahead of him wearing her finest clothes but that she may not speak to him until he speaks to her.) Here is the difference between Enide's situation and Guivret's, for, faced with the imperative of Erec's command, Enide has two choices: to obey or disobey it, to warn Erec of the knight's approach or to keep silent (3714). (Guivret, we will recall, is not presented as faced with a choice of fighting or not fighting when Erec appears, but rather as swinging into action as soon as he sees the stranger.) That is to say, Enide can respond directly to the challenge of experience as it is perceived (as Guivret unreflectively does) or she can evaluate experience in the light of her established relationship with Erec, and be bound by the terms of that relationship rather than by her impulse to give warning of the fast approaching attack. The combination of critical choice and limited time in which to make it gives the moment terrible personal urgency and makes it for Enide a more demanding, even more subjective *kairos* than it is for Guivret.

And yet—to complicate *our* response to the moment even further—it has a symbolic and ritual quality as well, for Enide has already been placed in the position of making an urgent choice several times in the story: first unintentionally, when she discovers that Erec's view of their marriage is destroying his reputation, then intentionally, when Erec arranges their passage through the forest-world of adventures so that Enide rides in front and must repeatedly warn him of the approach of robbers.[23] Thus the scene before us depends for its impact on Guivret's unreflective aggressiveness, but also on Erec's very conscious structuring; both responses to reality contribute to Enide's anguish. Our reaction to the scene balances our sense of it as a unique, personal crisis and as a deliberately repeated thematic *exemplum*. Insofar as Enide is *our* surrogate, we are caught up in the scene's drama; insofar as we are conscious of Erec's artifice in arranging the scene, we respond to him as Chrétien's surrogate and experience a more detached sense of admiration for the art of the creation, as opposed to its content.

Having, at line 3714, stated to herself the crucial question of whether she should warn or obey Erec, Enide moves to the third stage of her response (the first being physical shock, the second, 3708–14, a despairing recapitulation of the condition imposed on her which would prevent her from telling her husband): she takes council with herself—"A li me͏̈ismes s'an consoille" (3715)—and prepares to speak, having, it seems, made a quick decision. But speak she cannot, for her teeth clench and her mouth shuts from fear, so that the voice cannot issue from within her (3718-23). This image of enclosure recalls Guivret's tower and its enclosed fortifications from which Guivret rockets forth. The contrast clarifies the difference between the liberation of unreflective action and the restraints imposed on willed behavior by the complexities of personal history (Guivret, we recall, has no prior history for us) and by resultant inner awareness of one's situation and the consequences of one's deeds.

The disappointment of audience expectation and the use of an image of imprisonment as a contrast for Guivret's release of energy signal a combat, not of charging knights but of opposed intentions within Enide (3724f.). By such parallelism, Chrétien opposes inner and outer experience, yet links them as equally crucial spheres of human activity. We see now that on the outcome of the inner battle will depend the result of the outer.

The narrative mode used to express Enide's inner process of decisionmaking is the Ovidian monologue, developed in twelfth-century courtly narratives like the *Roman d'Eneas* and *Narcisus*. Chrétien modifies the function of the monologue here, for Enide is not scrutinizing her thoughts and emotions to see if she loves Erec (as is usually the case with such passage in earlier works), but rather trying to decide whether to show her love on this occasion by obeying or disobeying her husband. (Compare the Ovidian monologues on the same subject earlier in the romance, 2827f. and 2959f.) She compares the effects on her of the courses of action open to her. To lose Erec through a surprise attack would be terrible (3725-28)—so she should warn him. But she cannot, because, in his anger, he would leave her to fend for herself in the wilderness, "seule et cheitive et esgaree" (3735).

At this point, using the device, common in such monologues, of the statement repeated as a self-directed query, Enide rejects

making her decision on the basis of its immediate effects, declaring, "moi que chaut?" (3735), for she realizes what terrible
long-range effects may attend obeying Erec's order:

> Diax ne pesance ne me faut
> ja mes, tant con je aie a vivre,
> se mes sires tot a delivre
> an tel guise de ci n'estort
> qu'il ne soit mahaigniez a mort.
>   [3736-40]

Enide confronts her *kairos* by balancing her knowlege of
what, in the long run, she wants or dreads against the potential
consequences of her response. She also maintains her awareness
of the present moment and its demands:

> Mes se je tost ne li acoint,
> cist chevaliers qui ci apoint
> l'aura einz mort que il se gart.
> . . . .
> Lasse, trop ai or atandu.
>   (3741-45]

In Chrétien's world, arriving at a personal decision of great
importance requires simultaneous recognition of the significance of both the smallest and the largest units of time: a few
seconds within which to decide and act, and a lifetime in which
to live out the personal consequences of an action. Enide's de-
liberations confirm what Guivret's actions have suggested,
namely, that reality is sequential and unfolds toward moments
of interaction which are crucial for *individuals,* not, as in epics
or salvation history, for all mankind. (We may call this a distinction between subjective and objective *kairoi;* examples of the
latter would be the fall of Troy or the Last Judgment.)

The sense of urgency generated in Enide by a combined awareness of time and of personal interest, together with her observation that Erec is thinking about other things and "lui meïsmes
oblie" (3749)—that he needs her aid to assume the prowess-
identity necessary to survive the impending attack—leads her

finally to speak, to release the perception and conviction she has painfully constructed within her consciousness. This release in words forms a final parallel to Guivret's energetic charge out of his tower; more importantly, it dramatically defines Enide at this particular moment of her life, by her reaction to a crisis, and invites comparison with her very different reactions to the earlier, analogous crisis when she discovered that Erec's absorption in their married life was costing him his honor. (At that point she refrained from telling him out of fear of his wrath—a fear she has now learned to overcome in order to save him.) The fact that this inner crisis represents a "typological" repetition of the work's major turning point[24] reveals to us the intimate connection between the romance's cyclical structure, its adaptation of the chivalry topos to make the spouses' mutual responsibility the key to their happy chivalric marriage, and its attentive rendering of the causal relationship between personal awareness and appropriate individual action.

Once Enide tells Erec what she sees, the episode passes again into the outer world of physical action, there to remain until its conclusion. But Chrétien does not cease playing with and manipulating our responses. His terse description of Enide's words and Erec's response—"Ele li dit; il la menace" (3751)—suggests another crisis, but it never materializes, for we are at once told that Erec is not serious in his threat. He perceives that she loves him and loves her in return (3753-55). Enide has, in effect, passed a test by warning Erec. But if this is the episode's meaning, its climax clearly lies in Enide's monologue, which reduces the battle between Erec and Guivret to the level of anticlimax. Yet, in terms of the adventure plot and the interest generated by the figure of Guivret, the climax must be the battle, and all that precedes it contributes to maintaining and increasing suspense. From still another perspective, the prowess-challenge of Guivret, already ambiguous in meaning, now achieves yet another significance: it is an occasion invented by Chrétien for testing Enide and for revealing the fact of Erec's love for her, submerged though it is beneath the veneer of his displeasure. From this perspective, neither Guivret's motivation nor his emblematic function are crucial, and our attention is drawn away from him to the question, never directly answered by Chrétien, of why Erec has taken Enide off on those adventures, and why he is testing her, thus making possible (or necessary) the existence and peculiar impact of Guivret.[25] In short, as this specific Guivret-moment, or *kairos,* becomes clear from one point of view, it becomes complex and mystifying from another. Chrétien uses this technique to remind us that our perspective on the encounter is as limited, and thus as individual, as that of any of the protagonists.

We come then to the final part of the episode, the battle, with an ever more complicated sense of its meaning and importance, having already been made to consider it from at least three separate viewpoints: Guivret's symbolic significance, Enide's mimetic inner conflict, and the ongoing, emotionally intense but artfully structured relationship between Erec and Enide. The return from reflection and emotional encounter within to the outer world of physical action takes the form of a collision which finally fulfills the energy and speed evoked at the beginning of the episode by Guivret's horse. (Erec has also entered the episode at full tilt; see 3653, 3660.) The battle that follows is a glorification of energy transformed into aggressive and potentially lethal violence: the sparks flying off the helmets from the sword strokes (3776-77) recall Guivret's horse, and if the swords survive the shock of battle, the struggle will go on "tant que l'un morir covenist" (3786). But the battle is also a performance, which the narrator embellishes by means of ironic comments (the knights' shields aren't worth two *escorces* to them [3762-63]; it's hard to do battle without a sword, [3816-18]) and hyperbolic statistics (they fight from *tierce* to *none*).[26] And of course there remains the fact that all the violence is literally gratuitous, unmotivated, unexplained. (We may compare the *chanson de geste,* where the reasons for battle are clear and ideological, our allegiance clearly solicited, individual encounters shorter and, though vivid, less hyperbolic.)

To the extent that the battle between Erec and Guivret is an emblematic representation of male prowess, its ending (Guivret

hits Erec's helmet so hard he breaks his sword) suggests metaphorically the self-defeating (even castrating) implications of
Guivret's furious, undiscriminating action. Yet the scene invites
a different, less programmatic response by emphasizing, at
battle's end Guivret's thoroughly human, nonheroic emotions.
He throws the hilt of his now useless sword far from him in a
gesture of disgust ("mautalant," 3812), and then, in fear (3815),
pleads with Erec for his life. Impersonal, thematic statement
and personal, mimetic counterstatement coexist ironically even
at the episode's high point of action.

Enide, watching the battle, nearly goes mad from grief (3787-
88), and her uncontrolled behavior, aimed at herself (she tears
her hair, 3790-91), reproduces the equally uncontrolled violence the combatants aim at each other. (Again, Chrétien parallels personal and public experience, suggesting the radical
equality of both.) Typically, her violence is carefully motivated
and springs from her self-defining personal relationship with
Erec: she is a *leal dame* (3792), terrified at the possibility of
her husband's destruction. Furthermore, the narrator validates
our involvement in the scene via Enide's emotions by adding,
"et trop fust fel qui la veïst,/se granz pitiez ne l'an preïst"
(3793-94). Enide, in other words, is not only an audience within
the frame, directing our attention to the battle, like a border
figure in a Raphael painting; she is also an element of the total
battle scene, and the figure for whom, in her travail, we feel the
most sympathy. Chrétien has taken the emblematic lady of the
chivalry topos down from her tower[27] and placed her in the
field, thus symbolizing her entry into the world of chivalry not
simply as a distant goal or ideal but as a narrative focus for the
inner, personal realities which impart meaning to, but also offer
a critique of, the exercise of prowess in the external world.

Having thus led us to a very complicated reaction to a very
standard knightly encounter, Chrétien terminates the battle and
moves to the first use of dialogue between the characters. Erec
demands that Guivret admit defeat, and the little knight eventually does, with none too good a grace: "Merci! sire, conquis
m'aiez,/des qu'altrement estre ne peut" (3838-39). Then they

exchange names and reveal their ancestry and worldly estate. Guivret expresses joy at meeting Erec and offers him the hospitality which Erec refuses. Erec does, however, ask for Guivret's future aid if he is in need. The request is granted, and before parting the two men bind each other's wounds with strips torn from their shirts. Only after Chrétien has carefully removed the antagonists from their (and our) involvement in the spectacle of paradigmatic heroic encounter do they assume identities for each other as individuals defined by name, rank, and authority. (Aptly enough, Guivret's authority over his neighbors derives from his awe-inspiring prowess rather than from any hereditary right; 3848–55.) The effect is to emphasize the loss of personal identity (and of the reactions it might inspire) during a prowess encounter. Battle respects neither private destiny nor individual perspective; its only important criterion is strength, its only meaningful identities, winner and loser. Once the prowess world has ceased to exist, thanks to Guivret's surrender, its inhabitants can assume individuality and, on the basis of personal identity, come to terms with each other. Here, since each knight is a lord of comparable rank and influence, they can accept each other as peers on a friendly basis, and even forge an alliance.

Chrétien here makes two contrasting, even paradoxical, points about prowess which recur repeatedly in twelfth-century chivalric romance; (1) prowess is depersonalizing in a world where personal identity is crucial;[28] (2) nonetheless, adventure-prowess is not an ideological violence and, once it arrives at a decision in its own restricted world of experience, does not hinder friendship between combatants whose personal identities were, after all, obscured while they fought. We are not dealing here with a sequence of cause-effect (prowess causing friendship), but with a metamorphosis of relationship, from combat to friendship, once the prowess impulse in its raw state has been indulged and surmounted.

Chivalric prowess of the most basic type takes the form of an aggressive response to any other knight one encounters outside the confines of the setting that gives one social identity (Guivret's tower, in this case). To venture outside the tower is to reject life's protections—its schedules and rituals—for life's challenges (the forest of adventure),[29] and unreflective prowess meets these challenges with uniform violence, making no distinctions between friend and foe, that is, refusing to consider questions of identity before, as opposed to after, fighting. Adventure prowess at its most elemental does not even involve the affirmation of one's own heroic identity, as it does in epic. The knight may identify himself and take credit, or not, at the end of the battle; the option is his. In more motivated forms of prowess, identity is, of course, important, as something to be affirmed or obtained for oneself and recognized in others. By means of Guivret's unmotivated attack on Erec, Chrétien confronts us with the prowess impulse in its most basic form—indiscriminate, ethically neutral, mindlessly intent on self-aggrandizement but courting self-destruction instead—so that we can distinguish between the impulse itself and the personal motives or social norms that, when imposed upon prowess, make it a moral, beneficial activity.

The process of refining Guivret's impulsive prowess is underway by the end of the episode. Once he and Erec have established a nonadversary relationship in the present, on the basis of knowledge of each other's identity, they can create a paradigm of future relations between them in which prowess becomes subordinated to, and an instrument of, their friendship. Guivret will not fight Erec, but help him instead, if he is in distress. The friendship of Erec and Guivret, that is, will be tested in time. The medium of testing will be prowess, now operating as a prowess of *service,* based on the perception that an identified friend needs help, not simply as a visceral reaction to the appearance of it-matters-not-what knight. Thus Guivret's prowess, which first functions in *Erec* as the inadvertent instrument whereby Enide expressed her personal love for Erec by serving him, now is to become the deliberate instrument whereby Guivret expresses an analogous, personal, masculine devotion. For both Enide and Guivret, perception—an inner, subjective capacity—is the crucial element determining action that expresses or takes account of individuality. Enide, challenged by

Guivret's aggression, learns the nature of her self-defining love for Erec and perceives how to express it most meaningfully; Guivret, having come to know his victorious opponent as a particular person, will use his knowledge to modify and control his aggressive impulse in any future encounter with Erec.[30]

The more closely one examines the Guivret episode, the more complicated it becomes, and simultaneously the more interesting, for reasons of the parallels drawn between various parts of the episode, and the light Chrétien sheds on the different, yet linked, spheres of human experience represented by prowess and by the love relationship. In the course of the episode, prowess evolves from a random and potentially destructive force to a discriminating activity, potentially contributing to social bonds and the welfare of other, particular individuals. Seen in this light, the episode is a statement about the possibility of ordering and controlling an impulse. Instead of typifying the opposition of all men to each other, it demonstrates the allegiance of specific individuals to each other. In a sense, Erec's victory over Guivret is a symbolic victory of the knight over an impulse in himself; the chivalric protagonist, seeking to recover a public reputation he lost by opting for an exclusively private life, here conquers a type of prowess inimical to individuality and inner choice, thereby rendering the aggressive impulse capable of service as well as disruption. The metamorphosis of prowess underlies the contrast between Chrétien's image of Guivret riding forth to challenge Erec, and the later image, at the end of the episode, of the former opponents "par amor et par franchise" (3903) binding up each others' wounds (3904-06). Chrétien states the change clearly when he says, "onques de si dure bataille/ne fu si dolce dessevraille" (3901-02).

Between the initiation of the battle in Guivret's aggressive impulse and its outcome in the control of that impulse we are immersed in the (apparently) completely opposed world of a woman's inner crisis, springing from her love of her husband and her need to decide whether she can best serve herself and him by obeying or disobeying a command he has given her. By juxtaposing these two parts of the episode, and in fact making Enide's inner crisis its central portion, Chrétien explores the chivalry topos and re-creates it as a complex and nuanced statement about individuality.

What Enide must decide, prompted by Guivret's appearance, is what the priorities of her situation are; her awareness, stimulated anew by the impending attack, that she values Erec's life beyond her own security (or rather that Erec's survival is the basis of her happiness) leads her to warn him to defend himself. Her words to her husband also represent her triumph over the physical and emotional paralysis inspired by fear at the sight of Guivret. Her relationship to Erec has exposed her to the challenge of experience (in the form of the charging knight), and now her awareness of what she must do if the relationship is to survive endows her with sufficient self-control to master her emotions and meet the challenge effectively.

In Chrétien's presentation, prowess (now a symbol of basic, unrefined human aggressiveness toward the outside world and of the challenges that world thrusts at the individual) is no longer an idealized and playful form of masculine behavior which inspires love (as in Geoffrey of Monmouth's paradigm). Instead, as an intrusive fact of life, it complicates the love relationship, stimulating an inner crisis which forces the lover to a new level of awareness of his or her desire, to resultant choice between alternative actions, and then to self-control—all finally issuing in behavior which defines the nature and priorities of loving, as the individual understands it. Enide's warning is, in a sense, the core of the episode, for it is the moment of *choice,* forced upon one by a combination of unique past history and the event of the moment as perceived by one person. Enide's choice is both the full expression of her identity and the link between her inner world and the outer worlds of Erec and Guivret. That is, love does not simply inspire prowess, but contributes to prowess a reason for existence and thus aids in the refinement of aggression to incorporate elements of identity and service.

By witnessing Enide's response to Guivret's attack, we also

come to realize that the fact of prowess must be further defined in terms of the unique perspective from which it is seen by individuals, that is, persons whose response is based not simply on sensory perception or accepted behavioral code, but on the interaction of perception with the unique events of past personal history. Furthermore, we see that as each individual confronts the world outside himself, he must not only face the challenge to self-aware action but also face it at a specific time and place, so that decision making must take these specifics into account. Enide's crisis has two elements: the decision she must make and the crucial moment (*kairos*) at which she must make it. That is, hers is a *narrative,* not simply a moral, crisis. Earthly space and time become the medium in which Enide must act. But it is also clear that, in Chrétien's narrative moment, space and time derive their significance from Enide's situation; they have a subjective, rather than an objective, meaning here. The *kairos* represented in the Guivret episode is Enide's *kairos* precisely because of her personal history and relationship to Erec. The episode, in short, offers a working model of reality defined as and by the individual's unique interaction with the world around him or her, a model in which time and space are organized around and by subjective perceptions and reactions.

In the course of the Guivret episode, control is a key factor. Enide controls her emotions and arrives, in time, at a decision to tell Erec of the threat to him, despite his order enjoining silence. Then Erec, after defeating Guivret, creates an arrangement with him which controls and channels the aggressive impulse so that it can serve rather than (or as well as) threaten. Furthermore, Erec has exerted important prior control over the form the episode will take by placing Enide in a position where she can be his sentinel, and help him earn martial honor, yet simultaneously placing a barrier between her perception and her action, in the form of the command that she can only ignore after an inner struggle to decide whether obedience or assistance has priority in her relationship with Erec. By means of this *engin* Erec manipulates Enide in order to raise her consciousness about her feelings and duties toward the man she loves, so that she will not fail him (and herself) as she did, prompted by fear, when Erec was losing his honor by staying home with her.

By presenting prowess to us in the many ways he does in the Guivret episode, Chrétien states in effect that it cannot be assessed in one way only, but rather its meaning changes with the circumstances in which it operates and is perceived. Guivret's reaction to an armed knight entering his territory is very different from Enide's reaction to Guivret's appearance in her field of vision. Guivret's prowess means something different to Erec at the end of the episode than at the beginning, not simply because he has defeated it, but because he has enlisted its aid for future occasions. Guivret on a spark-surrounded charger impresses us differently from Guivret binding Erec's wounds. Chrétien's refusal to maintain a constant attitude or point of view—his insistence on presenting different perspectives *seriatim* or even simultaneously—reflects the assumption, implicit in the episode, that there is no objective meaning of reality, of deeds done, of time passing. Rather, each individual defining himself and creating his destiny by his interaction with experience will see "reality" and the deeds which comprise the chivalric narrative in a different way.

To the extent that the Guivret episode is typical of twelfth-century chivalric romance, it suggests that the romances are constructed of linked critical moments that define their characters as individuals by exploring the dynamic relationship, inevitably differing from person to person, between inner and outer worlds of experience. The most dramatic moments in chivalric romance are those *kairoi* in which self-awareness undergoes revolutionary change, leading to a profound modification of the basic desires which shape the actions and goals of a protagonist. That these moments are almost invariably purely private, having their effect only on one person—unlike some great turning point in an epic, where the fates of armies hang in the balance—means that they also become studies in individual psychology or pathology and greatly heighten our sensitivity to the domain of individual experience as it expands in every direction through the adventure world of chivalric romance.

The second paradigmatic episode I have chosen for analysis contains a revolutionary *kairos* and recounts a turning point in the career of its hero far more climactic than is the battle of Erec and Guivret for *Erec and Enide*. The episode is found in lines 5173–6234 of *Partonopeu de Blois*. It recounts the meeting between Partonopeu and Urraque, the sister of Partonopeu's mistress, Mélior, empress of Byzantium, in the waste forest of Ardenne, to which the knight has withdrawn in despair at having betrayed Mélior. Once Urraque recognizes her sister's *ami* beneath the appearance of the madman he has become, she pretends to be a messenger of reconciliation from Mélior and thereby dissuades Partonopeu from suicide. From this turning point emerge all the subsequent stages of his recovery, culminating in his winning a tournament of which the prize is Mélior herself—a model display of chivalry in action.[31]

The differences between this episode and the Guivret episode in *Erec* are immediately apparent. Chrétien builds his scene around a chance meeting of combatants, whereas here there is a meeting (likewise chance) of friends, linked by their shared bond to a third person. Chrétien, through Guivret, makes a statement about the socialization and control of elemental aggressive energy; the *Partonopeu* poet presents a hero who has abandoned even the desire to survive, and shows how the rekindling of a sense of self, and of a desire for and hope in eventual self-fulfillment, is the necessary prelude to the minimal aggressive impulse necessary to exist as something other than a self-destructive isolate. The logical conclusion of this episode lies not within it (as is the case with the Guivret episode) but at the end of the romance, when Partonopeu, his inner world restored, finds the instrument of fulfilled desire in the optimally controlled prowess of the tournament. Using a similar narrative movement from isolation to social incorporation, and betraying a similar interest in the relationship between external experience and the inner life, the two poets set problems which hinge, in a sense, on opposite phenomena: too much (or too uncontrolled) prowess versus too little. Both episodes, however, point us toward the same, individual-centered view of human experience.

The episode of Partonopeu's meeting with Urraque falls into two sections. The first part, preceding the forest encounter proper, explores the inner life of the protagonist, presenting a rhetorically copious, psychologically perspicuous picture of the effect of a love crisis on the awareness *and* behavior of a chivalric hero. (This part therefore forms a longer analogue to the section of the Guivret episode given over to Enide's inner crisis.) Partonopeu's sense of failure, loss, and guilt, after Mélior has angrily dismissed him from her castle in the fabulous Byzantine city of Chef d'Oire because he has tried, against her command, to see her face, prompts a mental and spiritual decline that isolates him from the world of friends and kin to which he has returned in France. In a soliloquy (5203-58) uttered as soon as he sets foot on French soil, Partonopeu sees himself as a self-betrayer ("Trahitres sui, si sui trahis," 5213), asks why he didn't die before meeting Mélior (5205-12), and contrasts his own viciousness with the virtues of his lost beloved (5214-24). His loss is such that he should be dead (5226); indeed, he is dead and alive, and it is fitting that one who has betrayed an *amie* should die (by remembering his treason) and live again:

> Ensi le doit la mors destruire:
> Sovent soit vis et sovent mors.
> Molt ait dolors et pou confors!
> Ses cuers l'ocie en ramembrant
> Sa trahison et son dul grant.
> [5252-56]

What has died in Partonopeu is the possibility of attaining the fulfilled self the vision of which he had within him—the inner image of himself knighted by Mélior and united to her in marriage, when he has come of age. The gap between present and future selves—always a point of tension in chivalric romance, as we shall see—has become apparently unbridgeable because of his act of *folie* (5225), which remains present to him through memory and grates terribly against his equally strong memory of Mélior's worth and his former happiness. (Memory is thus the catalyst of awareness as awareness is of despair.)

This key word, *folie,* which means both "folly" and "mad-ness" in twelfth-century French, links Partonopeu's betrayal of Mélior and his melancholy withdrawal to the forest, after he has gradually assumed the appearance of a madman (5392–404); the latter is an emblematic, external reproduction of the former— inner *folie* (the decision to try to see Mélior) acted out. In killing the possibility of imagined future happiness, Partonopeu has destroyed and lost part of himself; his identity is therefore not what it was before the crisis, and this fact, too, is mirrored externally in the change of his appearance soon after: with his long hair, uncut nails, and pale, dirty body, he is no longer ex-ternally "recognizable" as the young knight of Blois conducting his life in accord with his desired (and now impossible, he be-lieves) destiny: ". . . nus connoistre nel pooit" (5404).

In another respect, Partonopeu's withdrawal to the forest symbolically re-creates his inner state. Like the mad behavior of Chrétien's Yvain in an analogous situation which probably inspired the *Partonopeu* poet, it involves stripping away and fleeing from the accoutrements of civilization, to reflect the hero's alienation from the public, socially defined self which, entangled in past and present family and feudal relationships, betrayed the private self and its vision of future fulfillment. (Partonopeu has been misled by his mother, his king, and the bishop of Paris, all of whom believe they are acting in his best in-terest in convincing him Mélior is an evil spirit. They cannot understand his private world; they can only define him in terms of the received and social identity they have given him, not in terms of the inner, destiny-identity he has given himself by loving Mélior.[32]) There in the forest, alone, isolated from so-ciety by choice, the hero can act out the self-destructive im-pulse which has destroyed his "best" inner self by offering his entire person and life to the wild, destructive forces of nature. (Partonopeu announces his death wish in a soliloquy addressed to God and to death itself; the latter he blames for killing the good and sparing the miserable; 5417–80.)

In other words, Partonopeu's decline into a suicidal, melancholy madman in the forest expresses metaphorically his feelings about himself, and about the social milieu which has trapped him into self-betrayal. The poet here suggests that our inner awareness shapes our outer behavior in its own image—a conviction I have already suggested may underlie some of Abelard's apparent eccentricities in his autobiographical letter. As an image of inner awareness determining external action and conviction, Partonopeu's behavior is equal and opposite to Enide's salutary reaction to crisis in the Guivret episode. (It is interesting to compare the Ovidian, agitated inner dialogue of Enide with the bitter, plangent declamations of Partonopeu. The idiom of chivalric narrative was sophisticated enough to allow for different styles of mimesis for different inner states.)

Finally, Partonopeu's actions represent a negation or inversion of the chivalry topos: with love destroyed, the aggressive impulse to dominate through prowess, which love at once intensifies and focuses,[33] no longer has reason to exist. The suicidal impulse, or repudiation of even just enough resistance to destructive forces to survive, represents a radical excision of that aggressive instinct which interacts with love-awareness to form true chivalry. Denied both its love inspiration and (thanks to Partonopeu's rejection of the social bonds which betrayed him) social framework, the will to fight has, in effect, died within Partonopeu.

Weakened by grief and self-imposed hunger, Partonopeu escapes his household with the aid of his squire, a pagan lad he had captured in an earlier battle. The boy insists on going with his master, out of love, even to death:

> —Sire, ce li dit li meschins,
> O vos morrai, c'en est la fins.
> Certes je ne m'en puis partir,
> Ne por vivre, ne por morir. . . .
>   [5643–46]

Furthermore, Guilemot (the squire) offers to allow himself to be baptized as a way of winning Partonopeu's acquiescence:

> . . . me lairai je baptisier
> Por savoir se m'avries plus chier,
> Ke me laissies od vos aler
> Les mals et la mort endurer.
>   [5651-54]

Until now, Guilemot has resisted all attempts to convert him from his worship of Appollin, and his offer, like his desire to accompany his pathetic, deranged master to death, is a clear token of complete loyalty to Partonopeu, the significance of which I will discuss shortly.

Partonopeu accedes to Guilemot's requests but, after having had the squire baptized, tricks him by stealing away while Guilemot (now christened Anselot) is asleep. He rides into the wilderness alone and abandons his horse (5792), which is then attacked by a "grans lions" (5796). As the second, climactic part of this episode of *Partonopeu de Blois* begins, the horse's cries reach a ship becalmed off the coast; the unnamed lady of the ship and a sailor possessed of a magic charm to calm the beasts of the wilderness go ashore and discover Partonopeu. The lady pleads with the recalcitrant wild man to let her help him, but he refuses and will not even reveal his name. When the damsel tells him she is Urraque, he faints. Now she recognizes him and, when he recovers his senses, uses her ready wit to convince him he has done sufficient penance for his misdeed and can hope for forgiveness. Thanking Urraque for bringing him back to his former self, Partonopeu agrees to leave Ardenne for her island, Salence—a *locus amoenus* on which she has "molt bon chastel" (6209)—where he can recover his strength.

The recognition scene, often complicated by the hero's deliberate or (as here) unintentional disguise, is a stock feature of the romance plot in all ages. (One need think only of the *Odyssey,* Xenophon's *Ephesian Tale,* and Pasternak's *Doctor Zhivago* to realize its wide diffusion.) Wherever it occurs, it focuses our attention on the uniqueness of personal identity and the fragility of personal relationships, dependent as they are on perceiving identity despite circumstances that obscure it. The

Partonopeu poet enriches the encounter of Partonopeu and Urraque by the full exercise of his complex art, deliberately offering us a variety of perspectives on the moment of recognition in order to complicate our response to the situation and characters. This sophisticated treatment of a climactic, emotion-laden turning point in the romance heightens our awareness that any moment in life, however important, is susceptible of multiple interpretations reflecting the personal points of view of participants and observers. The "reality" of an event comprises the sum total of individual experiences and outlooks.

I distinguish *four* perspectives on the recognition scene in *Partonopeu*: *First,* a *structural perspective* based on direct and ironic parallels between the episode and earlier moments in the hero's life. (In the Guivret episode, there is a similar relationship between Guivret's approach and earlier challenges that prompted Enide to warn Erec, as well as a parallel between this situation and the one in which Enide failed to warn Erec of the subtler danger to his honor, uxoriousness.) *Second,* an *ethical perspective* arising from the episode's presentation of exemplary values and emotions and its exploration of their effect on human relationships which, in turn, determine individual self-fulfillment. (In the Guivret episode, this is the level at which Guivret is an emblem of prowess controlled and socialized, the result of love's self-awareness.) *Third,* a *mimetic perspective,* by which the poet uses the meeting and recognition to present a view of spatial and temporal reality dependent on individual perception. (Chrétien similarly exploits limited amounts of time and space, and Enide's perception of them, in the Guivret episode.) *Fourth,* an *artistic perspective,* embodying the poet's techniques for establishing atmosphere and regulating our involvement with or detachment from his fictional world. (Chrétien's artistry works similarly in the Guivret episode, as we have seen.)

1. The structural perspective of the Ardenne scene comprises manifold balancings and oppositions between it and other parts of the romance. First, Partonopeu's return to Ardenne to die brings him back to the place where his love affair with Mélior began. He thinks that the beginning-place will be the end as

well. As it turns out, the place of the birth of love will be for
Partonopeu a place of rebirth, thanks to Urraque. As Mélior
took the young hunter away from the hunt to the magical city
of Chef D'Oire, so her sister, Urraque, will take him to the analogously unusual isle of Salence. Urraque's ship thus recalls the
ship Mélior sent to Ardenne for Partonopeu. These similarities
throw the differences between the two key points in Partonopeu's life into high relief. At the beginning of his love career,
he was the naive huntsman, whose pursuit of the beasts in the
forest represented a state of unreflective confrontation of life
and the attempt to overcome it by external force.[34] This is the
state of what we might call pre-awareness, associated with those
who do not know love, its mysteries, pains, complexities, and
joys—those, in short, who have not discovered the existence of
the power within, awakened by love, to imagine a future self-
perfection, which must then be sought by means of self-control,
suffering, and constant dedication. When Partonopeu returns to
Ardenne, his self-awareness, in all its negative intensity, has
come to dominate his life and shape his actions. The hunter has
become the hunted, by his own desire, and wishes to be destroyed by the beasts he formerly conquered.

At the same time, the contrast between Mélior and Urraque is
also illuminating. Mélior used magic, the magic of the youthful
vision of love, shrouded in secrecy, avoiding the world, and
making absolute demands on the beloved;[35] eventually, the
magic failed and exposed the lovers to the daylight world and to
the misery of parting. Urraque uses what we might call the
"fallen" magic of *engin* to bring Partonopeu to rebirth and to
make the second Ardenne adventure a parallel rather than a
contrast to the first. Her use of *engin* derives from her pity for
Partonopeu and her desire to serve him and her sister. Her
benevolent dishonesty, furthermore, balances Partonopeu's
equally benevolent use of deceit to escape from his squire,
Anselot, so that the boy will not share what he expects to be his
fate in the wasteland. Partonopeu's "betrayal" of Anselot, who
loves him, recalls his earlier betrayal of Mélior, who loved
him.[36] Partonopeu has so poisoned his awareness of himself in

the first betrayal, that, in order to strip away all other relationships as a part of his self-punishment, he must repeat his failing with his last companion. By using similar deception to reverse Partonopeu's suicidal impulse, Urraque begins the process of his resocialization. Her motivation to use deception and Partonopeu's diverge, underscoring the way in which individual intention puts a personal stamp on each instance of a reiterated pattern of human actions.

The parallels and contrasts among Ardenne, Chef d'Oire, and Salence function analogously within the story. Chef d'Oire is a city full of marvellous palaces, containing all the goods and pleasures a sophisticated society can offer, while Salence is an isolated spot where fertile nature provides most of the beauty. When Partonopeu first saw Chef d'Oire, the absence of any other people gave the place an air of fantasy and also a suspicion of sterility or artifice, the exclusion of nature. Under the patronage of the forgiving, pitying Urraque, the world of Salence offers sympathetic, re-creating nature as an alternative to Mélior's glittering, fragile palace of enchantment and art. This is a fitting representation of the difference between Urraque's human affection for Partonopeu (see 6316–18) and her sister's soaring vision of love that demands from its adherents absolute obedience to extreme conditions—the lovers' ignorance of and isolation from each other—with total disaster as the price of failure.

The structural perspective of the Ardenne episode underscores the element of continuity in human life, suggests how even in apparently "cyclical" experience the effects of inner, private awareness and the influence of the unique individuals with whom we come in contact give linear and individual shape to our lives. Partonopeu descends into self-loathing and despondency, out of which, through the agency of Urraque's pity and human understanding allied with *enginos* shrewdness, he recovers a new vision of possible self-fulfillment and a consequent return of the desire to live and the impulse to work for reconciliation with the object of his desires. The chivalric poet has set up his network of correspondences and recalls within this

scene to demonstrate his subscription to the idea that the external world, as we experience it, takes on much of its meaning
because of the personal perspective from which we view it.
Partonopeu's despair transforms Ardenne from "adventure's
start" to "adventure's end," but Urraque's more potent virtues
transform it again into a place of rebirth, paralleling the beginning of Partonopeu's great love-adventure. (These radically
different perspectives on Ardenne reflect the participants'
radically different perspectives on the earlier scene that begets
this meeting: Partonopeu's attempt to see Mélior at Chef d'Oire.
To Partonopeu, this earlier moment is a permanent fall, a source
of irreversible self-hatred. Urraque sees it compassionately, as a
problem to be alleviated by *engin* and finally solved by Mélior's
forgiveness.[37]) Salence, on the other hand, reflects the fact that
Partonopeu has passed into the control of Urraque's benevolence and, through her assistance, has become reconciled to
himself to the point where, freed from despair, he is ready to
overcome obstacles in order to obtain the self-fulfillment he
had thought lost forever.

2. The significance of Salence suggests the second, ethical
perspective on this episode. The *Partonopeu* poet constructs a
paradigm in which human virtues, and the feelings on which
they are based, break the barriers enclosing the self and establish therapeutic personal relationships between individuals.
Strengthened by the sympathy and actions of another human
being, the hero can begin to control his innermost existence
and resume his private quest for self-fulfillment.

The ethical paradigm begins to take shape at a point in the
episode we might easily overlook, as it involves not Partonopeu
but his horse. To the horse, the world of the wasteland represents purely and simply a most hostile and threatening environment. Partonopeu has sought this world as a setting that mirrors
his loss of control over his desired destiny and therefore his loss
of his chosen identity; the beasts whom he expects to devour
him will only be reproducing his own self-destructive behavior.
The horse finds Ardenne unwelcome and is fearful—but this
fear stimulates the frantic courage and strength with which the
horse kills the lion that menaces it (5815–26).

Now the poet tells us, in a curious aside, that the lion needs to be angry to attack, so if he sees a peaceful beast (like the horse) he beats himself with his tail until he is angry enough to attack him (5801-14): "Tant est gentils et debonaire/Qu'il ne seit sens coros mal faire" (5807-08). The lion, that is, does not always rely on aggressive instincts. Faced with beasts who are *hardis* (tigers and bears, 5810-11) he responds to their *orguel* with a spontaneous desire to challenge them (we think of Guivret); but with the animals he needs to kill when he is hungry ("familhos," 5798), he must stimulate prowess as a matter of self-preservation. The horse and lion, then, represent two kinds of prowess: one stimulated automatically by fear, the other knowingly induced out of self-interest. Both contrast with the condition of Partonopeu, who, in abandoning his desire to survive, has placed himself below the beasts. Similarly, the love and loyalty of Partonopeu's infidel squire, Anselot, who will give up both his faith and his life for Partonopeu, serves, like the loyalty of Yvain's lion, to indict the Christian knight for having been disloyal to a woman who had offered him love and the promise of supreme private and public fulfillment—much more, that is, than Partonopeu offered Anselot.

Consciously or not, the poet is here making a very important point about his (and his age's) view of man. The discovery that the individual is a unique microcosmic unit with his own inner reality organized by private awareness has both positive and negative implications. On the secular plane of the romances, emphasis is placed on the lifelong striving for self-perfection and on taming basic impulses like prowess so that they serve this quest. But the discovery of individuality also brings with it a new understanding of the possibility of self-destruction when negative self-awareness (self-alienation), leads to a loss of the desire to strive, that is, when it leads to despair. In the state of despair the individual, aware that the perfected self he desired to become is now lost and dead, is ready, even eager, to allow the world to destroy the fallen self that remains. Between these two extremes a whole gamut of human response to awareness can be explored. Chivalry, with its control of experience and organization of impulses in subordination to the individual's quest for the highest fulfillment of *joie* in love, explores the upper reaches of the earthly perfection of the self. On the other hand, the horse and the lion, whose opposed but equally self-preserving forms of prowess contrast with Partonopeu's suicidal bent, clarify the extent to which the inner life of the individual can make external behavior descend to a level below the beasts. (The equivalents of these responses in twelfth-century religious experience are, respectively, the quest for union with God and despair at one's ability to be saved. The twelfth century explored both religious extremes; it also placed new stress on confession and penance, the sacramental means by which to escape from despair. The moment of contrition, when hope in God's love returns, is the religious *kairos* most analogous to the meeting of Partonopeu and Urraque, which reverses Partonopeu's decline by creating hope in Mélior's love.)

Partonopeu's self-induced, desperate situation can only be ameliorated by a change in self-perception. The poet now sets out to show how such a change can be brought about. The horse's instinct of self-preservation which leads to his conquest of the lion provides a starting point; his distress cries bring help to the scene. The implication is clear: desire for self-preservation is the necessary prerequisite to subduing the adventure world and establishing contact with other individuals.

The hero's meeting with another person who can serve him and affect his destiny is the next stage in achieving self-fulfillment. Urraque and her sailors respond to the horse's cries, and to Ardenne itself, as an occasion to help another (5851–68); the old sailor, Maruc, knowing how inhospitable the forest is to a lone wanderer, proposes:

> S'or volent nostre compaingnon,
> Si soient pris li aviron;
> Tost i seron ja al batel,
> Car tens avons suef et bel.
>   [5865–68]

Thus the impulse to serve and save is crucial as a moral, personal response to the enunciation of need by another. We may also note that the same incalculable fortune (*aventure*) which keeps the beasts from eating Partonopeu has becalmed the ship; if the sailors are to help whomever is in need, they must row, that is, overcome fortune's grip.[38] The desire to challenge Ardenne's hold on another mortal finds its reflection or metaphor in the charm of Maruc, which renders wild beasts harmless (5873–86). (His charm also recalls by contrast Mélior's magic, with its more personal end and antisocial manifestation: the empty, enchanted city.) Since, as we have seen, the forest represents, from Partonopeu's perspective, an outer analogue or expression of his own self-destructive impulses, which he is willing to have devour him (that is, bring him to the complete loss of the self and person he can no longer stand), the charm which calms the beasts, like the impulse to reach out to another, overcomes the effects of that isolation (physical or spiritual) which endangers survival.

It is worth noting that the *Partonopeu* poet is here expressing a paradox central to both the imagined world of chivalric romance and the world of the individual as it was emerging in the consciousness of twelfth-century society. The paradox is that the self can only survive and prosper as a private essence if it reaches out beyond itself, becomes social (through love, comradeship, bonds of mutual service), and thus orders the outer world in ways beneficial to inner and outer experience. (Saint Bernard states the same perception in religious terms when he stresses, in *On the Love of God* and *The Steps of Humility,* the love of all men in God as a necessary stage in the soul's ascent to the love of and union with God.) The alternatives are the external, prowess-isolation of Guivret, to whom all men are adversaries, or the inner despair-isolation of Partonopeu, who can no longer find a reason for survival.

Urraque's interest in and sympathy for the barely human creature she finds in Ardenne is thus a focusing of and response to Maruc's general impulse to help those in difficulty. As the party moves through the forest, the beasts watch, frozen in fear (5907–08; 5915–18); the poet dwells on the destructive and venomous forces here paralyzed, not by prowess, but by an "enchanteor" (5907) impelled by desire to help another mortal. However, it is left to Urraque to find Partonopeu himself, whom she discovers because of "un sospir qu'il a gete" (5951). Her first reaction is to shrink back in fear ("por paor un pou l'eschive," 5954), but then she comes forward and, finding him to be human, reacts in a way which moves the ethical perspective of the episode to its next stage: she overcomes her fear by the urgency of her concern for the stranger, as soon as she realizes he is no beast but "alcuns chaitis" (5974). The nature of her concern is manifested in her wish that God will save the being she calls her friend ("Amis, fait ele, Dex vos saut," 5975; compare 5980). She then begs him to tell her his problem, "por De amor" (5983), so that she may help him:

> Ne me celes vostre aventure;
> Sachies de voir, ja n'iert si dure,
> Ne vos en face alcun socors.
> > [5995-97]

Partonopeu refuses, again declaring that he is too far gone to be helped, that "J'ai deservi si bien la mort/Ke je n'ai cure de confort" (6001-02) and that he wishes only to be left alone to die, not bothered by her. Urraque now reduces her request to a desire to know his name and whence he has come (6007-12), and Partonopeu bitterly replies that his only and true name is traitor (6017-24); he does not wish to know hers. Undaunted, the damsel says she will tell hers; she is of royal lineage and deserves better of him than to cry over him and be thus rebuffed:

> J'ai d'un roialme la saisine
> Et sui bien pres d'estre roine.
> Et vos me faites ci plorer,
> Si me veez vostre parler. . . .
> > [6035-38]

At this point she names herself and the episode reaches its long prepared-for climax.

Aside from the scene's tantalizing suspense and carefully delineated momentaneity (or second-by-second rehearsal), its main feature is the confrontation, in all its tension, of two completely opposed responses to life, one self-enclosed in a shell of despair and self-hatred, the other reaching out in hope of touching and affecting the life of another person. Partonopeu's harsh manner and words—"Vos me destorbes malement;/Dame, car siwes vostre gent" (6005-06)—grate against Urraque's pleas, which are suffused with a glowing, almost sentimental tenderness. The audience's hopes and feelings are all with the woman, but her love and pity are thwarted, even in her attempt to coax from Partonopeu his name, the minimal confession of identity which will enable her to transform their chance meeting into a personal relationship. Only Urraque's determination leads her to speak her own name; the shock of recognition brings new grief to Partonopeu (6043), but also enables Urraque to come close enough to the unconscious man to detect Partonopeu beneath the raggedness of the recluse.

Urraque displays a combination of charitable sentiment and insistence upon making herself an individual to Partonopeu by naming herself (even if he refuses to do the same). The recognition which crowns her efforts is, however, no more than an opportunity: her pity can now be focused on doing something to save a man whose history, and therefore whose needs, she knows. We have again arrived at the moment of awareness—in this case, Urraque's awareness of who Partonopeu is and what she must do. At once she lies to him, and the long process of his remaking begins. Openness (Urraque's willingness to come ashore), pity, determination all provide the foundation of which *engin,* the ingenious manipulation of facts and lives to order and control reality, is the crowning virtue. It is also a thoroughly pragmatic virtue, involving not only the initial lie, but many subsequent, supporting falsehoods as well: Partonopeu asks Urraque if she is leading him into "falz espoir" (6088), and she replies "de mentir/Ne vos vuel je mie servir" (6097-98); later, she sends Partonopeu false letters, ostensibly from Mélior, to keep him motivated. But since Mélior does indeed still love Partonopeu (as she herself confirms, 6655-64), Urraque's *engin* is both deceitful *and* accurate, an ambiguity that makes it problematic as well as effective.

The progression of Urraque's personal qualities provides the antidote for the terrible effects of negative self-awareness, but only because they are coordinated within *her* and because their object is Partonopeu; the impact these characters have on each other depends on their uniqueness: particular past experiences, particular inner awareness, particular reactions to specific segments of time and space. This brings me to the third, *mimetic* perspective on this episode, the way in which the poet gives to his narrative turning point a context of experienced reality and makes us see Partonopeu's crisis as an expression of how the concept of the individual organizes the adventure-world of chivalric romance.

3. The mimetic perspective of the Ardenne episode comprises the poet's use of narrow mimesis to present the progressive stages and personal effects of the episode's central act of recognition. The *Partonopeu* poet, like the author of the *Life of Christina of Markyate,* apprehends human experience sensorily and shows how each person interprets sensory data in the light of his own history and situation. Put most simply, it is necessary for Partonopeu and Urraque to be precisely the people they are before the latter can help the former; whatever the combination of fortune and other factors (such as the horse's instinctive actions and the general benevolence of the sailors) involved, the meeting, when it comes, takes on a particular importance because of the subjective reactions and perspectives of its protagonists.

Partonopeu is where he is because of his past experience, while Urraque recognizes what he has become and why because of her personal involvement in Partonopeu's unique past. Urraque's tolerant benevolence, wisdom, and ability to control situations through *engin* can help Partonopeu now, in the wilderness, though she was unable to aid him at Chef d'Oire when he betrayed Mélior. The virtues Urraque possesses could not have the same effect on Partonopeu singly that they do united in her (note, for example, how Anselot's pity and devotion fail for lack of guile), nor could the same combination of virtues be as salutary for Partonopeu in a stranger who lacked the information about, and feeling for, the outcast that Urraque's special perspective gives her.

In other words, once again a woman must act at a specific moment—a *kairos*—to save a man. The importance of limited, human, individual perspective in the scene is underscored by Urraque's gradual discovery of Partonopeu's identity and by the effect on him of her own delayed identification. Facts emerge gradually, moment by moment, across a diminishing distance in space, and emerge from personal observation and revelation, not from "objective" data given us by the narrator at the beginning of the encounter. The sequence is as follows: first the landing party finds the dead lion and goes off to find the horse, leaving Urraque behind. Partonopeu sees them and expresses his displeasure in a sigh (5951), hearing which, Urraque perceives that something or someone is present. Looking intently at it ("Si l'a longement esgarde," 5952), she perceives next that it is "chose vive" (5953), and starts back in fear (5954). We, of course, know about Partonopeu, so our perspective on the scene is different from Urraque's, but the poet is making us experience the moment from Urraque's perspective—a device so common in novels and the cinema that we may not realize that it is foreign to the representation of reality in pre-twelfth-century medieval literature. Also, since we do not know who the lady is, we, too, have an incomplete perspective on the encounter. The passage of time, second by second, becomes a crucial factor in the episode, for each moment brings the characters—and the audience—to fuller perception and understanding of the scene in which they are taking part, while the scene itself begins to achieve its meaning from the perceptions, and consequent actions, of the participants: *it has no other meaning.*

As Urraque's virtues of openness and curiosity overcome her fear she moves closer, and sees better: "Puis vient plus pres et miech l'avise;/A l'entercier a paine mise." (5955-56). She now realizes this is a man, one whose face she still cannot see (5957-58). Her head-to-foot survey of him (5962-72)—the first such description of the melancholy Partonopeu that we have had, so that we experience it with Urraque—leads to his face (5973), and to her next conclusion, that he is a poor unfortunate ("chaitifs," 5974). At this point Urraque's pity and compassion take control in her attempt to comprehend and communicate with the wretch—but also the person—before her. Her virtues are triggered by, and are a function of, perceptions that accumulate within the temporal continuum of experience.

After the dialogue in which the two characters reveal their divergent responses to this chance intersection of their lives, Urraque names herself and, as Partonopeu faints, the poet returns again to narrow mimetic description, thus continuing the rhythm of this part of the episode, that is, alternating passages of perception and resultant reactions. Urraque lifts up the fallen man (an action emblematic of the entire scene) and finally gets a close enough look at him to see who he is (6045–48). At this central and most intense moment of the episode, we are made most conscious of limited, personal perspective. Having recognized Urraque at the same moment Partonopeu does, we experience excited hope for a favorable outcome; our knowledge of romance plots allows us to see now what the poet is about. From Partonopeu's perspective, however, the recognition of someone closely allied in his mind and memory with his great disaster has the opposite effect: "Ses dolz li est renoveles;/Torne les oilz, si chiet pasmez" (6043–44). Urraque's recognition of Partonopeu not only solves the mystery of his identity, but sharpens her awareness of the plight of this "chaitifs":

> Dex!
> Est ce li bialz Partonopez?
> Dex! Com tu es or empiries!
> [6047–49]

Finally, looking even more closely into his face, she decides he is in fact close to death; by combining with this perception her understanding of his inner state of despair and self-hatred (based on his words to her), she arrives at the knowledge which activates her power for moral *engin,* her equivalent of Mélior's magic and Maruc's enchantments:

> . . . Quide bien qu'il soit fines
> Si par li n'est reconfortes.

> Si fait une fause noveile
> K'ele quidoit k'a lui fuist beile.
> [6053-56]

Only the combination of prior knowledge, ability to understand, present perception, and innate gifts for moral manipulation of external reality which Urraque possesses enables her to
act successfully at this crucial moment; the *kairos* establishes
Urraque's individuality, and her response to it in turn confirms
Partonopeu's, effecting the reversal in his inner life that must
precede any change for the better in his external situation.
Urraque announces that Mélior, conscious of Partonopeu's repentance for the wrong he has done her, has pardoned him and
wishes him to be her lord (6057-76). Now he must become
happy, leave the forest, and come to recover in a secret place
she knows (6077-84). The "franchise" (6102) and "mesure"
(6108) (the ability to forgive and accept a less than perfect
lover) which Urraque attributes to Mélior are, in fact, a portrait
of her own tolerance, compassion, and realism. Partonopeu's
reaction is immediate: "Partonopeus a molt grant joie/De ce ke
li a dit la bloie" (6085-86). If Mélior can forgive him, and love
him, in spite of his treason, then he can dwell on her perfections
(6106-08) and on his memories of his happiness with her
(6109-12) without seeing an unbridgeable gap between love
and memory, on the one hand, and expectation of complete
personal fulfillment as her husband, on the other. Convinced
that his hope was doomed to frustration, Partonopeu had chosen
to destroy his mutilated inner self by doing away with its bodily
frame. Now, Urraque's news has revived expectation and knitted
up the breach in Partonopeu's inner life, and he announces the
reintegration of his identity in thanking her: "Car sol de ce ke
je vos voi,/Sui ge tos *revenus en moi*" (6015-16; italics mine).

At first, Partonopeu's recognition of Urraque only increases
his grief (6043), presumably because it thrusts before him with
renewed force happy memories and, simultaneously, the moment of betrayal (when he first met Urraque) that has poisoned
those memories.[39] Grief turns to joy with the news of Mélior's

forgiveness and the concomitant realization that it is possible to
construct once more a full inner life in which memory, awareness, and expectation all have something to contribute as Partonopeu attempts to shape and control his life. As he puts it,
responding to Urraque's tears of pity at his weakened state:

> Je fiz, fist il, la trahison,
> Asses ai je piz deservi,
> Ke onkes n'ou aillors n'ici;
> Mais cant li plaist ke j'aie pais,
> Bel m'est ke vive desormais.
>   [6148–52]

The complex awareness here—of sin, desert, dependence upon
another, and expectation of final "pais"—defines Partonopeu,
and him alone, at this moment in time. Yet it is an accurate
description only because he has encountered, at just this moment, the one person who can *resocialize* him. To function as
an individual requires recognition that one is not alone. Read
with different emphasis, the couplet I have quoted (6015–16)
sums up the paradox of the individual's need to redefine himself
through social relationships: "Car sol de ce ke je *vos* voi,/
Sui je revenus en *moi*" (italics mine).

In the poet's capable hands, a standard moment of romance
recognition has become a complex representation of the nexus
between a person's inner life and the external, moment-by-
moment situation—between self-defining awareness and self-
defining action. The scene also defines the human condition
as a fragile web of single threads which, properly interwoven,
can support each other without obscuring the individual character each possesses. His vision of love revived and strengthened
by Urraque, Partonopeu can now build upon his renewed impulse to survive, refining it into the controlled aggression of
chivalric prowess; his ultimate, successful synthesis of love and
honor, in the tournament at the end of the romance, ends the
movement whose beginning is here so carefully, circumstantially
depicted.

4. In referring to the artistic perspective on the Ardenne episode, I intend our own heightened awareness, as an audience,
of the poet's strategies at each stage in his presentation of the
crisis of his protagonist. Our changing responses to the poet's
mimetic art provide an extratextual parallel to the changing
responses of the characters to their circumstances and reproduce affectively within us the kaleidoscope of limited perspectives that define individual perception of reality within the
story.

Of the devices used by the poet to vary the atmosphere of his
narrative, some stimulate involvement, others distance, between
audience and story. In the former category must first of all be
included the use of the mysterious and uncanny. A masterful
instance is the description of how Maruc's charm renders the
beasts of Ardenne "trestos tremblans,/Tos pooros et toz en
pais" (5884-85). The suspended animation of a world of
destructive energy grips our attention by its simultaneous depiction of the unnatural calm and references to the usual dangers
now restrained:

> Li ors sont tapi as rochiers
> Et li dragon es noirs mortiers
> Et li lion es mons antis,
> Li liepar soz les boz foillis;
> Apoié sunt tuit en estant,
> As grans arbres li elefant;
> Es espoises li tigre mainnent,
> Ki come porc el tai se baignent.
> Li felon serpent sont es mons,
> Et les guivres es vals parfons
> Desoz les ewes tenebroses;
> Noires les font et venimoses.
>   [5919–30]

The simplified, paratactic syntax and singsong quality of the
end-stopped lines create an almost hypnotic effect. A similar
use of fairy-tale-like (but carefully contrived) naiveté and

wonder makes the important transition from the horse's cries of pain to the introduction of Urraque, the crucial figure, into the episode:

> La lune est halt al ciel montee
> Et pure et bele et alumee,
> N'en tot le ciel n'a une nue,
> La mer en pais n'est commeüe,
> Li tens est süés et seris
> Et beals et nes et esclaris.
> Li palefrois hennist tant cler
> C'on l'ot merveiles loins en mer.
> Une nef fu en la mer loign
> Ki del sejourner n'eüst soign,
> Mais cant el ne puet avoir vent,
> O veilhe ou non, illoc atent.
> En la nef ot une pucelle,
> Cortoise et proz et sage et bele;
> Cele a sa nef en sa bailhie:
> N'a nul ami ne n'est amie.
>   [5835–50]

The preternatural calm of the evening is balanced against the shattering cries of the horse; the becalmed boat has, as always in romance, overtones of mystery (and here we recall the mysterious boat which first took Partonopeu away from Ardenne to Chef d'Oire), and again there is a tantalizing, fairy-tale quality to the introduction of Urraque ("En la nef ot une pucelle," etc.). The maiden's virtues will, of course, be shown shortly to live up to the poet's enumeration of them (5848); more intriguing is the information that love is foreign to her (5850), which, in the light of her virtues and beauty, suggests delicately that she is not fully human—another fairy, perhaps, as Mélior first seemed to be. This deliberate mystification catches our interest and creates audience suspense as to what will occur when this world of mystery and magic (the enchantment) intersects the life of the wretched Partonopeu. Will he be saved? Ravished to fairyland like Marie de France's Lanval?

Once the scene has become a dialogue between Urraque and

Partonopeu, our involvement via mystery gives way to involvement in the moment-by-moment account of Urraque's perceptions and reactions, and in the sonatalike contrast between
Urraque's tender pleading and Partonopeu's harsh, self-hating
rejection of contact with another human being. But the poet's
continued refusal to name the damsel, along with the progressive building toward her naming herself, keeps alive within the
audience a spark of sheer curiosity—of involvement in an un-
raveling mystery.

Even as we are thus involved in the drama of encounter in a
world of mysterious possibilities and powers, we are kept by the
poet in an ambiguous state of response to Partonopeu himself.
When the squire Guilemot arranges for Partonopeu's escape, and
then for his own conversion, his love for and loyalty to his master make him the center of our sympathy; Partonopeu's "betrayal" of the young man when he leaves him behind, even
though it is to spare him death in Ardenne, creates a parallel
with his behavior toward Mélior. This parallel, together with the
contrast between the lion and horse, who fight to survive, and
Partonopeu, who will not, forces us to adopt a partly negative
view of the protagonist and to keep him at a distance. It is interesting that the most pathetic (and therefore sympathy-creating)
description of the state to which Partonopeu has been reduced
comes *after* he has regained the will to live. He tells Urraque
that he is too weak to leave the forest with her under his own
strength:

> Tant sui chaitis, flobes et las,
> Ke je ne puis aler un pas.
> A cotes et a genoz vois
> Querant herbetes par ce bois;
> Cant grant fain ai, ce me restraint
> Mes talens, et ma dolor vaint.
>   [6135–40]

This image of "talens" and "dolor" conquered by the will to eat
touches us as well as Urraque (see 6141), but earlier our reaction was not so simple.

Finally, there is an intrusive element in the course of the

episode which ultimately requires analysis in the light of the romance as a whole. When Partonopeu decides to seek death in
Ardenne, the narrator says that the hero's heart led him to this
decision (5501); he then appends a discussion of some thirty
lines (5502–34) in which he attacks clerks who attack women,
promises to disprove their malignant assertions on another
occasion, and includes extravagant praise of all ladies, since he
loves them all ("J'ain totes dames come moi," 5527). This
excursion into polemic and hyperbole, with its basis in the
narrator's supposed character and autobiography,[40] distracts
attention from the story, reminds us that it *is* only a story, and,
by its statement of extreme opinions in a rhetoric that partakes
more of lyric than narrative conventions, emphasizes the
artificiality of Partonopeu's lovesickness when seen from the
perspective of everyday, as well as parodistic, behavioral
norms.[41] The narrator's comments serve as a frame-device for
the story he is telling and heighten our appreciation of the
poet's artifice, simultaneously inducing the disengagement of
our sensibilities from the extreme behavior of both fictional
lovers: the narrator and his hero.

In the foregoing discussion of episodes from *Erec and Enide*
and *Partonopeu de Blois* I have tried to do equal justice to the
nuances of thematic intention and to the complexity of artistic
techniques, for both elements of chivalric romance represent
radical departures from the world of early medieval narrative.
Neither can properly be isolated from the other in assessing the
achievements of the twelfth-century poets. This achievement
may perhaps best be characterized in terms of paired impulses
coexisting and interacting in fruitful tension. For example, the
two chivalric poets here examined share a predilection for using
what we may call emblems to raise issues metaphorically or
symbolically: Guivret, his tower, his small size and enormous
horse; the battle between horse and lion; Maruc charming the
beasts. By means of such emblems, as over against direct,
homiletic statement, the poets comment on prowess, its ex-

tremes, and the relationship between it and social existence or personal happiness. Simultaneously, the narratives exhibit an equally strong attraction toward dramatizing characters' personal responses to the emblematic or metaphoric situations. Psychological analysis, narrow mimesis, and limited perspective are the tools for this part of the poetic endeavor, and its focus is the subjective *kairos,* the critical moment at which action issues from and reflects individuality and in turn determines the personal future of the actor. Partonopeu's *kairos* involves a radical reorientation of attitude, Enide's the making of a crucial decision.

The self-conscious artfulness of the poets underlies another pair of impulses in the episodes. As *actions,* the episodes move toward the establishment of control over forces and images of potential chaos, disruption, even destruction. Awareness, virtue, above all *engin* play their part in the successful completion of the action. From this focus, the characters are audience surrogates. We are involved in their efforts which express in imaginative form our aspirations to control our own lives. Yet the very centrality of *engin*—of deceit and manipulation of idealized and fantastic situations by witty characters—keeps before us images of human beings as problem solvers and creators of fictions—as artists, in other words, and surrogates for the author, moving through stylized *performances* peopled by knights, who are paragons or monsters of prowess, and superlatively beautiful and gifted damsels. Erec is a maker of processions and arranger of situations to test Enide; behind him, Chrétien is arranging situations to test and define both protagonists.

We see then that the path through the complex world of the chivalric romance leads us in one direction to the characters as individuals grappling with problems of personal fulfillment, and in the other to the poet as an individual grappling with problems of artistic creation. The moral and technical complexities of the Guivret and Ardenne episodes impel us simultaneously in both directions. Having discovered some of these complexities by intensive analysis of limited materials, we can now move on to confirm our findings extensively, ranging through a variety of twelfth-century courtly texts to study their presentation of the literary hallmarks of individuality: inner experience, subjective, mimetic representation of the temporal and spatial environment, and the use of human wit to facilitate the happy union of love and prowess proclaimed in the chivalry topos.

3: "ENGIN" IN TWELFTH-CENTURY COURTLY TEXTS

In every text with which I have dealt in any detail thus far in this study, the issue of how the protagonists use their intelligence and ingenuity to manipulate and control situations for their own advantage has come up again and again. Often it finds an echo in the manipulation of literary conventions by the author, in the interests of revealing his conscious artifice for our delectation. The faculty in question, described by the term *ingenium* in Latin and by its derivative, *engin* in Old French, is the subject of this chapter. As used in courtly literature, the word *engin* has a variety of meanings, applicable to human abilities of an intellectual rather than a heroic nature, but also to specific achievements that issue from these abilities: marvellous artifacts, war machines, and the like. The manifestations of *engin*—wit, shrewdness, manipulation, deceit—are by no means always admirable; often they leave the characters within a story and the audience outside it equally troubled or dissatisfied. Our reaction to *engin* embodies a profound ambivalence: *engin* complicates our acceptance of straightforward chivalric values (love, prowess, heroism) because it often makes those values work in spite of themselves, or criticizes them by exposing their inadequacy.

As we have seen in the preceding chapter, *engin* also self-consciously deflects our attention from the events of the story to the artfulness of the poet telling it, or to larger general questions about the role of art in creating "reality." Despite all these difficulties, characters and situations exemplifying *engin* have their own special charm—sometimes exhilarating, sometimes cynical, always profoundly human—as they embellish the world to make it better (or at least other) than it is and surmount life's obstacles by manipulation and circumnavigation rather than by brute force or irresistible goodness. *Engin* is the virtue par excellence of fallen man, who is weaker, perhaps, but more knowing as a result of that experience. His use of his knowledge to overcome the imperfections of his existence is also, as we shall see, a guide to our judgment of him as an individual.

By examining the role and dimensions of *engin* in a courtly but not chivalric twelfth-century narrative, the *roman antique* of *Enéas,* and also in Hue de Roteland's *Ipomedon,* I will try in this chapter to clarify the range of meaning inherent in the term, to explain our ambiguous reaction to it, and account for its use as a major element of the imagined world of chivalric romance. First, a few words about definitions of *engin* are in order.

In Godefroi's *Dictionnaire de l'ancien langue française,* the noun *engin* and related nouns, verbs, and adjectives are documented as possessing several basic meanings. *Engin* itself yields "habileté, addresse, ruse, fraude, tromperie, artifice, expédient." *Enginer* can mean "fabriquer avec art," "trouver a force d'habileté le moyen de faire quelque chose," and "tromper." Similar equivocations appear for *engigneor, engignement,* etc. *Engigneor,* for example, can mean a maker of machines, the planner of a project, and the devil (the great deceiver)! Finally, a proverb quoted from Wace's *Brut* further defines the concept by opposing it to another kind of behavior: "la vaut engins ou force falt."

The Latin ancestor of *engin, ingenium,* carries a smiliar set of meanings in DuCange's dictionary of medieval Latin: "machinatio, ars, fraus." In Lewis and Short's dictionary of classical Latin, however, the major meanings are positive: "innate quality, character, talent, genius." DuCange also lists a phrase, "malum ingenium," which presumably represents a transitional stage between classical and medieval usage; he also unaccountably omits strongly positive meanings for *ingenium* such as the one Abelard intends in his famous phrase opposing *usum* and *ingenium.* A final classical parallel to the range of meanings of *ingenium* is supplied by the Greek word *mēchanē,* and its derivatives, which, according to Liddell and Scott's dictionary, signify "an engine," "a contrivance or device," "art," or "a trick."

There is, then, a strong and old tradition for linking together in one word contradictory judgments on witty or ingenious problem-solving behavior and its physical embodiment in artifacts. In the twelfth century this tradition was revived and considerably strengthened by the intellectual, institutional, and social developments that I have already discussed in connection with the Latin personal histories treated in chapter 1. It remains to survey the role played by *engin* within the literature of courtly culture and to assess our reactions to its various manifestations in several texts.

Two main uses of the term *engin* are established early in the *Roman d'Enéas* (which I have considered briefly in chapter 2 in connection with its role in the development of the chivalry topos toward a plot). The first type of *engin* involves behavior and is illustrated when Paris judges the dispute over the golden apple (101–82), and again when Dido, exiled from her native Tyre, employs a strategem to gain enough land in Africa to build the city of Carthage (391–402). "Par grant engin" (131) Paris holds off his judgment to allow the rival goddesses time to approach him with bribes; "par grant engin" (393) Dido asks the "prince de la contree" to sell her as much land as a bull's hide will enclose. The prince, "qui de l'engin ne se garda" (398), agrees, and Dido, by cutting the hide into thin strips, makes a boundary large enough to enclose a city.[1] But the word *engin* is also used to describe the walls of Carthage, marvellously constructed of multicolored blocks (placed "par grant aning et par consoil," 424), and the capitol building of the city ("par merveillus angin fu faiz," 534), so engineered that even a whisper can be heard all over the central chamber (419–47, 528–41).

In a sense, *engin* presides over the opening scenes of the *Enéas,* giving it an atmosphere quite different from that of the

Aeneid: a compound of ingenious heroes and heroines and a city constructed with rare and marvellous artfulness.[2] *Engin* here connotes wit, readiness to take advantage of a situation, problem solving, manipulation of others, and shaping materials into unusual, effective forms—in short, the shaping of the human environment to one's advantage, not by force but by the gifts of the mind. There are ambiguities: Paris is a trickster the final fruit of whose *engin* is the doom of Troy (179-82). But his manipulation of the situation in which he finds himself is a triumph of ingenuity over both divine pride and fortune. In Dido's case, *engin,* cooperating with *richesse* and *proesce,* helps a woman who has lost her rightful station in life regain authority. (See 403-06: "Puis conquist tant par sa richece,/par son angin, par sa proece,/que ele avoit tot le pais/et les barons a soi sozmis.") The component of fraud in *engin,* forced on her by necessity, proves her worth. The combined effect of the Dido and Paris examples is to propose alternatives to Vergilian heroism and *pietas.*[3]

The *engin* to which the description of Carthage testifies, on the other hand, is an alliance of ingenuity approaching the marvellous with a striving for illusionistic effects. The birds, beasts, and flowers painted on the walls of Carthage (427-32) suggest a *locus amoenus,* but the walls themselves are thick and lined with magnets (*engins* in the attested sense of war machines).[4] The city, in short, is an artifact, embodying Dido's *engin, richesse,* and *proesce,* to which we respond with admiration.

More complex is our reaction to the tent-castle, with its tent-keep inside, erected one night by the Trojans during a truce in their war with the Laurentians (7281-356). Seen from the walls of Laurentium, the beautifully decorated tents seem really to be a stone castle such as would require three years to build, and not just painted cloth, about which the poet says, "n'iert noiant fet por forteresce/mes por biaute et por richese . . ./ne fu pas forz, mes molt fu biaus," (7303-04; 7330). Nevertheless, the sight of the tents frightens the Laurentians into blaming their king for not seeking peace with men possessing such a formidable ability to wage war.

In this incident, ingenuity, illusion, and beauty, coexisting in an "unreal" and occasional artifact, permit the Trojans to offer an illustration of the proverbial opposition of *engin* and force. (The poet provides another emblematic expression of this opposition in his description of Drances [6633-42], a sage and prudent Laurentian who "de parolle ert molt anginos,/mais n'estoit pas chevalleros," and who condemns Turnus's heroic folly.) The tent, *biaus* but not *forz,* is successful as policy. In responding to this paradigm the audience must balance elements of admiration for Trojan cunning, ironic laughter at the gullibility of the Laurentians, and detachment from an heroic situation (the Trojans' battle for national survival) which suddenly descends to make-believe. Indeed, by calling our attention to the illusory power of a beautiful but unreal creation, the poet reminds the audience that it, too, is being "tricked" into participating in the imagined world of the poetic artifact. At this point, by inducing a shock of recognition, the trickster-poet seeks our applause for his art instead of our involvement in his story. Such moments of self-conscious artfulness, in which the poet reminds his audience that he is the creator and master of a fictional world of beauty, ingenuity, and events unbounded by the limits of the possible, are relatively frequent in the *Enéas.* Two others that illustrate the poet's sense of his own artfulness, and suggest that he revels in its ability to transform a sometimes harsh reality into something beautiful, striking, unreal, and praiseworthy precisely for its unreality, describe the tombs erected to hold the remains and honor the memories of Pallas (6409-518) and Camilla (7531-718), who have been killed in the battle between the Trojans and the Latins. These structures, which have no counterpart in Vergil, are marvels of architectural fantasy, but also marvels of ecphrastic virtuosity on the part of the poet. Through his elaborate description of the tombs' improbable architecture, rich decorations of sculpture and painting, and panoply of miraculous features—among them a mirror which will detect the approach of a besieging army from far enough away to allow the city's defenders time to arm and make provision—the poet effectively disguises the fact that these are monuments to early death (both Pallas and Camilla have been cut off in youth) and metamorphoses the atmosphere of the narrative from extreme grief and pathos to wonder and delight.[5]

One source of the wonder is especially instructive. The poet tells us that Camilla's tomb is built in stages, held up by pillars, with each stage wider than the one below, giving the effect of an inverted pyramid (7615-28). The poet's remark, "Grant mervoille sanbloit a toz/que graindre ert desus que desoz" (7629-30), guides our response to his art as well. It is an art of the impossible, to be savored for its upending of gravity and reality alike, making pleasure out of mourning and romance out of epic. Here courtly artifice is acknowledged as escape and becomes laughable; simultaneously, however, the skill of the poet demands the delighted acquiescence we give it. He, rather than his characters, becomes the audience's surrogate: he is man the manipulator, constructing a highly individualized version of "reality" and imposing it on an audience that esteems him for the very brazenness of his self-aggrandizing imagination.

One last example of *enginos* behavior in the *Enéas* looks forward to chivalric romances, for it shows *engin* working in harmony with the assumptions of the chivalry topos. Lavine, needing to communicate her new love to its object, Enéas, both to inspire him in his single combat for her against Turnus and to discover if he returns her passion,[6] wraps a love letter around an arrow and has it shot at Enéas as he passes her tower.[7] Lavine is prevented from overtly encouraging Enéas (her mother opposes the relationship) or testing his devotion (denied by her mother, who insists that Enéas is a homosexual). But she has come to the point of self-awareness where she knows that only his love, or knowledge of its impossibility, will satisfy her, so the poet and his heroine press ingenuity into the service of love, and thus of chivalry, through the clever expedient of the arrow. In the process, Geoffrey's lady-in-the-tower is transformed from beautiful flirt (like the ladies who watch the jousting in Geoffrey's *Historia*) to witty conspirator. But once again our response to the episode is ambivalent, for the arrow shot for Lavine recalls love's arrow and its wound, a metaphor exploited by the poet (see 7975-92, 8057-67, 8168-69). Metaphor becomes strategic action, but action in turn becomes part of a world of image and art. Here too there is tension between our admiration for love-inspired decisiveness and wit and our admiration for the poet's witty blurring of the line between symbolic and exemplary behavior in an obtrusively fictional, "designed" world.

The liberal and varied use of *engin* by the *Enéas* poet reflects interests shared by himself and his courtly audience. The first is the role of wit, ingenuity, manipulation, and the creation of illusion in the accomplished individual's successful encounter with a potentially (or actual) adversary world. In a literary universe not presided over by an active, all-controlling God, *engin* is humanity's substitute for providence—the gift which makes things turn out better than it seems they will, given the "facts." This ability to create an advantage by calculation, manipulation, and the use of illusion is particularly admired and cultivated in a courtly society, where it is the only power available to most. (In the sixteenth century a similar, even more nuanced form of artfulness is praised in Baldassare Castiglione's great courtly dialogue, *Il Libro del Cortegiano,* where it is called *sprezzatura.*) In both twelfth-century and sixteenth-century courtly society, virtue (and personal desires) cannot simply be enunciated or practiced without forethought for the reactions of those with whom one is dealing. A climate, pattern, or structure of limited possibilities must be created by ingenious manipulation of the materials at hand, within which pattern other people do or learn what you want them to. This will result when, as is often the case with *engin,* they do not realize at the beginning that you have led them into a situation that limits their freedom of action or reaction and thus controls their responses. When recognition finally comes to those on whom *engin* has been practiced, the result can be salutary—or the reverse. *Engin,* that is, can deceive, improve, or educate, depending on the intent of the *engigneor.* Here we see how *engin* contributes to the sense of the individual in the chivalric romance; personal motive, consciously decided upon and expressing personal values or needs, determines our response to any particular use of this basic human capability.

The second interest of poet and audience revealed by *engin* is that of artistic self-consciousness, that is, fascination with the power of man to create and order his world, like a substitute God, making of reality as he finds it a new, artificial, sometimes illusory world. This is what the artist does in creating a fictional narrative, and what his characters do in creating "fictional" situations, in making others the characters in their own plot, the happy ending of which is personal fulfillment (or national fulfillment, in the case of the *Enéas*). Beyond this, the places in courtly narratives where description of marvellous artifacts or creatures are inserted for the delectation of the audience are also self-conscious assertions of the poet's power to create an imagined world and assume the function of the visual artist in describing it.[8] The interaction between the vocations of courtier and artist was much more discussed and used in the sixteenth century; parallel vocabulary described courtly and artistic self-consciousness.[9] Here again the twelfth century offers a precedent, albeit without the critical vocabulary and theory to describe it, in courtly and chivalric narrative.

In turning from *Enéas* to the romances of Chrétien de Troyes, we find that, as the romance plot has given a new importance to the chivalry topos as the medium for exploring the nature and problems of individual destiny, a fortiori it integrates *engin* more closely into the plot as another human area of activity (aside from love and prowess) which, by its very nature as an intellectual activity, impinges upon and affects the less reflective impulses toward dominance and fulfillment. In fact, the way in which *engin* is motivated and used vis-à-vis the chivalry topos from romance to romance determines to a considerable extent how we react to that topos and judge the hero's quest for self-fulfillment and/or honor.

Using a distinction made above, I can say that in *Erec, engin* is most importantly used to educate, in *Cligès* to deceive, and in *Yvain* to improve the chance of satisfactory resolution in extremely problematic situations involving both the protagonists and other characters. In every case, it contributes to our understanding of the limits and possibilities of the chivalry topos as a model of individual self-definition and happiness. In

Erec, engin is least central to the plot and is used in support of the successful exercise of married chivalry. When Erec leaves his father's court after having been awakened (literally and metaphorically) to the consequences of abandoning prowess for uxorious love, his intent, as the audience gradually discovers, is both to prove his worth in adventure (and thus reestablish his honor or lost identity as Erec the brave knight) and to teach Enide that if she does indeed love him she must show it by saving and warning him, even risking his displeasure in the process. Enide is to define her special contribution to the marriage by paradoxically asserting her autonomy and affirming the importance of her individual perceptions and resultant personal awareness, rather than by subordinating her experience to what she thinks will please her husband, thus submerging her identity in his.

Erec's method in achieving this double end is to establish a paradigmatic and exemplary placement in space of himself and Enide which will provoke and control desired responses from Enide and from the adventure world which, he now realizes, is the proper setting for the marriage relationship. (That is, marriage, like the lonely search for adventure, requires openness to experience rather than avoidance of it.[10]) Enide, riding ahead of Erec in her best clothes, draws adventure to him by making herself an inviting target and advertising his presence. Her existence in his world thus becomes an impetus for brave action, rather than for avoiding exposure to action, as was the case when he first married her and retired from public life to dote on her in privacy. In other words, Erec's ingenious arrangement makes Enide a test of his prowess and insures his full involvement in the quest for honor (through openness to life's adventures) because of, rather than in spite of, his married state.

Other, subordinate instances of *engin* fit in with this use of it in *Erec*. In turning aside the threat posed to Erec by the foolish, vain Count Galoain, who wants her love because he feels he deserves it and is quite willing to kill Erec to get it, Enide must resort to trickery. She convinces the count that "Je vos voldroie ja santir/an un lit certes nu a nu" (3390-91) and that he

should wait until the next morning to kill Erec in an under-
handed way (see 3377–86). By falling in with the count's plan
to betray her husband, she actually betrays the count; Chrétien
makes much of the fact that behind the illusion of treachery lies
her loyalty to her husband.[11] By fooling the count, Enide is
able to save her husband from death. Enide's *engin* (here in the
simplest form of deceit) is thus highly moral: "mailz est asez
qu'ele li mante,/que ses sires fust depeciez" (3412–13) and it is
effective because she is dealing with a *bricon* (3411) whose
vanity makes him as easily duped as he is prone to evil. His flaw
is the lack of awareness both of the wrong he does in plotting
to kill Erec and of the possibility that Enide might love Erec
more than himself. Accordingly, when Erec, forewarned by
Enide, defeats and wounds the count the next day, the latter
undergoes a revelation of awareness reminiscent of Erec's earlier
awakening (3618–46),[12] and repents what he now understands
to be his earlier treason. Enide's *engin* thus serves as an educative
vehicle for the count, as Erec's does for her. As Galoain puts it:

> esploitie ai vilainnement:
> de ma vilenie me poise;
> molt est preuz et saige et cortoise
> la dame qui deceu m'a.
>
> [3630–33]

The conversion (as it were) of the count is a typically inner
process of rejecting the old self from a position of heightened
awareness—a change of identity—which occurs alike in twelfth-
century chivalric romances and religious works as part of the
age's new conception of the individual. Enide's doubly effica-
cious *engin* confirms the role of human wit in advancing both
man's attempt to overcome his natural environment without the
guidance of all-encompassing providence and his inner progress
toward full self-awareness and thus control over his inner impulses in the service of moral self-realization.[13]

In *Cligès*, on the other hand, *engin* is no longer chivalry's
servant, enhancing its basic effectiveness in the ideal love-
prowess relationship evolved by Erec and Enide. Instead, it is

chivalry's master and substitute. Within the peculiar world of *Cligès,* prowess, because it is enmeshed in feudal politics or tyrannical social norms, is largely irrelevant or misdirected where the inner world and personal desires of the protagonists are concerned. Alixandre's heroic deeds at Arthur's court, pre-serving the king from vassals who have rebelled against him (a situation reminiscent of Geoffrey of Monmouth's Arthur or of the "epic of revolt" type of *chanson de geste*),[14] do not help him win the love of Soredamors because he is too shy to speak to her and she is too proper to speak to him; the queen must finally bring them together like a knowing teacher instructing two favorite pupils.[15] When Alixandre's son, Cligès, falls in love with Fénice, the damsel chosen to be the wife of his usurping brother, Alis, he does so only after he has won her for the usurper in bloody battle with the duke of Saxony. Both Alixandre and Cligès resort to *engin* at a climactic moment in their respective martial careers: each disguises himself in the armor of an opposing warrior to confuse the enemy, penetrate the hostile ranks, and add the element of surprise to the force of blows. But in both cases the ingenious gambit has unexpected consequences that symbolize the counterproductiveness of the hero's overall reliance on prowess. Not only do Alixandre and Cligès fool the enemy—they also confuse their own followers, who believe that the missing (because disguised) knight is dead.[16] The suggestion is clear: *engin* linked to prowess that is not in the service of individuality—that does not help attain the inner fulfillment and perfected identity of love—subverts that prowess by revealing its suicidal tendencies.

Later, Cligès goes to his great-uncle Arthur's court to prove his prowess and thus earn an identity in Britain based on prowess instead of descent. Again, *engin* is involved: Cligès fights on successive days in different suits of armor, defeating the heroes of the court while confusing them as to his natal identity until he has proven his qualitative identity through martial deeds. Again the problem is that there is no relationship between Cligès's prowess or the *engin* that turns it into a virtuoso performance, and his love needs; Fénice is not the tournament prize. Cligès's other deeds of prowess with Arthur only keep him away from Fénice, and eventually he returns to her no better off than before he left.[17]

The association of *engin* with thwarted prowess and, by extension, with death finds its fullest expression in the false death of Fénice, staged so that she can enjoy her lover Cligès without (as she feels) committing adultery against her husband Alis. (Alis, meanwhile, has enjoyed only the illusion of carnal love with his supposed wife, the result of a potion given him on his wedding night by Fénice's servant Thessala, on whom see below.) The ironies and parodistic elements of the heroine's false death (which deliberately recalls the passion, death, and resurrection of Jesus) have been discussed by Haidu, Owen, and others;[18] the secret love of Fénice and Cligès inside a tower— where Fénice, supposedly dead, must remain—continues for fifteen months, during which she never sees the light of the sun. The lovers, with the help of Jehan, Cligès's serf and builder of the tower, now remove to a garden supposedly securely walled against discovery. However, they are soon accidentally discovered by a knight chasing a hawk.

The effect of these episodes—Alis's illusory love, Fénice's false death (which, because of a potion she has taken, temporarily fools Cligès as well), the love-tower which is also in effect a tomb cut off from the light of nature, and finally the ostensibly protected garden—is to suggest that the love relationships in the romance are all illusory and that love as Cligès and Fénice must practice it is a trap, a death of the individual to society and the external world, the appearance of a private, self-fulfilling relationship without the reality of security or legitimacy. There is, finally, a radical dichotomy between the public activities and situations—the outer identities, in short—of the major characters and their inner, imagined fulfillment. In this sense, Cligès and Fénice share the anti-romance situation of Tristan and Isolde, whose fate Fénice is so anxious to avoid.[19] The two parts of the chivalry topos never come together; Cligès fights against his own interest (winning Fénice for Alis) or irrelevantly (at Arthur's court), instead of forwarding his love quest, which itself is a tissue of illusion.

With both parts of the chivalry topos rendered ineffectual and illusory by the poet, the story of *Cligès* is held together by the *engin* of two ostensibly subsidiary characters, Thessala and Jehan, two servants who are (and are called) the "masters" of the plot and its protagonists.[20] As Haidu points out, Thessala and Jehan are magicians, creating a world of illusion which will not survive the influx of reality (represented with deliberate banality by the knight Bertrand shinnying up the garden wall in search of the lost hawk).[21] But they are also—especially Jehan—artist figures. Jehan's tower is a marvellous artifact created with great *engin*, like the tombs and tents of the *Enéas*, and like them it calls attention to Chrétien's own "magic" in creating the circumstantial yet exotic Byzantine world of *Cligès*. The tower is filled with beautiful works of art ("ymages, beles et bien anluminees," 5492-93) and gives aesthetic pleasure to its visitor as the romance does to its audience. (When Cligès has seen it, "si li a molt la torz pleü,/Et dit que molt est boene et bele," 5500-01.) But it also contains secret chambers, known only to its maker (5508-15), that give it higher significance (as a hideaway for Fénice) when they are revealed to Cligès. This secret, "thematic" dimension of the tower further buttresses the parallel between Jehan and Chrétien, who can, by his art, endow courtly narratives with higher, metaphorical significance. In Jehan's case, however, the transformation of art into magic (and therefore failure) is the consequence of the complete inability of the protagonists to order their lives satisfactorily by the control and synthesis suggested by the chivalry topos. The illusion involved in Jehan's *engin* is therefore that it *is* magic, that it alone can make up for the failure to surmount problems in the lovers' total situation. Cligès cannot fight for Fénice, nor is she free to encourage him to do so and still avoid the fate of Isolde. When *engin* attempts to fill such a gap, its apparent success is tinged with magic, and, like magic, proves illusory.

Cligès, in short, is about the ironic and flawed results of *engin* attempting to do its ordering job and chivalry's as well in a radically unchivalric world. It is apposite here that *Cligès* is of all Chrétien's romances the one most anchored in the political and geographic realities of his day.[22] Chrétien is perhaps suggesting that the individual freedom which chivalric romance assumes can be earned is in fact very difficult to achieve in a world of historical and political constraints—an interesting and self-conscious comment on the asocial, ahistorical conventions of most romances. In the absence of chivalry's balance and control of impulses, we are left with personally unsatisfying, even self-destructive aggression; imprisioning, deadly passion; and dishonest, self-defeating *engin*. Through Jehan the serf, Chrétien may intimate that his own art will be false if, in search of freedom, it abandons the conventions of chivalry for pseudo-historical fiction. Interestingly enough, in just such a pseudo-historical courtly narrative, the *Eracle* of Chrétien's contemporary Gautier d'Arras, the hero's one failure, as we shall see, is in respect of the love affair of the empress of "Rome"— actually Byzantium—that is, of Fénice's precise analog. The ending of *Cligès,* which states fancifully that because of Fénice all subsequent empresses of Byzantium are guarded as in prison by their husbands, suggests by means of this cynical etiology that love and imperial politics are perpetual enemies.[23]

In *Yvain,* as I have mentioned, Chrétien did not abandon the chivalry topos but made particularly free and problematic use of it, as though his aim were to complicate in every possible way our response to the conventions of chivalric romance. The place of *engin* within the process of testing chivalric assumptions is illustrated by Lunete, *demoisele* of Laudine de Landuc, whom Yvain loves, marries, and abandons. Lunete is one of Chrétien's most attractive characters—knowing, witty, moved by noble motives, and thoroughly dedicated to the use of quite outrageous *engin* to bring together Yvain and Laudine, not once but twice in most unpropitious circumstances. The most famous use of *engin* in all Chrétien's works occurs in the episode where Lunete first helps Yvain to win Laudine, whose husband he has just slain in battle at the magic spring. Yvain is here doubly incarcerated, both by the effect of his prowess and desire for honor (which has brought him into prison in Laudine's castle) and by love (which keeps him there willingly). Chrétien invites our laughter at the ironies of Yvain's situation and at the extremity of his devotion for the least obtainable of all love objects. Meanwhile, Laudine's violent grief borders on the comic, as well as the pathetic, in its intensity.[24]

In this most unpromising situation, Lunete, realizing that her former benefactor loves her mistress, persuades the latter to accept Yvain as husband on the grounds that (1) he must be better than her former husband, since he defeated him; and (2) the spring needs a new defender, with Arthur and his court on the way to test it. In other words, Lunete analyzes and capitalizes on the reversal of roles, within the chivalry topos, of the protagonists: Yvain, having arrived at Laudine's castle in search of honor (vengeance for Calogrenant, proof of bravery for slanderous Kay), now seeks love, while Laudine, moved to grief by love of her husband, now seeks honor in the person of a new defender of the spring.[25]

Many critics have found this scene puzzling or a negative comment on Yvain or Laudine.[26] The absurdities of Yvain's passion, the brazenness of Lunete's trickery, and Laudine's calm acceptance of her husband's killer as new husband, while she manipulates her councillors to accept him also—all create difficulties. But Lunete is not a Jehan figure, working for his own freedom, nor the type of cynical, acquisitive go-between who appears in other romances and whom we shall see at work in Gautier's *Eracle*. Her motives for helping Yvain are gratitude and a desire to save him from the excesses of uncontrolled, unrequited passion.[27] She is also loyal to her mistress and manipulates the *usage* of the fountain by means of *engin* to create a relationship which, if it has love mostly on one side, has at least erased the negative results of Yvain's prowess: grief, imprisonment, and the possibility of further death (Yvain's, at the hands of the lady).[28] Lunete supplies a way out of a situation where prowess has failed and, paradoxically, honor remains possible for the hero only through love: Laudine's acceptance of Yvain brings him honor among her people (2166–71) and the chance of honor at Arthur's court, by his defense of the spring against Kay.

Our response to this episode is highly ambivalent. We sense the

difficulties not resolved, the coolness of Laudine, and the defi-
ciencies of prowess, kept before us by the references to Laudine's dead husband.[29] Even as we minimize Lunete's *engin* by
these reflections, we experience some exhilaration that, stimulated by a desire to serve, not cheat, *engin* can bring at least a
tentative harmony out of a situation scarred by violence and
grief. The ironies of the scene makes us see how fragile Lunete's
achievement is but do not destroy the satisfaction we derive
from a clearer sense of our capacity to order even circumstances
like these in support of private and public fulfillment through
wit and ingenuity. Lunete's triumph of manipulation is Chrétien's as well, as he ingeniously brings his hero through near-
disaster and a complete change of orientation (he will now
suffer indignity and death for love who before saw vengeance
and honor as his highest goals) to a moment of triumph in
reconciling older social and new personal desires.[30]

In the latter part of the romance, two more instances of
engin suggest a transformation of the world of the romance, in
keeping with the hero's new knowledge of his needs for self-fulfillment. At Arthur's court, when two sisters engage Gawain and
Yvain as their respective champions to settle a disputed inheritance, the knights battle in disguise to a standstill, and then,
learning each other's identity, refuse out of love for each other
to fight any longer. To settle the dispute, Arthur tricks the
older, unjust sister into confessing her guilt and thus reconciles
the sisters in a relationship of mutual respect and service.[31]
Then Yvain goes to the magic spring, ready to make it storm
until Laudine accepts him back, and is met by Lunete instead of
a knight. She persuades him to come quietly, and once again she
tricks Laudine, this time by obtaining from her the promise to
do all she can to effect a reconciliation between the Knight of
Lion (whose other identity Lunete knows, but not Laudine) and
his lady, in return for his agreement to guard the fountain. Laudine then discovers that she has unknowingly pardoned her
repentant husband.[32]

In both these episodes, prowess situations are transformed by
love through the revelation of individual identity and the desire

to serve. The knight's impulse to gain honor cedes to love as Yvain and Gawain almost emblematically offer to lose the battle in which they find themselves, each for the sake of his dear companion's glory; and the storm-causing fountain calls forth an apostle of reconciliation rather than a practicioner of knightly violence. A new hierarchy of values emerges from experience, and the prowess that ruled the fictional world in all its amorality and violence (symbolized by the fountain) is now definitively subordinated to the characters' desire for harmony. One can almost put it typologically: the temporary triumphs of love over honor when Yvain falls in love with Laudine, and when he realizes that he has lost her, are the types of this final resolution.

But the taming of prowess is not enough by itself. In order to solve the problems that remain between individuals (the two sisters arguing over their inheritance, Yvain seeking forgiveness from Laudine), some other instrument than weapons must be found. For both Arthur and Lunete at the end of *Yvain* that instrument is deceptive, manipulative wit, which makes possible the reconciliation of kinsmen and lovers. Because of the deceits practiced on the older sister by Arthur—he not only extorts an unintended confession of guilt from her, but threatens (untruthfully) to declare her champion defeated, in order to scare her into acquiescence in his settlement of the quarrel—we feel some sympathy for her; similarly, we agree with Laudine when she exclaims that she has been caught in a trap by Lunete in agreeing to help one knight who turns out to be another.[33] *Engin,* that is, solves problems but does not resolve doubts. We experience some satisfaction that things turn out as they do in *Yvain,* but no exhilaration. Chrétien does not allow real joy at the end of this difficult romance (as he did in *Erec*) but instead stresses the attainment of pardon and peace (the word *pes* is reiterated at 6769, 6783, 6789, 6801). The reason, I think, is clear: all human relationships are rendered difficult by our failings, and in *Yvain* we find *engin* taking the role of neutralizer or transcender of failings, bringing about what harmony—and peace—is possible in a fallen, "postchivalric" world.[34]

At the beginning of *Yvain* Chrétien gives us two examples of
openness to the sense of life as an adventure, an exposure to
personal risk for the sake of personal betterment, an acceptance
of the challenge to *become,* not just to *exist.* Such an openness
holds within itself the beginnings of the emergence of the indi-
ividual—the man who seeks his private destiny. Of these two
examples, one, Calogrenant, is unthinking and unable to match
desire and performance. (He seeks out the magic fountain only
to be ignominiously defeated by its guardian.) The other, Yvain,
is misdirected, succeeding only too well in an objective (victory
through prowess) which he then discovers is not only not what
he wants, but harmful to what he wants, namely, love. Openness to adventure and heightened awareness of personal goals
(that is, self-consciousness) are necessary but not sufficient
stages for the hero. They bring him to the kind of realization
which is, by itself, frustrating (Yvain imprisoned) or maddening
(Yvain realizing he has lost Laudine by staying away too long).
The human capacity for wit and manipulation dedicated to the
service of others—what Lunete has in *Yvain,* what Urraque
possesses in the analogously fallen world of *Partonopeu*—is
necessary to the individual, given his flaws of performance, judgment, and vision, if he is to achieve self-fulfillment. The knight's
forceful confrontation of public reality, however moral its
motive, and his maintenance of a private vision of happiness—
the life, in other words, of pure chivalry—cannot, without the
catalyst of *engin,* bring about outer or inner peace, by which
Chrétien ultimately intends the bridling of the strong impulses
toward disorder and chaos in man and in society. The permanent presence of these impulses in the world of *Yvain* (as represented by the storm-causing fountain, a natural phenomenon)
gives the romance its darker cast, while the repeated use of
engin to correct the imperfections and inadequacies of chivalry
holds out the hope that man, as a free and intelligent individual,
neither controlled by providence nor defeated by circumstance,
can achieve the personal goals toward which desire and imagination lead him.

My last example, Hue de Roteland's *Ipomedon,* dazzles by the audacity, variety, and centrality of the *engin* used by its main characters. Hue's interest in *engin,* like Chrétien's, centers less on artifacts of rare accomplishment, more on wittily deceptive and manipulative behavior. The special feature of *Ipomedon* is that the hero is the prime *exemplum ingenii,* whereas in *Cligès, Yvain,* and *Partonopeu* supporting figures employ this method of surmounting obstacles. (Erec is another exception, but his *engin* is staid and limited compared to Ipomedon's.) *Ipomedon's* heroine, La Fière, has her share of ingenuity early in the romance, but Ipomedon himself soon dominates the action as much by his tricks and illusions as by his formidable prowess.

Because Hue's plot exposes the *folie* of his characters at every turn, and because his humor is often reductionist and cynical,[35] it is easy to decide that the entire romance is burlesque or satire, with *engin* but a part of the joke,[36] or to regard the arbitrary turns of the plot, resulting from its hero's penchant for witty deception, as Hue's self-advertisement of his control over a fantastic world created for delight but not involvement. But such views are oversimplifications. By means of *engin,* Hue is able to communicate important reservations about chivalry, and able to help us understand the role of delusory appearance in our life. The educative function of *engin* (and, by extension, art) is uppermost in Hue's scheme, and its effect is therefore to heighten awareness and remove obstacles placed in the way of self-fulfillment by ignorance and incorrectly ordered values. At the same time, *engin* itself finds an intermediate place in the hierarchy of human values or impulses that represents optimal personal interaction with and control of experience, that is, the model of human life as an adventure quest for individual fulfillment. Rational awareness and analysis issuing in ingenious manipulation of the environment count for much with Hue but cannot by themselves bring the individual to his chosen, imagined goal of self-perfection, represented here, as always in chivalric romance, by attainment of the long and perilously sought beloved.

Ipomedon, as a young squire (like Partonopeu), falls in love with the duchess of Calabria, called La Fière (*pucelle*) because she has vowed to marry only the knight who can defeat all others and win supreme *los* and *pris* wherever he goes (105-59). This is, of course, an extreme and programmatic theoretical statement of the chivalry topos, stemming not from experience (La Fière has not seen and fallen in love with such a paragon of prowess before making her statement) but from a fixed and abstract opinion of one's worth and deserts—a result, one might say, of too naive an acceptance of the literary convention of chivalry as a way of actually conducting one's life. Although La Fière begins to feel passion for Ipomedon, who has presented himself to her as a huntsman-squire rather than as a fledgling knight, she is ashamed to violate her public vow, and so indirectly warns him to leave her court and undertake adventures. Stung, Ipomedon leaves Calabria, even as La Fière realizes her mistake and decides, too late, to ask him to remain with her. The parting of the protagonists accomplished, the rest of the romance tells Ipomedon's adventures and especially his two great triumphs in La Fière's behalf.

The first of these triumphs of arms occurs in a tournament, the winner of which is to marry La Fière. She has summoned the tournament as a strategem to buy time in the face of her barons' demand that she marry; she hopes her vanished *ami* will rescue her from what she now realizes are potentially contradictory obligations: her public and "theoretical" vow to marry the best knight and her subsequent, private, and experience-prompted vow to marry no one but her unknown beloved who has fled her. Ipomedon competes and wins, but fights every day in a different suit of armor (compare *Cligès*), sends La Fière half-true, half-false messages concerning his identity and intentions at the end of each day's fighting, and meanwhile leads a double life as *le bel malveise* (3267), a prowess-scorning huntsman who has come unannounced to take up residence at the court of Sicily. (We recall that Ipomedon had earlier come to La Fière's court in Calabria disguised as a hunter; later in this episode Ipomedon draws ironic parallels between chivalric prowess and the huntsman's "quest" to dominate not knights but beasts.) To this twofold deception Ipomedon adds yet another by winning from the king of Sicily the boon of leading the queen to and from her chamber each day and permission to kiss her once on each such occasion. Because of these privileges he will be known (inaccurately, of course,) as *dru la reine* (3071). (Hue is here recalling, and burlesquing, the romance convention of the boon granted to a knight by a monarch; compare Kay and Arthur in *Lancelot,* Guinglain and Arthur in *Bel inconnu.*)

When the tournament is over, Ipomedon reveals his true (and many false) identities, but only by messenger, and only after he has left the court to embrace once more the life of adventure. La Fière is miserable, and so is the queen, who had come to love her pretended *dru* but was afraid to reveal her feelings because of her shame at his apparent rejection of prowess.

Ipomedon's second encounter is a single combat with the huge, evil, pagan knight Léonin, who has come to Calabria to force himself on La Fière and has issued a challenge to anyone who would dispute his claim to her (7685–90, 7711–15), in accord with her own former public avowal. (Now, of course, La Fière is doubly regretful of the vow, both because of her love for another, and because of Léonin's extreme hatefulness.) Returning to the Sicilian court disguised in the tattered garb of a fool-knight, Ipomedon undertakes the rescue of his *amie,* again as the result of a boon begged from (and contemptuously granted by) the king, who, with the court, ridicules the apparent fool. He fights Léonin wearing the same armor as his opponent and, defeating the proud invader, pretends to be him, thus convincing La Fière that all is lost. She begins an escape into exile, and Ipomedon prepares to return to his adventures. The story seems destined to continue indefinitely, but suddenly Capaneus, a Sicilian knight who had earlier befriended Ipomedon, appears, challenges and nearly kills the exhausted hero, and at the last moment sees a ring on Ipomedon's finger which identifies him as Capaneus's hitherto unknown half-brother. The reunion between the knights is quickly followed by Ipomedon's recon-

ciliation with La Fière, and finally by his coronation as king of
Apulia.

I will concentrate here on the role of *engin* in the tournament
episode, with a few references to other places where it is intertwined with chivalry.[37] It should be noted that Hue's hero and
heroine show progressive maturation as they fulfill their "ortho-
dox" roles within the chivalry topos—Ipomedon's prowess
assuming larger dimensions of social service, La Fière's love becoming increasingly unselfish and faithful, no matter what the
cost to herself.[38] The effect of this progress is that the critical
function of *engin* is directed at a relationship which, in terms of
chivalric convention alone, must be called successful and which,
at first appearance, is frustrated rather than aided by Ipomedon's deceptions. Only in appreciating the metaphoric and
epiphanic (that is, educational consciousness-raising) role of
engin for the romance's world and its audience can we fully
understand what Hue is about.

Hue emphasizes the uniqueness of Ipomedon's ingenuity by
prefacing it with La Fière's less attractive, more self-serving
version of the same quality. Her ruse for nipping the young
Ipomedon's love in the bud (she delivers a rebuke clearly intended for him to another squire, her cousin, in Ipomedon's
presence) exemplifies the fate of *engin* tutored not by inner
awareness of ultimate personal priorities but by shame (the
desire to be thought well of by others, and thus the willingness
to let others define one's values, goals, and, in short, identity):
such ingenuity serves folly instead of combatting it, and en-
slaves instead of freeing, because it impedes the attainment of
personal fulfillment instead of aiding it. Ipomedon is impelled
by La Fière's ingenuity to leave her, an outcome which, once it
happens, La Fière realizes to be the opposite of what she really
desired. After she has achieved this first level of new awareness,
under the tutelage of nascent love (a process that shows her to
be the lineal descendant of the heroines of the Ovidian *contes*
mentioned in chapter 2), she appreciates the necessity to protect her new, private vision of future happiness and uses her resources of wit more beneficially, to hold off the demands of her

barons and to find a solution (the tournament) that may bring her her *ami* without exposing her to the shame of marrying for love and disregarding her vow to marry only as the chivalry topos dictates. La Fière confides to her damsel, Imeine, in outlining her plan and motives:

> Certes, Imeine, ço n'est pruz,
> Idunc s'en gabereient tuz:
> Quant si riche vou ai voe,
> Si avrei' un vadlet ame,
> Ke unc ne fist chevalerie,
> A tuz dis serreie hunie.
> Pur deu, Imeisne, ore entendez:
> Si jeo mesdi, nel me celez:
> Se peusse tant bel preer
> E vers le rei si engigner,
> K'il feist aukes de mun pru,
> Pur meintenir mun riche vou,
> K'a un terme vousist attendre
> E un turnement ci prendre,
> Ki sulement treis jurz durast;
> Ke le pris d'iloc en portast,
> Certes, jol prendrei' a seignur,
> Ja n'atendreie avant un jur;
> Kar, se mis amis est en vie,
> Jo ne quit pas, k'il le lest mie,
> K'il ne venge, se deu me salt,
> S'il nulle ren as armes valt;
> E s'il ne vent, dunc sai jo ben,
> Ke de pruesce n'i ad ren:
> Ne jo dunc par nulle destresce,
> S'il n'ad en sei mut grant pruesce,
> Ne l'amerai ja a nul for,
> Mes q'hum me deust crever le quor;
> Certes, Imeisne, ben vus di,
> U il del tut le ferunt si,
> U jo tut le pais perdrai,
> Autrement seignur ne prendrai. [2477-508]

La Fière's attempt to trick the king (2486) relies on the chivalry topos because she still cannot face the consequences of earlier *folie,* even though she now recognizes it as such. If she admits publicly that she loves an untested *vadlet,* she will be shamed forever (2482); the tournament will bring him to her if he has any martial virtue at all (2498), and if he does not, she will love him no more (2503). This last remark shows that at this point La Fière is still blinded by her foolish vow to the magnitude of her desire. Her *engin,* therefore, remains problematic, because it is both self-interested and self-deceiving. As Hue says,

> Femme set ben fere sun bon,
> E dunc ne sunt femmes mut pruz,
> Ke si engignent nus trestuz?
> Veer poez qe mut sunt sages,
> Quant li reis e tut sis barnages
> E li chivaler de deus regnes
> Sunt deceu sul par deus femmes.
> [2574-80]

Ipomedon's strategems, on the other hand, elicit Hue's repeated praise;[39] but our initial reaction to the tournament in which we see them at work is to ask why *engin* plays a part at all. Ipomedon could, after all, enter the tournament *in propria persona,* and, having won the prize, stay to enjoy it. Instead, Hue chooses to follow the convention of the disguised hero, familiar to us (and presumably to him) from *Cligès, Lancelot, Yvain,* and *Partonopeu.*[40] The device of having the hero fight incognito and only reveal himself after his final victory expresses metaphorically the gap between the hero's experiential situation and his love-inspired vision of his "true identity," that of a self perfected and fulfilled. However, Hue immensely complicates the metaphor by having Ipomedon assume two mutually contradictory disguises—the *bel malveise* and the unknown prowess hero—and then splits the latter into several apparently different identities, each distinguished by a different color of armor. As *bel malveise,* Ipomedon denies his abilities and prompts social scorn (the Sicilian courtiers mock his cowardice); as three knights in one, he misleads the contestants in the tournament, La Fière, and all other observers by fragmenting his abilities to invite incorrect assessments of them. He even calls attention to his method by setting up a further, obviously false identity as *dru la reine.* (Creating a gap between name and reality is a frequent trick of Chrétien's; here the hero, not the poet does it.[41] Ipomedon is here an artist-surrogate, and his *engin* points to Hue's. There may also be in the name *dru la reine* a comic reference to and repudiation of the adulterous chivalry of Lancelot and Tristan.)

Moreover, Ipomedon's *engin* encompasses deceit via obsessively public behavior and equally obsessive private, or secretive, behavior. As *bel malveise* he creates and stages processions like the novel one in which he arrives at the court of Sicily (2635–711),[42] or his departure for the "hunt" each morning of the tournament (3527-44). Simultaneously, and indeed under the cover of these ostentatious displays of hunting procedures (which awaken, and thus annoy, the courtiers each morning), he creates a system of arriving at and leaving the tournament unnoticed each day, and spends his days there, as we have seen, in a series of different disguises.[43]

In his daily dealings with La Fière, even the discarding of disguise becomes part of Ipomedon's *engin,* for he couples it with a false announcement of his imminent departure from her land (4149-62, 5185-200, 6301-24). Finally, by using a friendly innkeeper as *nuntius* (6651f.), Ipomedon can reveal his campaign of double deceit and still avoid the harmony and reconciliation which normally accompany such revelations in romance. Astonishing the work's internal audience (the other characters who have observed him in his various roles) and defeating the expectations of its external audience (whose knowledge of romance leads to certain assumptions about the consequences of such revelations of the truth), he shows his mastery of his world (which in turn shows Hue's manipulative mastery of the chivalric romance form) by postponing the satisfaction of its yearnings for losses restored and sorrow's end.

Why this centrality of *engin*? Ipomedon's many staged processions are *semblants*—the word is Hue's preferred one for
behavior inspired by but concealing *engin,* and appears like a
leitmotif throughout the episode[44]—which hide the real man
and his purpose (battle) behind a screen of formal pageantry
and organized activity. But so, we realize, is the tournament and
its *semblant* of chivalric order directed to a noble end (the
winning of La Fière) a screen for the violence which Hue so
graphically describes, and which, taking control of men, puts a
new perspective on their quest:

> N' i ad si membre ne si sage,
> Ki gueres penst de mariage;
> Tel i pert le pie u le poing,
> Ke vousist estre d'iloc loingn;
> . . . .
> Teus quidout espuser la fere,
> Ke l'um d'eloc porte en sun bere.
> [4933-40]

(Hue comments further on the violence of the tournament and
resultant human damage in several other passages: 3885-912,
4821-44, 4915-42, 6161-68).

All of Ipomedon's deceptions taken together create a *semblant* of reality which traps people into reactions that reveal
their true emotions and the assumptions underlying them: the
despair of La Fière at losing Ipomedon, the derision of the
courtiers, and the shame of the queen at the antics of the *bel
malveise-dru la reine.* The epiphany with which Ipomedon ends
the episode reveals that what others considered reality was a
performance, and that their reactions, treating illusion as
reality, convict them of *folie.* (Of course, the episode is also an
exercise in showing the negative effect of multiple, limited perspectives on "reality" which isn't reality at all. Comparison of
Ipomedon's *engin* with Guinevere's manipulation of Lancelot
and its antisocial effects, as well as its creation of multiple
perspectives, in the tournament at Noauz [see chapter 5] is
useful in forming an adequate understanding of Hue's positive
use of *engin* in the tournament scene.)

Ipomedon's *engin* does not solve problems, as does that of La Fière or Lunete or Urraque; it converts an exercise in chivalry—the tournament—into an exercise in consciousness raising. (Again, in this respect, the hero and his creator are closely linked, for it is from Hue that all lessons ultimately proceed.) The main fact we learn through this exercise is that we *all* create a false reality—through *folie,* not *engin*—when we so completely accept a restrictive social code as to distort our understanding of individuality, of the complexities of motivation within each person, and can only judge by the *appearance* of whether a person or deed conforms to the precepts of a code—in this case the code of heroic prowess. (That is, we define people socially and thus deny them the possession of a unique identity which may show its uniqueness and its self-awareness in ways not easily assessed by means only of conventional social codes.) Ipomedon's ridiculous assumption of the title *dru la reine,* based on the appearance alone of such a relationship with the queen, acts out for the court its own folly in dubbing him *le bel malveise* and censuring him because he prefers hunting to killing in jousts, one kind of mortal game to another. (Ipomedon's descriptions to the court each night of his supposed daily hunt are comic allegories of his adventures in the tournament, thus paralleling the two activities; see 4415–30, 4445–52, 6504–18. His description of how he was wounded while hunting tricks the courtiers into mockingly praising him for receiving his wound in the tournament, that is, for telling the truth under guise of jest. See 6552–54.) The court has sinned against his individuality by being able to assess him only by matching him to a dominant ethic, not by judging him in terms of the personal goals and identity he has set for himself.

Furthermore, to accept the false reality of a code which judges men by the apparent conformity to that code is to injure one's own interests. The queen of Sicily exemplifies such *folie* when she conceals her love for her "dru" out of shame at his refusal to conform to the accepted prowess code. (Hue offers touching descriptions of her contradictory emotions: 4431–42, 4509–18.) Hue's attitude toward this *folie* is succinctly and saltily put at 4311–12: "Amur ne quert fors sun delit,/Mut valt

le juster enz el lit." This had also been La Fière's failing, as I
have already observed: she attempted to impose upon her inner
feelings and desires, that is, on the indices of true personal fulfillment, an external, "received" fulfillment based on prowess.
Léonin's appearance in the latter part of the romance demonstrates the magnitude of this *folie*; that one who meets the
conditions of her earlier vow should be so hateful to her means
that her love for Ipomedon has brought her to awareness of
the irrelevant and potentially disastrous nature of her earlier
confusion of illusory (conventional) and real (personal) satisfaction. Léonin's name—the lion was a common medieval
symbol of pride[45]—and his description as *orgeillus* from the
moment he enters the story (7674) also suggest that Hue wants
us to think of him in part as a personification of the queen's
own pride come home to roost and of the self-endangering
nature of the *fole* choice of external as opposed to internal
control over personal destiny.

From another perspective, Ipomedon's *engin* is directed at
himself and at all others who submit their lives to the norms of
chivalry (functioning here as a metaphoric image of all attempts
to mold experience to our desires through forceful confrontation). Allegiance to the restricted code which La Fière imposes
on Ipomedon as the price of her love destroys all other values
except victory and sets all men equally against each other, without regard to motive, character, or bonds of relationship. Hue
makes this point, which I have discussed in connection with the
Guivret episode in chapter 2, by means of the battle between
Drias and his brother, Candor, who are on opposite sides of the
melee during the tournament. Drias "out mut grant envie"
seeing Candor's prowess on the field, and, not recognizing
him, attacks and kills him (5991–6068; note the contrast between this outcome and the near-repetition of the same catastrophe later between Ipomedon and Capaneus, averted by
recognition of the ring given by their mother). Also, Ipomedon
fights his feudal lord, Meleager the king of Sicily, who does not
recognize him (5093f.). As all men are judged by the same
external touchstone, private identity is in effect lost. Hence

Ipomedon's decision to fight anonymously and in a different disguise each day dramatizes his loss of all other identity than that bestowed by his armor and his performance. Throughout his adventures, in fact, Ipomedon fights anonymously; he even refuses to be crowned king of Apulia when his father dies (7201–26), "K' il volt uncore de terre en terre,/aler ses aventures quere" (7219–20). In such a life, kingship is meaningless; when chivalry is the yardstick, all identities are indistinguishable and thus interchangeable. The ultimate statement of this damning truth comes in Ipomedon's greatest battle, the single combat against Léonin. By donning the same armor as Léonin, Ipomedon removes all grounds for choice or distinction between the contestants except that of prowess, despite their complete divergence in moral worth and motivation.[46]

Ipomedon's *engin* thus dramatizes his alienation from himself and victimization by prowess, the foe of individuality, and justifies the condemnation which the *bel malveise* directs at prowess and at the winner of each day's jousting, that is, at himself.[47] (In Ipomedon's descriptions of his supposed daily hunts, the best hunting dog is given the same color as the armor he wore that day. The *bel malveise* also declares, "Mut tenc ces chevalers a fous,/Ki tut de gre suffrent teus cous,/De grant folie s'entremistrent" [5461–63].) As a result of the curtailment of identity which results from submission to the chivalric conventions of the adventure quest, neither Ipomedon or any other participant in the tournament can be said to be fully human, fully an individual with private destiny and personal identity.

The paradox of Ipomedon's situation is that although his *engin* and its *semblants* stimulate the comprehension of his plight, they cannot release him from it. (This is very different from the problem-solving use of *engin* in the imperfect, chivalric world of *Yvain.*) The chivalric quest imagines the triumphant attainment of love and self-fulfillment but, logically, to suspend the quest for *los* and *pris* is to leave oneself open (like Erec after his marriage) to the charge of *recreantise* and, in Ipomedon's case, his nonfulfillment of La Fière's vow;[48] there will always be someone else to fight as long as one sees battle as the validation of one's deserts in love, and therefore as the guarantor of one's personal destiny. Chrétien broaches this same logical flaw in the chivalry topos too strenuously applied, through the predicament of Mabonograin, the giant knight in *Erec* who is trapped in the magic garden (symbol of the love relationship) and cannot leave it until he loses a battle, which his pride will not let him do intentionally. When Erec defeats and frees Mabonograin he uses prowess, inspired by love in a free relationship, to overcome prowess forced by love into a constraint which denies freedom and ultimately individual identity: Mabonograin is nowhere known by his name since he never used it as a squire and has not had a chance to use it since he became a knight because he was immediately imprisoned in the garden by his *amie*.[49] Hue, pushing beyond Chrétien, does not allow prowess to solve what prowess has caused.

Engin clarifies the dilemma of the hero trapped within chivalry, but cannot, by understanding it, resolve it; Ipomedon's art has great power, but also clear limits. His last abandonment of La Fière, by its postponement of the reconciliation we have twice been led to expect, coopts us into disgruntlement and disillusionment about chivalric adventure: we want the romance to end at this point, the more so as we have now become fully aware of all the faults of the chivalry which has sustained the plot. That is, we now see the difference between chivalry as a conventional system and the individual's search for fulfillment, which chivalry does not seem able to bring about.

Capaneus now appears, and, by discovering another contact between men besides that of clanking steel—the kinship revealed by the ring—makes possible Ipomedon's liberation, and thus La Fière's, and thus their union and self-realization as individuals. The all-important ring was given to Ipomedon by his dying mother, whose gift incorporated into the chivalric world a legacy of love, passed from one generation to the next, which, if not disguised by the armor of prowess, will bring men harmony and fulfillment via the recognition of individual identity and therefore the potential of personal relationships based on things shared between individuals. Capaneus only sees the ring when the armor enclosing Ipomedon's hand is struck off (10,200f.), and after Ipomedon reveals where he got it both knights drop their swords and shields to the ground (10,285–88), symbolically ending the reign of depersonalized prowess by the recognition of private identity. Only on this basis can Hue show us, as he does, the heroic, adversary vision of human relationships superseded by a sense of shared humanity which forms a basis for reconciliation. And this metamorphosis in perception of the norms governing the knight's meetings with others in the course of his adventure quest for personal fulfillment makes possible that fulfillment—figured as the union of man and woman. We respond to Ipomedon's manipulations of reality to create epiphanic paradigms of experience and its pitfalls with profound sympathy for the abrupt and artificial turn of events which brings *Ipomedon,* against our expectations, to a happy conclusion.

The very artifice of the ending of the romance deflects our attention (and gratitude) from the characters to Hue who, through his *engin,* has, Godlike, created and saved Ipomedon, his abilities, and his world.[50] We stand poised between the ironic dismissal of chivalry and sincere acceptance of its transcendence by love, as we stand poised between acceptance of Hue's final comic perspective on his extravagant and fantastic ensemble of heroism and *engin* (see his closing obscene remarks) and the conviction of having looked deep into the well of human experience and seen reflections of our talents and *folies.* Such a balanced response is an important correlative to the balanced art of twelfth-century chivalric romance.

This deeply rooted double perspective on chivalric romance as literature parallels the double perspective on *engin* about which I have said a good deal. Through *engin,* characters and authors of chivalric romances are repeatedly shown to be at work gilding over intractable realities with a facade of chivalry and idealistic love. At one extreme, the self-conscious audience sees the self-conscious artist as a teacher and a standard-bearer, expressing their courtly aspirations through his art better than they can, and thus encouraging them toward perfection. But at the other extreme, the artist is a deceiver, a dealer in images that falsify reality, or that occupy a never-never land toward which the proper response is healthy, skeptical laughter.[51] What we witness in assessing the impact of *engin* is a society attempting to come to grips with artfulness, with those abilities whereby man does not simply endure reality heroically, but attempts to mold it to his inner vision. The ambivalence of the self-conscious individual toward his own vision of self-perfection and final happiness underlies ambivalence toward *engin* and the romances that rely on it. On the one hand, the vision is the essential prerequisite to a meaningful attempt to live life as an individual, as someone who makes choices and shapes his behavior to fit his sense of himself, instead of merely attempting to conform to a pattern of life imposed from outside: ritual observances, acts of public penitence, prescribed feudal duties. On the other hand, the vision is always in danger of degenerating into fantasy, or escape from reality, and of thus becoming a source of entertainment and relief—a welcome interruption from the demands of prescribed routine, but of no more effect on "real life" than dreams and pretty paintings.

On the subject of audience response to poetic achievement in a chivalric romance it will be useful to adduce the one place in Chrétien de Troyes's poetry where we find depicted the actual reading of a romance. The moment comes in the course of Yvain's adventure at the Castle of Pesme Avanture (5101f.). Yvain arrives at the castle seeking lodging for the night and is warned by the villagers that he will find only shame there. The porter repeats this threat but the undaunted Yvain enters the castle, only to find three hundred maidens living in abject poverty, imprisoned in a fenced yard where they spin fine cloth for the profit of the lord of the castle who keeps them there (5182f.). Having learned from the maidens the reason for their plight and the terrible custom of the castle, which will force him to fight for his life against two vicious "filz de deable" (5265), Yvain moves on into a garden within the castle keep. There, in an idyllic setting, he finds the lord and lady of the castle, sitting in elegant idleness while their beautiful teenage daughter amuses them by reading a romance—"ne sai de cui," Chrétien says. (5360). The lord greets him politely and entertains him, but the next morning, as promised, Yvain and his lion must defend themselves in the manner predicted. By defeating their opponents, they free the three hundred damsels and break the evil usage of Pesme Avanture.

Chrétien's point may seem at first reading to be that romances (including his) provide escape from the sordid realities of the world, represented by the imprisoned damsels and the horrible custom of the castle, rather than instruction in how to overcome them. But this is not really the case. Chrétien is not, I believe, equating his own art with an undistinguished anonymous story by which the innocent damsel entertains her parents and helps them to disguise the cruel nature of their society. On the contrary, by giving the moment so little attention (almost pointedly, we might say)[52] and by avoiding any response to it that would, like the *Enéas* poet's comment on his tombs, prompt us to identify it with Chrétien's own work, he is opposing this inoffensive, immature, ineffectual art to the excitement, variety, suspense, and essential morality of his own version of romance, of which this very episode—with its juxtaposition of the miserable, very real damsels, the golden conventionality of the garden, and the threatened encounter with devilish opponents—is a complex example. By placing the conventional, detached, and minimal use of romance as entertainment in one corner of his own larger vision, Chrétien both appropriates its effect as one part of his own and shows how much more he can do. (One thinks of the contest in book 4 of Ovid's *Metamorphoses* between the ineffectual mythological storytelling of the daughters of Pierus and the richer, more Ovidian art of the Muses, whom they have foolishly challenged to a contest.[53])

Chrétien has chosen to make this comparative claim for his art in a setting which stresses the individual's power to overcome social restrictions through personal virtue. In the hands of a master, chivalric romance, far from distracting attention from evil customs, offers exemplary encouragement to break the coercive, exploitative hold of *usage* on the "artist" in all of us (represented by the weaving damsels) so that we can be free to "weave" our own lives,[54] into a form that will bring the personal enrichment of self-fulfillment, the same enrichment being actively sought by Yvain, whose fortitude on his lonely quest (aided by the loyal lion) results in liberation, and thus proper personal recompense, for the imprisoned maidens.[55]

It is possible to argue that even when most attentive to its own artificialities and unreality, chivalric romance never abandons its commitment to images of individual excellence. The great reliance placed by the poets on a new battery of techniques to render the environment, and the characters' interaction with it, palpable to the audience helped them to ground their works solidly in the reality of personal experience. The next two chapters will be devoted to extensive consideration of some of these mimetic techniques.

Among the representational innovations of twelfth-century chivalric romance, perhaps the most revealing, in terms of the emergence of the individual, is its treatment of time and space. In the romance genre generally, man is defined in terms of *becoming*, not *being*; that is, what he is is a function of what time brings him. The sequence of events whereby protagonists are separated from and then returned to their "normal" world, or grow from helpless children to capable adults, shows them (and us) what they can do and presents them as the sum total of their experiences, as more than they were when they started, even though in a physical sense they remain the same person. (I will say more about identity paradoxes in romance in chapter 6.) The passage of time brings discovery, recovery, truth. But if time shapes man, man shapes time: it is the individual life at the center of a romance which gives to time the meaning it has. We see and apprehend the passage of time—often in large parcels of decades and generations—from within the hero or heroine, or at least from their perspective. Time exists, in effect, to let man grow and experience; it is the medium of his dynamic definition. Larger temporal frames of reference than the biographical—the rise and fall of nations, the control of all human history by divine providence, the division of the world into a specific number of ages—are not determining facts in romance; what matters instead is the time it takes a man to return home from the war, or to pass from untested youth to seasoned adulthood.

Now, if time takes its effective meaning in a narrative from the "biography" of the protagonist, rather than from a larger, world-historical scheme or social-historical unit, we can call time, as a plot factor, "subjective," to distinguish it from time schemes which are "objective," that is, which preexist or are valid outside the particular experience or career of an individual.[1] And a fortiori the crucial periods in the time-continuum of a biographically centered narrative—the turning points, and especially the occasions when a decisive action, to be decisive, must take place within, or before the expiry of, a certain specific segment of the time-continuum—are also "subjective." They are crucial because the career and the perspective of one protagonist (or a few) make them so. (Witness the crises of Enide and Urraque.) At those critical moments, or *kairoi,* we are aware of the passage of time not simply as the medium of experience, but as its organizing force, compelling an individual into situations where what must be done cannot be determined without considering when (and how quickly) it must be done. (As the Greek proverb puts it, ὁ χρόνος ἐστὶν ἐν ᾧ καιρός, καιρὸς ἐν ᾧ χρόνος οὐ πολύς: time contains critical moments, but critical moments don't contain much time.) By means of the *kairos,* the writer of biographically centered narrative shows how the personal experience of time shapes responses which contribute to self-definition, and, in the long run, impel the individual toward or away from self-fulfillment.

As a narrative device, creating suspense and forwarding a plot, the *kairos* ultimately derives its validity from the irreversible biological processes of life, from the fact that we move forward in time from birth to death and cannot turn back to undo or redo a moment. Thus the crucial fact of *any* moment of life is its uniqueness; all "biographical" or "subjective" time is, logically, a sequence of *kairoi,* and the few *kairoi* of a particular romance are therefore exemplary of a basic fact of all human life.

It is also possible to interpret human life from a perspective outside the individual, to look beyond biological irreversibility and biographical uniqueness for the grounds of life's meaning and to concentrate instead on other, objective criteria. Examples would include (1) showing how any one life recapitulates universal processes that render time and experience cyclical (as in seasonal myths and rituals); (2) defining human existence in relation to a normative set of events that impress upon all history a definitive pattern and thus render the subjective perception of time irrelevant (as in a chronicle organized according to the Seven Ages of the World, or historiography like Bede's offering a national version of salvation history). In other words, the meaning and use of time in a narrative is not an isolated or random choice made by the author, but a reflection of a view of personal experience and its significance. The use of critical moments in a narrative to show how the passage of time gives meaning to, and derives meaning from, specific, unique, autonomous lives implies the presence of the concept of the individual at the center of the writer's mimesis. The absence or violation of a strict temporal sequence organized around biological (irreversible, cumulative), biographical (personal, as opposed to national or universal) and subjective (valid only for the protagonist) *kairoi* implies a perspective on reality stressing collective or universal rather than personal or unique experience.

The role of time, and of events in time, in chivalric romance vis-à-vis earlier medieval narratives illustrates this general opposition of uses of time and supports my claim that twelfth-century chivalric romance peculiarly embodies its age's discovery of the individual. Further examples from romance (to corroborate the inferences about time I have drawn from the Guivret and Ardenne episodes) and contrasting examples from early medieval narratives are now in order.

In most early medieval narratives the passage of time is not presented with much concern for the sequence of events in time which make up the earthly experience of the characters. Time, as men experience it in their lives, moment following moment, is seldom carefully represented with a view to making the audience feel its impact, or to exploiting its ability to focus the perceptions and emotions of characters. *Beowulf,* for example, in presenting its memorable picture of a hero and of the pre-Christian heroic age, uses many romance-plot devices (journeys, gaps of time, the isolation of the hero) but remains an archaic epic to which we respond very differently from the way we respond to chivalric romance. Much of the peculiar effect of *Beowulf* is traceable to its use of time. John Burrow has pointed out that *Beowulf* is the kind of work which tells its "facts" by lumping together narration, recall, and prediction—by leaping from present to past or future and back without warning, and sometimes without immediately apparent reason.[2] (Thus the proliferation, some years ago, of critical literature arguing about the relevance of the digressions in *Beowulf,* most of which involve such leaps forward and backward away from the main story to recount others.[3]) Opposed to this procedure is one in which an author parcels out his facts in accord with the time sequence experienced by the protagonist. In this scheme, the hero, the audience, and the narrator all know the same amount about the story as it unfolds. Mystery and uncertainty are, as a result, dominant characteristics of the narrative.

In *Beowulf,* on the other hand, a sense of doom is propagated by the constant referrals forward in time—to the burning of Heorot, possibly to the strife between Hroþgar and Hroþulf, to Grendel's destruction when he approaches Heorot for the last time, to Beowulf's own death when he goes forth to confront the dragon. The sense of doom is but one form of awareness on the part of the audience that the characters are partaking in a temporal scheme and fatal process larger than themselves, often beyond their control. The final part of the epic, recounting Beowulf's last battle, is constantly punctuated by accounts of wars between the Geats and Swedes stretching back over several generations; as a result of these long-past events, Beowulf's death will mean disaster for the Geats, and the messenger who brings them the news of their leader's death confidently predicts a time of exile and misery for the survivors. Here our gaze is swept forward, well beyond Beowulf's death, making the warrior's fall part of a continuum of events in the ongoing life of a nation. In this part of the epic there is also a description of the last survivor of a long-gone civilization saying goodbye to his race's treasure. This is the treasure the dragon will guard, the ancient dragon who seems to represent the logical curse of time itself—of history gone wrong, as it must go wrong and destroy all men when it is not perceived to be organized by the Christian providential scheme which gives a hopeful, positive direction to time.[4]

The *Beowulf* poet is attempting in his epic to recapture the virtues of the heroic age while putting it in perspective as a time when men were ignorant of God's purposes. To underscore this latter point, he not only uses formulaic half-lines which stress the ignorance of the Danes (for example, 49-51, 119-20, 162-63, 180-83; the basic formula is, *x ne cunnon* [*or cuþon*]), but also uses violations of the narrative present to establish the audience's knowledge of events and outcomes as superior to that of the characters. When Wealhþeow, queen of the Danes, bestows a rich necklace on Beowulf, the occasion of the gift allows the poet to leap backward in time, to compare it with Hama's famous robbery of another fabulous collar, and then at once forward, to show us what will happen to Wealhþeow's present: Beowulf will give it to Hygelac, who will lose it when he is killed on a raid into Frankish territory; it will then pass into the possession of a lesser warrior (1192-214). Thus the necklace is placed in double perspective: one heroic (consider the *scop* who compares Beowulf's deeds to Siegmund and Heremod, 874-915), the other ironic and subversive of the symbolic function of treasure in heroic literature.

The nature of oral culture is such that all deeds can only be evaluated by comparing them with the legacy of stories about past deeds. Thus the measure of tribal reality in such a culture is not the individual but the body of tradition into which the individual and his deeds must be fitted. Accordingly, the movement of time in oral (or archaic) literature will be constantly interrupted by digressions, excursions into the past intended to help the audience give meaning to men and deeds—meaning they do not fully achieve until they are matched up with and inserted into the continuity of tradition. But since surviving oral-influenced literature is about an age now over (the age of oral culture), there is inherent in it an elegiac component, a sense of decline and ephemerality, which coexists uneasily with the celebration of the past. This sense is expressed by another kind of violation of time sequence, the prophecy, such as the Geatish messengers or (more troublesome to critics) Beowulf's prophecy-description of the failure of Freawaru's peace-making marriage to Ingeld and the rekindling of the feud between Danes and Heathobards. To ask how Beowulf could know this is to ask a question based on literary assumptions not shared by the *Beowulf* poet. We can only object to leaps backward and forward in time, beyond what the hero could know by experience, if the poet's art aims at representing moment-by-moment experience of time as the norm for our understanding of the unfolding narrative.

The *Beowulf* poet, instead, sees the continuum of time as an opportunity to make points about the nature of heroic society and about how human existence should be seen. God's battle against the forces of evil in the world—Cain's kin, the race of giants—goes back in time far beyond any one human life or national career; the sword hilt which Beowulf offers to Hroþgar after killing Grendel's mother bears a record of the earlier stages of that battle and is both a guarantee and an image of history itself. As a decorated object, a product of high art now devoid of an effective cutting edge, it is also an image of the heroic tradition, magnificent but useless in the face of the Christian view of history which is implicit in it, but not, apparently, understood by Hroþgar.[5]

The poet, then, must both expose the limits and ignorance of the human condition and give us a larger perspective, and more information, so that we can judge his heroes. The inevitable result is a disjunction between the characters' involvement in time and our own, larger involvement. This fact, added to the oral-culture necessity to assess men (and celebrate their deeds) by referring to the record of past *res gestae,* results in the constant juxtaposition of past, present, and future as the narrative moves forward on what appears to be a biographical track, but is in fact antibiographical in most of its tendencies. The critical moments of the plot—Beowulf's three great fights—display some features of the romance *kairos*; but in the dragon fight the momentaneous quality of the encounter is radically undermined by the poet's introduction of Wiglaf's history. Grendel's entry into Heorot is rightly famous for its tremendous tension and ironies, but we have been told Beowulf will win (696–700). Also, as the monster approaches (rendered by triply repeated "þan cwom" sentences),[6] his moment-by-moment advance is balanced by the poet's linking of the angry Beowulf, waiting inside Heorot, and God's well-known (*yldum cuþ*) protection of the Geats (705–09). This kind of involvement-distancing alternation should be compared to the kind we have seen in the *Erec* and *Partonopeu* episodes, where the shifts are accomplished by introducing ironic perspectives into the scene, not by looking beyond or outside it to a higher level of meaning known to an omniscient, post-heroic-age narrator. Very rarely does a chivalric poet interrupt the temporal development of a scene to introduce information or reflection on its ultimate results later in the hero's life, or its ultimate significance from a Christian or other perspective. (There is much analytic and generalizing comment on the characters' inner states, especially love, as in *Yvain* or *Cligès,* but this deals with psychological meaning, not with history or the character's fate.[7]) In short, the hero's consecutive, progressive experience of events in the context of his own temporal perspective is normative in most chivalric romances in ways that it is not in *Beowulf.*

An analogous, though differently motivated and expressed violation of temporal sequence occurs in the other great archaic epic of the early Middle Ages, *La Chanson de Roland.* (The dating of the *Roland* is disputed; it may have been written down in its Oxford MS form as late as 1100, or even later.) I need spend less time making this point for the *Roland* than for *Beowulf,* thanks to Auerbach's superb study of paratactic style as a distinguishing feature of the mimesis in this epic.[8] There are practically no retrospective scenes in the work (only brief descriptions of Roland's past deeds of heroism and pride by

himself and Ganelon), and only one prophecy, that of Charlemagne on the effect of Roland's death on the peace of his
empire. The laisse structure, moreover, breaks the narrative into
small units, each of which brings it to a complete, or nearly
complete, halt by means of the sententious or exclamatory last
line. The sweep, in other words, is not too large, as in *Beowulf,*
but too small, too fragmented, too jerkily climactic to represent
reality as seen within the continuum of an identity—a personal
experience held together and unified by memory, desire, and
biological integrity.

Furthermore, the poet's technique in using laisses is often to
repeat the same basic laisse two or three times, varying the information in it a bit. Related to this is the device of looking
at the same moment in different ways, or, more precisely,
breaking it down from a complex whole into component parts,
in successive laisses. Auerbach begins his discussion of the
Roland by considering such a scene, that in which Roland is
nominated by Ganelon to lead the rearguard and, in consecutive laisses, exults in the responsibility and proclaims his hatred
of Ganelon as a betrayer (751–65; laisses 59 and 60). These
feelings need not be contradictory, nor require excision of one
or the other from the text, but they do entail the presentation
of viewpoints as separated, autonomous statements which presumably coexist in Roland's mind in complex relationship.

The result of this use of laisses is to ignore, or at least dis-
count, the irreversible integrity of passing time. Nor is this
method an artful attempt to present multiple perspectives on an
event or moment in order to show that all human perceptions
of external reality are limited and partial.[9] As opposed to the
manipulations of a Chrétien, the poetry of the *Roland* is not
self-conscious, not interested in devices which call attention to
themselves, not involved in making its manner an intrusive element in the scene's meaning. There is no analogue between the
poet's technique and the hero's behavior, as in *Erec* or (as we
have just seen) *Ipomedon.* The time-scheme (or supertemporal,
providential scheme) which to the poet is irreversible and normative lies beyond the life of any person in the epic, except

perhaps Charlemagne—and he is not its master but its slave, as we see at the very end of the epic.[10] That scheme is the realization of God's will on earth through the actions of the *ecclesia militans.* It is a scheme so great in extent and duration as to dwarf all normal mortals and even the crises of the earthly, feudal society which is its custodian. The work moves in a kind of eternal present; it opens by telling the audience that Charlemagne, our emperor, *has been* in Spain for seven years.[11] As opposed to the opening of *Beowulf,* which distances us from the *geardagum,* that of the *Roland* destroys historical distance. Unlike *Beowulf,* where the narrative is centered on a life, and ends with it, here the hero dies less than two-thirds of the way through the story, and what we see for the rest is the way in which God's chosen society overcomes the internal and external obstacles to its functioning, metes out revenge to Saracens and domestic traitors—and must then stagger on to its next task within the providential scheme, weakened but left no choice.

On the one hand, then, the temporal context in which the world of *Roland* is ultimately set dwarfs all individual lives, all personal desires or awareness. (Charlemagne has an angelic hotline to the top, where alone there is an absolute and objective perspective, and all others in the system take orders from him, betray him, or, like Roland, in effect do both at once, yet die serving God.) On the other hand, the "building blocks" of this immense, providential time scheme are the laisses, subepisodic fragments which impart to the narrative the character of a flow of discrete particles. Because of laisse construction, events in the *Roland* are juxtaposed to each other sometimes sequentially, sometimes simultaneously. They lack both the continuity and the logic possessed by a fictional reality perceived consistently through the eyes of one or more characters having a personal point of view which colors their perception of time's passing.

Finally, the critical moments in the narrative action of the *Roland* contain elements which similarly depend upon perceptions of time outside or beyond the personal. The moment in which Charlemagne discovers Roland's death and realizes that he must avenge his fallen warriors seems to offer the monarch a challenge to act effectively within a given, limited time (before the Saracens' escape) or add the disgrace of failure of revenge to the calamity of defeat. But as Charlemagne offers pursuit, an angel lengthens the day for him, allowing him to reach and destroy the pagans (2418-75). The effect of this divine intervention is twofold: by establishing a typological parallel between Charlemagne and Joshua, the Franks and the Israelites, it denies the uniqueness of the moment, and in effect suggests an objective historical system which gives meaning to events in time; and by showing God's control over the very passage of time from moment to moment, it undermines the concept of ὁ καιρὸς ἐν ᾧ χρόνος οὐ πολύς (the critical moment in which there is not much time [to act]). If God wills, there will be time enough.

A related technique (and underlying view of human action in time) is manifested in the battle between Charlemagne and Baligant, when an angel arouses Charlemagne as he seems about to be defeated by his Saracen *semblable* in the crucial encounter of the whole Spanish campaign (3602-14). The protection and inspiration offered Charlemagne from on high does not make the moment less crucial, but does make it clear that events happen as God wills and as part of (indeed in illustration of) an objective scheme controlled in time and space from outside personal experience—the scheme summed up in the stirring declaration which echoes through the poem: "paien unt tort et chrestiens unt dreit" (1015; compare 1212). This fact, while abundantly proven by the events of the epic, does not take form as specific human beings respond to specific crises within suddenly perceived critical moments. Rather, it exists outside and beyond any one human life, is guaranteed by God and systematically proven by him over immense stretches of time. Similarly, God's power and plan underlies the success of Thierry, the very ordinary, antiheroic Frankish warrior who defeats Pinabel and justifies Charlemagne's authority. (Thierry is described as neither too big nor too small, slender, and somewhat swarthy, 3820-22.) The ending of the poem makes it plain that Charlemagne, too, must bend his will to God's intentions for

the *ecclesia militans* and its warriors. From this divine ordering
of events it follows that even Roland is expendable (painful as
his loss is to the Franks), and what might seem to be the work's
one real, human *kairos*—the moment in which Roland refuses to
blow his horn—becomes ultimately irrelevant. Roland chooses
heroism over feudal responsibility, but thereby neither chooses
his own death (the Saracens cannot kill him; he destroys himself
by blowing the horn when it is too late to save his men, an
emblematic act of heroic self-destruction), nor dooms the Christian cause which, as we have seen, God controls by manipulating time and events.

The urgency of Roland's decision not to blow the horn lies
in his relationship with Oliver (whose perspective on the claims
of duty in the moment when the pagan ambush is discovered
differs sharply from Roland's), and, by implication, his relationship with his fiancée, Alda, Oliver's sister. The poet's
introduction of this personal level (like his introduction of the
enmity between Roland and Ganelon) complicates the picture
of a nation-*ecclesia* fighting to realize God's plan for history. We
find these personally based conflicts and tensions the most
attractive and meaningful parts of the poem, which shows how
thoroughly we have assumed the view of individual-centered
experience and reality purveyed by the chivalric romances and
their successor genre, the novel. This is not to say they are not
in the poem, nor that the *Roland* poet did not want his audience
to see and feel them. His intent is to show how a system—feudal,
hierarchical, superpersonal, guaranteed by God, in short, objective—contains within itself the seeds of subversion, tension, even
destruction, but cannot avoid its ordained place in carrying out
God's scheme.[12] It is as though the poet, perceiving the concerns of a new age with personal fulfillment and personal experience as the measures of all reality, adopted traditional material
and an archaic poetic form to explore both the end of an era
and the inevitable tension between personal perspectives or
motivation, on the one hand, and the imperatives of a rigid,
Christian-providential view of reality and life's meaning on the
other. I say "as though" for, in the nature of the case, these are

unprovable assumptions that argue for a poetic consciousness which I do not believe the poet possessed. Still, some such double perception or interest underlies the brief, pathetic appearance of Alda or the presentation of Oliver and Roland. (I cannot call the process dialectic, for there is no synthesis in the epic that I can discover, only a sense that God's demands are inexorable and that man is subordinated to them by a social, rather than personal, system of values and actions.) The important thing is that, in terms of time, the poet does not come to grips with personal experience as the norm.

In two other narrative genres, historiography and hagiography, similar judgments on early medieval views of time obtain. C.W. Jones has shown how early medieval chronicles—non-narrative, year-by-year accounts of noteworthy events—were usually the fruit of an impulse to illustrate some large theological principle about universal or Church history, or to keep a practical record of the passage of years in connection with monastic liturgical observance.[13] Hagiography, on the other hand, was an edifying and exemplary, rather than a biographical or historical, genre. The history which mattered in the lives of the saints was salvation history, centered on the life of Christ and recapitulated in the life of the saint. The accounts of such early medieval saints as Martin and Benedict, emphasizing features already present in Athanasius's *Life of Saint Anthony,* ignored biographical continuity and precise temporal relationships in their fragmented narratives of miraculous incidents.[14] In the *Voyage of Saint Brendan,* the wanderings of the saint and his disciples are controlled by, and made to represent, the cycle of the liturgical year, itself a symbolic, recurrent observance of the universal landmarks of salvation history.[15]

Bede's *Ecclesiastical History,* perceptively analyzed by C.W. Jones as a "national hagiography," shares with hagiography proper a lack of concern with presenting events in temporal sequence reflecting a personal experience of time. Bede's indifference to earthly time and commitment to a larger, normative Christian view of history reveals itself in the first book of the *History,* where the conflation of material from

Gildas and a *Life of Saint Germanus* raises insuperable problems of chronology—insuperable, that is, if one is trying to piece together an account of what happened in what order in the course of post-Roman British history. If, on the other hand, the point of this section of the work is to show the sinfulness of the Britons, and thus to justify their loss of Britain to the Saxons, and in turn to justify the progress of Rome-based Christianity and its usages (as opposed to Celtic ones) in England, then chronological order is not important. Being drawn from a hagiographical source, the Saint Germanus episodes are especially lacking in what we might call temporal logic (*Ecclesiastical History* i. 17–19, 21). This does not make of Bede a negligent or credulous historian; it simply shows that pegging events precisely within a time continuum—a necessary prerequisite of a biographical narrative like romance—is not important to him.

It is against this literary background (and underlying cultural assumptions about man and time) that the novelty of the chivalric romance stands out so clearly. The romances contain abundant evidence of a new interest in, even intoxication with, time as moment-by-moment sequence; time as critical moment; time as organizing factor in an heroic life; and, underlying all other perceptions, time as subjective, perceived in terms of its unique impact on each individual life. There is, for example, Chrétien's interesting creation, as it were, of new, subjective, and existential time schemes in the course of *Yvain,* to reflect the hero's personal crisis and self-liberation from social pressures seeking to control and thus define him. At the beginning of the romance, Chrétien locates the scene in time by a reference to Pentecost, on which day Arthur is holding a feast for his court. There is no indication of where in the course of Arthur's reign we are; as a reign it has no history (unlike Geoffrey's Arthur, who is very much a king of the Britons and whose great crown wearing comes at a specific point in his reign). The temporal indication is drawn from the Church calendar, which means that it has symbolic resonances of inspired unity (Pentecost being the birthday of the Church, when the Holy Spirit descended on the Apostles and formed them into a cohesive unit, enabling them also to appear to men of all nations with their message of salvation), here treated ironically by Chrétien, since the court is clearly in disorder. (Arthur leaves his knights unexpectedly to go to bed with the queen, and in his absence there are squabbles and a tale of knightly failure told by Calogrenant.) Beyond this, however, as a feast in the liturgical calendar, Pentecost recurs yearly, and therefore has cyclical implications as well. The next temporal reference is to the seven years that have elapsed between Calogrenant's defeat by an unknown knight at the magic spring and his narration of this adventure to the court. Given the long interlude between what seems a trivial, albeit unpleasant, incident and its airing, Yvain's sense of urgency to avenge his cousin is ludicrous; clearly, the world of the romance adventures, as first presented, does not move quickly toward crisis, or demand hasty responses. The next reference to a moment in time is the Feast of Saint John Baptist, by which Arthur expects to arrive with his court at the magic spring. While some critics find baptismal imagery implicit in this juxtaposition of the fountain and Saint John, I am more inclined to stress the connection between Saint John Baptist's Day and the Midsummer revels held on that day (and night) throughout medieval Europe. Arthur, that is, wants to treat his court's trip to the fountain not as a perilous (and personal) adventure, but as an occasion for social gaiety, part of the celebration of the seasonal cycle.

The cumulative effects of these early references is to suggest a world whose cyclical and expansive time schemes are at odds with Yvain's chivalric urgency. And indeed, after Yvain has married Laudine and is persuaded by Gawain to go off tourneying, the hero's urgency (which had found its parallel in the urgency of Laudine to find a defender for her magic spring before Arthur arrives at it with his court) seems to give way to the cyclical and especially the leisurely perspective of the court world: he takes a full year's leave from his new bride and then forgets about the passage of time altogether and does not return to Laudine on the appointed day. That is, in breaking his word Yvain not only places the pursuit of honor above love, thus demonstrating ingratitude and cruelty to the woman he has chosen to love; he also loses his realization of the importance of time and the awareness of its passage as ordering elements in personal experience. For these faults Chrétien then proceeds to show his hero punished in a highly appropriate manner: Yvain becomes trapped in a series of situations where the passage of time, and deadlines in time, become crucial factors in his successful exercise of a new, moral chivalry of service.[16]

The latter part of *Yvain* is full of crises resolved by the exercise of virtue at the critical moment. Such moments, critical only for Yvain and for the characters he is serving, make personal awareness of the passage of time the basic temporal ordering force in the romance world. Yvain must, for example, defend the daughter of Gawain's cousin from the lustful demands being made on her by the giant Harpin—but if, in doing so, he is delayed so that he cannot arrive back at Laudine's court by noon on a certain day, Lunete, his benefactress, will be burned at the stake as punishment for her dereliction of duty toward Laudine. Time, as much as Harpin, is against Yvain, and Chrétien revels in the narrow margin by which Yvain succeeds in performing both deeds.[17] A similar cliff-hanging moment comes when Yvain's lion must dig his way out of a room in which he has been enclosed in time to help his master in the latter's fight against the two fiendish enemies for the release of three hundred damsels imprisoned in the forecourt of a castle by the lord of Pesme Avanture (5588–623).

These crises involving crucial, absolute deadlines for key actions are the staple of all adventure fiction and movies, and we tend to take them for granted. But we must remember that underlying them is a sense of the importance of earthly time, conceived of as irrevocable sequence, and of the primacy of individual experience, in which the personal (not collective) *kairos* is an organizing and defining element.

There is, however, an even more interesting innovation with regard to time in Chrétien's ordering of his hero's adventures. From the Harpin adventure onward, the poet inserts several references to Gawain's and Lancelot's quest for Guinevere (the plot of Chrétien's *Lancelot*), which unfolds in time simultaneously with Yvain's quest and in part determines Yvain's actions.[18] We see here that Chrétien is creating a temporal, linear history for Yvain's world by relating one set of adventures to another, day by day. Lancelot's adventures are an external referent by which a hypothetical observer can "date" Yvain's exploits. What makes Lancelot's adventures important for Yvain is their direct impingement upon his own (if Gawain is off with Lancelot, he cannot defend his kin, so Yvain, his friend, must, etc.), not their provision of an absolute or cyclical touchstone, such as a Church calendar or chronicle of salvation history would provide. Neither Lancelot nor Gawain is a "type" of Yvain; his adventure does not fulfill or complete theirs. Rather, they are individual knights having their own sequence of adventures, and their progress serves as a relative (not absolute) standard by which to place Yvain in time. Chrétien is here playing with the fact of *simultaneity* (that many individual adventures can happen concurrently), which, like narrow mimesis, calls our attention to our personal, moment-by-moment experience of time. Biological and biographical *perceptions,* not theoretical or doctrinal *schemes* of time, control our response to the story.

Still, Chrétien's use of time in *Yvain,* as I have just described it, is sufficiently different from the individual experience of time in the Guivret and Ardenne episodes, discussed in the last chapter, to require further explanation. The temporal correlation of Yvain's adventures to Lancelot's, and the deadline by which Yvain must rescue Lunete, involve an element of abstraction about time which is lacking in the *Erec* and *Partonopeu* situations. It is one thing to realize, on the basis of seeing a knight galloping toward you, or by holding an unconscious wretch in your arms, that you must act at once, or within a brief interval of time, to avert disaster. In these cases, the senses deliver the information necessary to heighten one's awareness of the passage of time and of the critical moment. But in the case of a deadline of noon the following day (as with Lunete), Yvain must treat time intellectually: he must understand how the day is divided into hours, when noon comes, and how to judge the passing hours and minutes so that he can be at the right place at the right time. He cannot "see" noon the next day as Enide can see Guivret approaching.

Similarly, the matching up of the adventures of Yvain and Lancelot implies (though Chrétien does not develop this) the keeping of "records" in the mind about *what* happened *when*; that is, it implies that memory can be organized by the intellect into a calendar system, precise to the day and founded upon the events of personal experience, not upon such objective recurrences as Church feasts. But is this not also an "objective" time—a system of time-telling equally valid for all? It is indeed, but of a radically different nature from that of early medieval narrative, by and large. M. Bloch points out that in the early medieval period the passage of time was a relative concept; the length of the "natural" hour changed with the seasons and few people knew about or were concerned with what we might call "well-tempered" time, that is, time divided into standard units which did not vary with the season or other circumstances.[19] The "objective" time scheme of this period—salvation history— was revealed by faith and theology, and it was *accepted* as real and all-important. Earthly time was incidental, a feature of man's exile from God, organized by the liturgical year in cycles, and by the seasons as well. Each man's experience of it was personally felt, of course, but not considered important enough to organize carefully except in monasteries, where the service of God was carried out at regular intervals. And as we have seen, early medieval narratives did not organize themselves around the personal perception of time's consecutive, irreversible passage.

Now, the *analytical* division or measuring of time, such as we see in King Alfred's device (extremely unusual for the early medieval period) of burning candles of equal length to divide his day, regardless of season, into equal temporal units,[20] involves the application of *ingenium,* intellectual order, to our perceptions, so that we may then further order our *actions* in accord with our perceptions. Alfred's candles are a unit of measurement, a least common denominator, a building block; using such blocks, Alfred could then order his day quite precisely: so many candle-lengths for reading, so many for his council, etc. He could also derive the time necessary for important actions in the same way, and plan accordingly. In other words, by analyzing and ordering our perception of subjective time, we arrive at a system of measuring it which is, in a new sense, objective, that is, it gives units which all can take as basic. But, unlike early medieval "objective" time, it does not offer a system of absolute time to be accepted. Rather it offers the opportunity to shape one's own temporal scheme, to express and obtain one's personal goals, etc. Early medieval objective time is collective, Platonic—a reality beyond and overshadowing the un-regulated subjective perception of time, an organizing scheme which renders personal time irrelevant. Twelfth-century "objective" time (underlying Yvain's deadlines and the matching of his adventures with Lancelot's) is analytic, reductive, intellectual—an application of *ingenium* to earthly time to give it a standard meaning, to allow us to organize it, and thus more fully to express our uniqueness by our free use and manipulation of personal time. This Aristotelian scheme elevates the importance of each individual's temporal experience by offering tools whereby to perceive it more accurately and thus control it more advantageously—to make our use of time more an expression of who we are and wish to be. This it does by expanding our ability to plan in crucial situations which extend beyond our immediate sensual perceptions. Such planning is part of the control of the personal environment at which chivalric romance aims.

This excursus seems important, as it explains the bases for the manipulation of time in chivalric romances and relates that manipulation to other high medieval developments of analytic, "least common denominator" systems built up from minimum units (such as the *summa* of knowledge or philosophy starting from individual definitions and propositions, or the units of measurement and combination of parts in the Gothic bay, itself the basic "unit" of an architectural system). In these systems each individual part achieves its importance from its place in the system, as each second and moment does in the continuum of biographical time. An even more interesting parallel lies in music, where the rise of polyphony, in which separate lines of music, usually sung by individuals (as opposed to the choral singing of monophonic plainchant), played off against each other as equals (like Yvain's and Lancelot's adventures), required the development of precise rhythmic notation, that is, an analysis of temporal units and the creation of an intellectual system of notation from which it was possible to plan ahead how voices would work together in time, second by second, to get desired intervals and cadences.[21] Here, too, agreement on standard modules of time (the rhythmic modes) and a notation for them made it possible for the composer to express his precise desires for performing a piece and thus establish his musical "identity." That is, exact rhythmic notations minimized the scope for improvisation which would give a piece a new personality (at least in part) with every performance and violate its integrity as a particular composition of a particular composer. (We might compare the difference between oral poetry, changing from performance to performance, and the written poetry of a single author.)

At a point in *Partonopeu de Blois* after the Ardenne episode, the poet again attempts a narrow mimetic reporting of a key event, this time in a more ambiguous manner and with more complex results. Partonopeu must be knighted by Mélior if he is to keep an earlier promise to her, but he does not want her to see him until he has made up for his earlier betrayal by winning the tournament for her hand; it is this tournament which makes it necessary that he be knighted. So Urraque arranges that Partonopeu will be presented to Mélior along with a group of young squires whom she is to dub; all will wear their helmets (according to the usage of the times, the poet laughingly tells us, 7433), so that he will not be betrayed. The young men enter the palace, and Partonopeu falls in with them from his hiding place (7425–32), past which they go. As they come before Mélior (7442), Partonopeu looks at her and goes into a kind of trance at the sight of her beauty, which recalls both her goodness and his "meffait" (7450). Now he looks in her eyes (7451) and presses closer to her in the crowd (7452). Grief seems to impel him onward, and he seems on the verge of doing something by which he will betray himself to her:

> Molt l'ocit qu'il li a meffait,
> Et nonporquant mais pres s'en trait;
> Por pou qu'il ne li vait al pié
> Querre pardon de son pechié.
> [7455-58]

Urraque sees Partonopeu about to lose his self-control and, as she did in the wilderness, acts to bring him back to himself from the *folie* to which grief is once again leading him (sacrificing the image of future fulfillment on the altar of harsh memories):

> Si s'estut halt por amembrer
> Et por lui faire revenir
> En son sen et por avertir.
> [7460-62]

But Partonopeu pays no attention to her gesture, and continues to act "que toz i fust aparceus" (7466).

But all is not lost. Having brought us moment by moment and step by step, almost, to this point of crisis, the poet cleverly, even outrageously, gets out from under the tension he has built up by declaring that all the other young men were so affected by Mélior's beauty that Partonopeu's reaction did not stand out! There follows a long catalogue of her beauties and dress which brings the action to a halt and submerges Partonopeu's unique perspective on the scene—the clash within himself of desire and memory—in the general response to her beauty.

At line 7515, after ending the interlude with a repetition of the information that Partonopeu is acting no more foolishly in his adoration than "si per" (7514), the poet returns to his hero, who, his head lowered, comes to Mélior "parmi la presse" (7516). Mélior fastens the sword, the details being fully recorded:

> Et Melior saisist s'espee,
> Si li a bel del col ostee;
> Des rainges l'a par des flans çaint
> Et fer noëe et bien estraint.
> [7519-22]

The crucial moment of encounter passes in a flurry of carefully observed detail and Mélior's smooth, assured movements. Now they are moving apart, but Partonopeu lingers and sighs (7524-26); Mélior looks and listens, and, although she does not recognize him, says to Urraque: "Cil chevaliers semble un petit/Des bels oelz vairs et de façon . . ." (7532-33). She does not finish, but looks at the receding figure, and almost calls him back (7536); however, her memory and grief take over, and she almost faints. Partonopeu retreats, "molt regardant" (7541), and ready to come back if she wishes it. Again, we seem to hang in the balance on the brink of a reconciliation or reunion, and again the poet breaks the spell of his suspenseful, moment-by-moment account of the simultaneous movements and feelings of the protagonists. The narrator breaks in to rhapsodize about his own unobtainable beloved (7545-52), and when he returns to Partonopeu, the latter is alone, and announcing his faith, using the "classical" chivalry topos.[22] The momentaneous mode has been dropped.

It is clear that, in this episode, the poet is teasing his audience by raising and then thwarting expectations which are evoked with special force by the technique of narrow mimesis. The realization of the dubbing scene so precisely in time and space—the meeting of eyes, the long second of hesitation when Partonopeu *may* throw himself at his beloved's feet, or when she *may* call him back to look at him closely—as the protagonists themselves experience it *should* lead to a personal encounter (like that between Urraque and Partonopeu) which will confirm the uniqueness of the moment to them as a subjective *kairos.* But this is not the moment in the plot for such a reversal or revelation, so the poet switches techniques and nullifies the built-up tension inherent in the intersection of individual careers in highly realized time and space. The lowering of intensity follows directly on the descent into techniques of description and soliloquy in which the passage of time, and placement in space, are not key elements. The clear nexus between technique and effect illustrates the value of individual-centered time and space to the chivalric poet.

The treatment of space in terms of a minutely observed earthly reality, perceived as if from individual perspective and inhabited by bodies of specific and limited volume, complements the representation of time in twelfth-century chivalric romance. In early medieval thought and imagination, earthly space was most frequently the realm of the Christian's pilgrimage, the place of exile from God; in the romances it becomes instead the indispensable physical setting for subjective time and personal *kairos,* the medium in which bodies are precisely placed so as to highlight personal uniqueness of identity and destiny. Brief reference to some standard attitudes toward and representations of space in early medieval narrative will throw the twelfth century's achievements into clearer light.

A common early medieval narrative treatment of space is to divide it into the limited, known, secure space and the surrounding unknown (or threatening) unbounded space beyond the walls. (The relationship between this scheme and the uncertainties of political or social existence in an age of barbarian migrations and invasions is too obvious to require comment.) The world of *Beowulf,* especially the first part, is a typical example: Heorot, the island of light and mirth, and outside the "enga anpaðas, uncuþ gelad" of a world inhabited by the likes of Grendel and Cain's kin. Beowulf, it is true, has his heroism in part defined by his willingness to leave the comforts of the hall for this threatening world outside; he goes to the underwater anti-hall of Grendel to destroy the monster's mother, and swims in the sea on a dare, battling sea monsters as he goes. But the important point (from my perspective) is that these external spaces are seldom realized with any descriptive precision. For example, after being dragged down to the bottom of Grendel's pool by Grendel's mother (or perhaps along the bottom; see

1495-96, 1506-07), Beowulf perceives that he is in an un-known hall, free of water, illuminated by bright firelight. There is no description of his passage from outside this hall to within it; it seems to materialize around him like a fantastic dream-location of indeterminate size and shape, definable only in terms of dryness and illumination—that is, in terms of its effect on his senses (1512-17).

Indeed, there is a similar imprecision about most of the epic's limited and secure spaces as well: scholars have argued for generations about where Hroþgar stands with relation to Heorot when he gazes on Grendel's hand, because the poet's depiction of the moment is spatially vague. (925-27: "Hroþgar maþelode—he to healle geong,/stod on stapole, geseah steapne hrōf/golde fahne ond Grendles hond ̣. . ."; see Klaeber's note to line 926). Spatial uncertainty on a smaller scale marks the de-scription of Beowulf's grasp on Grendel at the beginning of their climactic wrestling match (745-49); the poet does not know how to describe, or is not interested in describing, pre-cisely the distribution in real space of two bodies. Consequently we are not sure who grabs whom first, nor what position is implied in the half-line "ond wið earm gesæt" (749b)̤

Since Beowulf's heroic feats clearly transcend what normal men can accomplish, his movements in space are used by the poet not to describe space as individuals perceive it, but as a quasi-symbolic medium, existing to demonstrate Beowulf's extraordinariness. Water, for example, is Beowulf's chosen medium, in a sense, but the poet does not render it with pre-cision: the murky pool of Grendel exists for the hero to dive down through for over a day, in order to reach the monsters' anti-hall; the stormy sea functions as an image of the stream of life, as it were, in which a brave man battles against tremendous odds (the monsters) to postpone his day of doom (553-81).[23] There is no room or need, in such a view of external reality, for precise descriptions; indeed, it has often been noted that there are no good descriptions of sea-voyages in *Beowulf,* only de-scriptions of preparations and shore meetings. (See, for example, the voyage of Beowulf to Denmark, 217-24.) The sea stands for the mysterious world beyond man's knowledge, when Scyld's funeral ship journeys off into it: no one knew who received that cargo, says the poet, although we—and he—know it was God.

In other words, in the world of *Beowulf* places and areas have a kind of "objective," symbolic value in terms of their social role or as reflections of the motives that underlay their construction. (Heorot, for example, is a place to give gifts, and therefore has the same social meaning to everyone except Grendel, though he, too, is a "hall-thane" who wants gifts, but the wrong ones: the lives of men, which the poem tells us Hroþgar could not give out.[24]) Likewise, an area receives an "objective" value from its relationship, or rather the relationship of its inhabitants, to God. Thus the *mearcstapa* Grendel inhabits a part of the world where those exiled because of sin (*forscrifan*) live apart from men and their halls (103, 106). When Grendel enters Heorot, the hall becomes infested and must be purged, not simply liberated (*faelsian*, 432, etc.).

A similar attitude toward earthly geography underlies the shorter Anglo-Saxon poems, *The Wanderer* and *The Seafarer*. In the former, the exile of the narrator is described at the beginning of the poem in terms of a few vague actions—"he . . . sceolde/hreran mid hondum hrimcealde sæ,/wadan wræclastas" (3-5)[25]—and his speech is given over to a description of his longings for the hall, his lord, and the society which is his no more. The *state* of exile is what matters, not its itinerary. In *Seafarer* there is much atmospheric writing about both sea life and land life, but these exist as a symbolic pair of opposites setting up the didactic opposition between the joys of heaven (earned by treating this world as a place of exile) and the "dead life" on land. To live on land, in other words, means to treat earthly existence as a home, a condition of life with which to become involved for its own sake. The Seafarer, like the Augustinian *peregrinus,* sees earthly life as a harsh state of exile from God; he endures, but also shuns it and seeks out its harshest aspects, in order to avoid becoming ensnared in the *civitas terrena.*[26] Here again, the ideology of earthly existence militates against precise rendering of given spaces or of our passage through them as individual, integral bodies. So the descriptions of the sea in *Seafarer* are formulaic, atmospheric set pieces stressing discomfort and hardship, not giving an account of where the Seafarer went or what his ship looked like, foot by foot. (Similarly, the geography of *Beowulf* is very vague, and it is impossible to tell where countries lie in relationship to one another just from the text.)

This is not to say that there was no sense of geography, or interest in its portrayal as places arranged in fixed relation to each other on a real earth. The addition King Alfred made to his translation of Orosius, being a description of Scandinavian voyages of two travelers who came to his court, shows such an interest. But, as we have seen with respect to time, Alfred was unusual for his age in being interested in earthly reality (and its measurement) for its own sake or because of advantages to be derived from the manipulation of one's world on the basis of a careful analysis of its components.[27]

To realize the lack of precision and individual perspective in early medieval spatial and topographic descriptions, one need only compare any passage from that era with the description of a marvellous artifact in a twelfth-century *roman antique,* such as the tombs of Pallas and Camilla, discussed above,[28] or of Gawain's approach to Bercilak's castle in the fourteenth-century English romance *Sir Gawain and the Green Knight,* which preserves much of the spirit of twelfth-century chivalric romances. Not only is the castle described sequentially (as Gawain looks at it) from bottom to top, and with great detail, but also more than once, and with different effect, as Gawain sees it first from afar and then close up.[29] I will say more about this type of multiple description of an object or situation, as an invention of twelfth-century chivalric romance, in the next chapter. I mention it here simply to show how unspecific, and un-individual-centered, early medieval descriptions are.

A passage in Bede, indeed perhaps the most famous passage in Bede, provides a last useful perspective on early medieval views of the physical world as the envelope for human activity. The

image of a sparrow flying into, then out of, the lighted hall at
night is adduced by one of King Edwin's councillors to urge the
king to adopt the Christian religion (*Ecclesiastical History*
ii. 13). The sparrow comes in from the cold world outside,
warms itself briefly by the fire, and then blunders out again into
the forbidding night. The inhabitants of the hall know neither
whence it came nor where it goes. Similarly, man on earth has
only the brief, bright moment of his life, and that moment is
surrounded by darkness shrouding his origin and final destina-
tion after death. If the new religion explains such things, it is
to be embraced.

The doctrinal message here is couched in symbolic geography;
we are told that what lies outside our ken is to be accepted on
faith, as a system of belief that we cannot fully explore or
analyze. The image of the sparrow reinforces that sense of space
on earth as divided into small centers of life surrounded by
expanses of unknown darkness. The impact of the sparrow on
Edwin and us depends upon our seeing our physical environment not as a place we must confront and explore in our search
for fulfillment, but as something too dangerous (or irrelevant)
to know by experience, an area of mystery to be transcended
by recourse to a higher form of truth than that offered by the
senses. This is, in other words, a Platonic approach to experience, in which earthly geography becomes a symbol of the
insufficiency of human knowledge. In such a scheme, the precise portrayal of how the world appears to us and is sensorily
experienced by us becomes irrelevant.[30] As Bede tells us in the
sparrow image, where we come from and are going is the same
for all of us; the precise, experiential path by which each of us
travels from one end of life to the other—our personal encounter with a physical environment that impinges on us
constantly—does not much matter. The crucial moments take
place as we attempt to reproduce in our own life Christ's
struggle against the devil; these are the moments which will
enable us to share the life of the saints, and which Christian
literature places in symbolic spaces like Saint Anthony's inner
mountain and great desert.

The basic shape of a twelfth-century chivalric romance plot offers a very different view of man's experience of and in earthly space. The difference is highlighted by an opening scene common to several romances from the twelfth century right through to *The Faerie Queene*.[31] In Chrétien's *Lancelot* and Renaut de Beaujeu's *Le Bel inconnu* (and in a parallel scene late in Hue de Roteland's *Ipomedon*) the scene is set at Arthur's court (or the court of an analogous monarch), at a time of social revelry or well-being. Unexpectedly, an unknown figure enters, bringing news or a challenge, the upshot of which is that one member of the chivalric community must leave the comforts of the court and go off on a perilous adventure. The intruder may be a defiant knight (as in *Lancelot*), a quasi-monster (as in *Gawain*), or a damsel in distress (as in *Ipomedon* and *Le Bel inconnu*); in the latter two examples, the arrival of the damsel is preceded by the arrival of a new knight who will shortly undertake the challenge of adventure. In every case, whatever serious, comic, or ironic point the poet may wish to make, the parallel with the sparrow simile is clear: a stranger sweeps into the court, remains briefly, raising an important issue, and then departs as suddenly. The difference, however, in terms of the value placed on the world of earthly space outside the hall court, is even more striking: whereas the sparrow's flight into the hall stands for the human condition as a universal phenomenon, bounded by areas which we can never explore but can only understand as part of an act of faith in a whole providential system which gives answers to all questions, the brief appearance of the messenger-challenger in romance stands for the challenge to each of us offered by life, a challenge unique to each individual (the intruder either asks for a specific respondent, singled out from the court society, or it happens that only one person is willing, or has a right to the adventure, on the basis of prior promise by the king). Furthermore, the individual so isolated by this call (which therefore symbolically expresses his vocation), can only pursue it—and thus his destiny—by accepting the additional challenge of the world outside the walls, a world to be experienced, not to be taken on faith.

That is, exposure of one's life and body to the great world of earthly space is, in this symbolic scene, good and necessary—the medium for self-improvement.

This episode at the beginning, or at a turning point, of a chivalric romance confirms the world we do not know—the external environment as we confront and encounter it in any new situation—as the proper, potentially beneficial medium of self-fulfillment which, moreover, we must face individually, not as part of an elect society such as the *civitas Dei*. Implicit in such a presentation of the world as our personal, defining space is the recognition that individual perceptions and experiences of the world through which we move (as opposed to an inner world of faith or imagination) are valid and important and are to be represented as such rather than ignored. The actual treatment of earthly space, and movement through it, in chivalric romance makes this recognition explicit, as the following examples (all, I believe, of a type not usually found in early medieval narrative) will testify.

First, just as the chivalric poets show themselves sensitive to the second-by-second experience and importance of time at key points in each individual life, and reproduce that experience as part of an individual-centered narrow mimesis, so are they sensitive to occasions on which the finest gradations of space, in conjunction with time, become crucial, subjectively, to a particular person.[32] That is, they love narrow escapes, that hoariest of adventure-story devices, which raise and exploit our awareness of how important it is that our physical selves occupy just so much space at just such a time and place. In Chrétien's *Lancelot,* for example, after Lancelot has ridden in the cart of public disgrace (which he mounts after a crucial delay lasting just long enough for him to take two steps), he arrives with Gawain at a castle presided over by a damsel. When it is bedtime, two beds are prepared in the hall for the knights, and nearby there is a third bed, more sumptuous than the other two, but which, the damsel tells them, is only to be used by those who merit it. Despite her denial that Lancelot, disgraced as he is, could possibly deserve the bed, he insists on lying in it.

At midnight, a lance comes down from the ceiling, intended to pierce the knight through the flanks and trap him in the bedclothes. A flaming pennon attached to the lance sets the bed afire, but the tip of the lance just misses Lancelot, grazing him. He puts out the fire, throws away the lance, and goes back to sleep (459–534).

In addition to its symbolic content as a representation of Lancelot's avoidance of self-destroying lust in his passion for Guinevere, whom he is trying to rescue, this episode combines two devices for its effect. The first is that of the chosen knight who, because of special merit, can sleep in the special bed. The lady denies Lancelot's merit, but he, by his courage and determination, proves her wrong and establishes his unique status among knights. In this regard the bed is symbolic and represents Lancelot's individuality. (In a later episode, 1856–954, Lancelot proves his uniqueness more explicitly by lifting a tombstone said to be moveable only by the knight who will rescue all those imprisoned in the land of Gorre.) The narrow escape, on the other hand, is experiential rather than symbolic: it evokes the sense of a human body occupying a specific space and the importance of its not being any larger or otherwise disposed on the bed. This aspect of the scene is mimetic rather than thematic, though of course the poet uses this evocation of space in such a way as to increase Lancelot's stature and importance in our eyes. His importance, however, is clearly that of a person moving in a very palpable spatial environment, in which his personal choices (to occupy the particular space of the bed) have consequences crucial and unique to him and his destiny.

An even more obvious use of bounded space as a crucial ingredient of a personal, self-defining quest occurs in *Yvain* when the protagonist, in pursuit of the knight he has wounded at the magic fountain, rushes after him into the latter's castle (876–961). Chrétien very carefully describes the gate to the castle: it is high and wide but with a very narrow entrance way, so that two men on horses cannot enter comfortably together (907–12). The portcullis above, activated by trip-levers in the ground, has a sharp edge, made to cut and mangle anyone it falls on. Precisely in the middle, adds Chrétien, is the narrow path between the hidden levers, and exactly on this path the wounded knight enters the gate. Yvain rushes after him, so close behind that, reaching forward, he grabs the other's saddle. Yvain's horse activates the lever, the gate comes crashing down and cuts the horse in two, but because Yvain was leaning forward holding the knight's saddle, the gate only touches him, grazing his back and shearing off his spurs(!). He falls to the ground, the wounded knight carries on, and another gate falls in front of Yvain, trapping him in the narrow space between. The appearance of Lunete then moves the narrative into its next phase.[33]

It is clear how completely this moment depends on a precise imagination of space, and of individuals' placement in it, for its effect. It is almost like a sermon on the potential importance for our destiny of exactly where we are at any given second. The pursued knight must find exactly the right narrow ribbon of space to avoid the trap; Yvain is saved—but just—by leaning forward. Space and our perception of it matter (and of course time—the split second—matters too).

The fact that this exciting moment ends with Yvain imprisoned within a precisely defined, very limited space provides a transition to another feature of space as used in chivalric romances, albeit one I shall discuss in more detail in a later chapter. If the enclosed space functions often in early medieval narrative as an image of light, security, and social joy, in chivalric romance it functions more often as a place of imprisonment or limitation. *Yvain* and *Lancelot* are full of such imagery including that of the three hundred damsels imprisoned in a "sweatshop" within a castle, and the imprisoned lion digging his way out from under the doorsill in order to help his master. At the center of *Lancelot* we find Guinevere's bower represented as a barred prison into which Lancelot must break to sleep with her. (The reversal of the expected image of breaking out marks Lancelot's disorientation by a passion which turns the world upside down.) In the middle part of Gautier's *Eracle,* the emperor's wife meets her young lover secretly in the narrow house of an old crone and makes love with him in a shallow cellar dug beneath its floor—a superb image of the imprisoning aspect of the love affair which is supposed to be her liberation from the forced imprisonment under which her jealous husband has placed her. (On this episode of *Eracle,* see below, chapter 5; the cellar is described at 4481f.) The tomb-hideaway in Chrétien's *Cligès* which Jehan builds for Cligès and Fénice, into which no sunlight can enter, has similar significance. And, of course, in all of Chrétien's romances the court is often presented as a kind of social prison, a place of restraint or frustration for the adventure hero, who must escape from it to prove himself or win his private destiny.

In other words, enclosures which determine and limit the spatial environment limit as well the hero's possibilities for free and full interaction with the world of human experience, for the *kairoi* which will prove personally crucial. Lancelot, imprisoned in a tower by Meleagranz, cannot get back to Arthur's court to fight Meleagranz at the promised time (a year after their first battle) to decide once and for all which of the two shall keep Guinevere. In order to meet the temporal deadline, he must be free to move in space. Lancelot's liberation from imprisonment embodies not an early medieval, Augustinian flight from entanglement in the *civitas terrena,* but a more positive faith in the ability, and the readiness, of the lone knight to find fulfillment and triumph as a result of accepting what unlimited exposure to experience will bring him.

A final note: just as, within the analytically rationalized time scheme of the world of romance, the principle of subjective time makes specific time sequences important to particular individuals, so with regard to space, the exaltation of earthly space into a medium worthy of precise observation and measurement serves as the context within which individual perspectives endow any given space, and the movement within it, with different meanings and significances. I am thinking particularly of the magic garden where Erec has his last adventure, the *joie de la cour.* The episode takes place in a "magic space," a garden without walls, blooming and fruitful all year round, yet one which can only be entered and left by a narrow gate, and the fruit of which can only be enjoyed within the garden itself.

Furthermore, medicinal plants, growing in abundance, mark the garden as a place of healing. Yet in its midst is a gigantic knight who challenges and has killed all knights who dared to enter the garden for many years past. The garden, which Erec enters eagerly and in search of joy,[34] is a place of sadness to King Evrain, in whose land it lies. Yet by defeating Mabonograin, Erec transforms it into a place of joy (except for Mabonograin's *amie,* who has shut him up in the garden with her by extorting from him the promise not to leave it while he is unbeaten). The garden, in ceasing to be a place of death, becomes a focus of joy for the court. It ceases to be a prison for Mabonograin and becomes a place of mourning and loss for the *amie.* And it becomes the triumph of Erec, the end of his quest for personal fulfillment and *joie.*

Clearly, the garden is a symbolic place, representing marriage, or rather the love relationship, as seen from both personal and social points of view.[35] Chrétien has situated it within the romance so as to allow himself to pull together strands of meaning and perspective which he has spun out through the adventures of Erec and Enide. The contrast between the garden and a place like the lake in which Grendel lives in *Beowulf* is instructive, for the latter has a symbolic value, but a univocal one, clearly relating to the objective world view that underlies the poem: the world is divided into territory where men obey God and places where sinners have been exiled from God.[36] In *Erec,* on the other hand, we see that even a highly metaphorical place will not mean the same thing to all who see or enter it, and the dominance of one or another viewpoint in the garden (as represented by the victorious knight) will endow it with its social meaning, as well. The way in which both Erec and Mabonograin see the garden results from (and indeed stands for) their unique personal relationship with a woman. So even though Chrétien is dealing in the *joie de la cour* episode with a space he has invented, rather than with the observation of space as people experience it sensorily, his method depends once again on the basic assumption that external reality is endowed with significance by individual, not universal or absolute, perspectives.

5: THE INDIVIDUAL AND MIMESIS, II: MULTIPLE PERSPECTIVES ON REALITY

The *joie de la cour* episode in *Erec* offers a good example of what I call the multiple perspective on reality in romance. As I have already explained, I mean by this phrase the way in which an episode means different things to different characters. I have also suggested, in dealing with the Guivret episode, that the poet can analogously force us to see the unfolding sequence of actions in his romance from a number of different perspectives—as he does, for example, by manipulating our responses to Guivret's prowess. The concept of multiple perspective is a keystone in the interpretative edifice I am here constructing; my realization that it was a principle of narrative frequently resorted to by chivalric poets of the twelfth century first forced me to consider that they were making serious statements about the autonomy, and subjective limitations, of individual experience within the deceptively fantastic world of chivalric adventure.

In the examples gathered for analysis in this chapter, I will be expanding my definition to include not only a particular moment or action that is interpreted (or experienced) differently by different characters, each of whom contributes by his response to the scene's total impact, but also events or situations which, because of the characters' movement in space or time, are presented in accord with an evolving, changing point of view and state of awareness. In either case, we are made to realize that "meaning" is subjective, depending as it does on individual response, but also that the "meaning" of events is finally collective or cumulative, the sum total of partial (in both senses of the term) impressions. In an individual-centered world, the subjective interpretation of reality is both normative and limited. From this paradox proceeds much of the complexity, problematic quality, and potential irony of the twelfth-century chivalric romance.

The trick of letting the audience watch the action of a narrative unfold through the eyes or comments of characters within the story is no twelfth-century discovery. Many of the most compelling moments of Ovid's *Metamorphoses* depend on our experiencing with a character, and through his perception, the change he has undergone. The story of Actaeon, for example, focuses on Actaeon's realization that he has become a deer, and his inability to communicate the fact that, internally, he is still Actaeon. Unable to pronounce his own name and thus save himself, he is torn apart by his own dogs, who are urged on by his fellow hunters; the hunters, unlike Actaeon, can communicate his name—they cry out for him to join them—but cannot perceive their friend in the body of the beast. Ovid is here contrasting the limits of his characters and his own ability, in telling the story, both to perceive and communicate how experience changes men.[1] *Beowulf,* which anticipates the forms and techniques of romance in so many ways (perhaps because, as some scholars think, it was given its final shape at and for a sophisticated court), plays with the technique of multiple perspective in the scene of Grendel's last visit to Heorot, but is too committed to the point of view of the historically (and theologically) omniscient narrator to use it consistently. At the very beginning of Western literature, in the third book of the *Iliad,* Helen's appearance atop the walls of Troy to watch the battle between Paris and Menelaos is commented upon by the Trojan elders, and she then comments to Priam on the Greek leaders whom she and the king can see from her vantage point, characterizing them to the aged monarch on the basis of her former experience and observation of them.[2] In this last example, the technique is beautifully, almost cinematically, used for ironic effect, that is, to create an atmosphere of expectancy and personal involvement centered on the hope that the winner of the duel between Paris and Menelaos will keep Helen and the fighting between Greek and Trojan armies will end. The perspectives of the elders, of Helen, of Priam, are then rendered anticlimactic by the inconclusive duel, which Aphrodite frustrates by whisking Paris away to his bedchamber, there to sport with his stolen wife.[3]

In twelfth-century chivalric romance, however, there are no gods who seal the fates of individual quests, as they do those of heroes and civilizations in the *Iliad*. Lacking this level of fate, the chivalric poets use the device of observing through the eyes of their characters as a way of communicating the complexity, not the fatality, of experience, and the subjective, but not insignificant, nature of human perspective. A comparison between a chivalric romance and an epic more contemporary with it may make this distinction clearer.

In the crucial scene of the *Chanson de Roland,* where Roland refuses to use his horn to summon Charlemagne and the main body of the Frankish army, he does so because he must be consistent with his past career if he is to retain his reputation. He resists change, and we know at once what the result will be, for the inevitable behavior of the Saracens, within the Christian-pagan war context, gives the episode and the entire epic "objective" meaning. Everyone's perspective on reality is the same; the Saracen warriors, we recall, are mirror images of the Christians: they have different gods but the same feudal relationship to those gods until they fail, and they have the same warrior virtues. Thus the poet can say of the Saracens that they would be wonderful if only they believed in the Christian God. Only the reactions of Roland and Oliver differ to what both know will be the outcome of the battle: much slaughter and suffering. The *Roland* poet sums up the difference between the two warriors when he says, "Rollant est proz et Oliver est sage;/ Ambedui unt meveillus vasselage" (1093-94). The two warriors exemplify different virtues but share a basic commitment within a definitive system of feudal relationships. The *Roland* poet is interested in the paradoxes of heroism within that system, as well as in other internal social tensions that threaten the doing of God's will by Charlemagne and the Franks. But characters like Roland and Oliver take much of their identity from the feudal order which God guarantees and makes objective in the epic. Roland, *proz* as he is, sees himself as Charlemagne's vassal and, in his dying gesture, ultimately as God's vassal, just as much as do Oliver and Turpin.[4]

It is impossible to sum up the meeting between Partonopeu and Urraque in the forest of Ardenne by having recourse to univocal value-words like *proz, sage,* and *vasselage.*[5] The chivalric poet includes in the recognition scene elements of personal experience and perspective, momentary perception and action on the basis of perception. Each actor in the drama has an isolable wholeness which is foreign to the "paratactic" world of the *Roland* with its lack of interest in inner motivation and its concentration on the clash of legal systems and the allegiances of men who follow them.[6] The *Roland* poet exploits a tension between the hero's singleminded devotion to his code (and to the avoidance of shame) and the more sensible, and by definition less heroic, outlook of those for whom he is at once the chief support and main vexation. These different attitudes (which we find in the *Iliad,* represented by Achilles and Phoinix, or Hector and Poulydamas) are stated and exemplified by the epic poet and form part of the working definition, as it were, of the hero. The chivalric poet is reporting the fact that characters perceive reality differently according to their personal situation or awareness; no evaluation is involved, but rather an observation of how difficult it is to make valuative assumptions, or determine what is really happening in the world, given the limited perception of individuals particularly placed at particular moments.

Roland's (or the *Iliad*'s) juxtaposition of epic attitudes within an immutable world picture and the multiple perspective of chivalric romance are poles apart in narrative technique. Somewhere between these extremes comes the structural ambiguity, and resultant ambivalence of values, in *Beowulf.* If the Old English epic is bipartite, contrasting youth and age (as Tolkien argues), it is a study in balance. If, with Rogers, Barnes, and others, we see it as tripartite, we can regard it as a study in decline.[7] The tension between the two implied structures puts great ironic weight on concepts like treasure, and indeed on characters like Hroþgar, so that we cannot be sure what they stand for—their significance changes with their narrative context. But again, there is an implied objective level here, that in which kingdoms fall and God imposes his will on the world. Further examples drawn from twelfth-century romances will help differentiate the structural-thematic ambiguities of *Beowulf* from the individual-based ambiguities of chivalric narrative.

The chivalric poet's main stylistic and narrative techniques are liveliness of action, variety of momentary effect within a continuum of conversational, run-on couplets, and attention to detail. In a paradigmatic scene from *Erec,* they fuse exquisitely in a moment of humorous, sympathetic multiple perspective, quite unlike anything found in early medieval literature. Erec has arrived at a strange town in pursuit of the unknown knight who has disgraced him and the queen. Needing a resting place for the night, he approaches a seemingly genteel but poorly dressed *vavasor* who promptly welcomes him into his home. The host calls his wife and daughter ("qui molt fu bele," Chrétien tells us in an omniscient aside, 398). The ladies enter, and there follows: (1) a brief antithesis contrasting the daughter's old clothes and the beautiful body they barely conceal (402–10), ending neatly: "povre estoit la robe dehors, /mes desoz estoit biax li cors"; (2) a more elaborate description of the daughter, using a variety of common rhetorical devices, including the topos that nature outdid herself in forming such a beautiful creature (411–23),[8] a favorable comparison of the daughter with standards of beauty both human ("Isolz la blonde," 424) and inanimate ("flors de lis," 427; "estoiles," 434), and a repetition of the uniqueness topos, this time giving God instead of nature as the creator who has outdone himself (424–36); and (3) a brief section in which the narrator, his rhetorical tricks exhausted, as it were, admits defeat ("Que diroie de sa biaute?" 437—another rhetorical trick, often used in chivalric poetry), but tries a last comparison, of the lady with a mirror in which the beholder sees himself (438–41); a reference to the Narcissus myth and to the power of the love object to heighten personal awareness).[9]

Throughout the narrator's self-conscious rummaging in his bag of descriptive tricks the narrative has remained frozen in suspended animation, as we see if we compare lines 401-02—"La dame s'an est hors issue/et sa fille . . . [i.e., from the next room]"—with line 442, of the daughter, "Issue fu de l'ovreor." The narrator has held a character before us and examined her from several rhetorical angles, ascending in complexity from the easy, offhand comment of line 398 to the stylized despair and striking conceit of the mirror image (which, we later realize, anticipates the unwelcome knowledge of himself which Erec will gain after their marriage, seeing her grief). Now the action begins again, the girl's entry into the room, halted for forty lines, is completed, and the narrator abruptly abandons rhetorical for narrative description: we see a series of reactions, physical and verbal, as the narrative asserts its independence from the narrator's powers of *amplificatio* by the concrete actions of the characters.

The daughter sees the stranger and immediately takes a step backwards, precisely because he is a stranger, blushing as she does, but saying nothing (443-47). Erec, for his part, is also surprised, or more properly astonished, at the beauty of the entering girl (448-49); like her, he says nothing. In contrast to, and balancing, these strong but silent reactions is the quite unruffled voice of the *vavasor,* instructing his daughter precisely on how to care for the unexpected guest's horse (450-58). From his perspective, his daughter's arrival on the scene is a completely ordinary event, and his words to her—a cheerful babble of equestrian jargon—dissolve the tension generated silently by the first meeting of the romance's protagonists: "ostez li [the horse] la sele et le frein,/si li donez aveinne et fein" (455-56). The semi-comic undercutting of a moment still dear to the writers of popular novels, makers of movies, and composers of sentimental ballads—the moment at which hero and heroine first lay eyes on each other[10]—is quite conscious, even outrageous: the first words of the *vavasor* seem to forward the emotional and narrative implications of the meeting, raising our expectations: "Bele douce fille, prenez/ce cheval . . ." (451–52); the use of enjambment places additional force on the *rejet,* and the *vavasor* seems to be saying, "prenez ce chevalier." But of course he is not; the joke is on us, and the accumulated tension disappears. The father is not, of course, being cruel or meddlesome; we have abundant evidence elsewhere of his warm feelings for his daughter (for example, 533–46). Rather, he sees this moment in completely different perspective from either Erec or Enide, just as they, we might say, feel its impact with an immediacy quite foreign to the verbose narrator, who seizes on the girl's entrance as the occasion for a display of virtuosity.

What marks this scene, then, is first its concern with the details of human action and response caught at a specific second in time, forming together (Enide's blush, Erec's astonishment) a representation of interaction between characters at the level of personal perception and instant response; and second the existence within the scene of a separate viewpoint—that of another character who misses the personal significance of the meeting. Both these features are thrown into sharp relief against the narrator's stiffer, nonmimetic, conventional description of Enide. Taken together, they underscore the individual nature of the meeting for the future husband and wife within a larger world defined by the sum total of reactions to any given moment. This scene, unimportant as it is narratively, testifies to the interest in individual experience—the conviction that it is the norm by which to approach and judge reality—underlying the whole romance.

Comparison of a roughly analogous scene in Geoffrey of Monmouth's *Historia regum Brittanniae* confirms Chrétien's innovativeness. In book 8, Uther Pendragon, king of the Britons, sees and falls in love with Ygerna, the wife of the duke of Cornwall, at a dinner. Here again, a beautiful woman appears before the man who will ultimately marry her, and Geoffrey describes Uther's behavior quite fully as the king tries to captivate her and call attention to himself by such strategies as sending her choice dishes.[11] But there is no attempt to render Uther's (or Ygerna's) responses at any given second, to savor the scene as a moment of personal intensity, instead of as an important incident in the narrative of British history.

Halfway between Geoffrey's report of an historically important meeting (from which Arthur is ultimately born) and Chrétien's presentation of a personally important one is a first encounter in the *Roman de Thèbes* (ca. 1150?), representing an earlier stage, within vernacular, courtly literature, in the development of the chivalric romance's representation of reality. When King Adrastus of Argos welcomes the exiled Polynices and Tydeus to his court, he has an intuition that they may be the men whom a goddess has predicted his daughters will marry. He calls his daughters to him; after a brief description of their appearance and clothing (951-56), the poet continues,

> Quant eles virent les marchis
> que a veoir n'orent apris,
> vergoigne orent, ne fu merveille;
> la face leur devint vermeille.
> Eles ne sevent qui il sont;
> quant les voient, grant vergoigne ont.
> Color commencent a muer
> et leur pere a regarder.
> Eles vindrent tot droit au roi,
> il les assist dejouste soi.
>
> [959-68]

This is clumsy and repetitive stuff, but the poet attempts to imagine, and represent, the scene by portraying specific, momentary, and as it were emblematic reactions, that is, to locate the first encounter of the princesses and their future husbands in time as it is experienced by the individual, through perception and instantaneous response. Their blush and instinctive glance at their father gives the moment an intensity—an individual identity, distinct from that of the moments around it—not by evoking historical or thematic consequences, but by letting

the audience experience it vicariously and subjectively, as a personal response to a new element in the sensorily perceived environment of specific characters. The *Thèbes* poet moves on to
a conventional, anticlimactic catalogue of the ladies' beauty
(compare the advantage Chrétien gains by putting this descriptive element first in his presentation of Enide and then undercutting it); even the moment just described is lessened in
intensity by the narrator's intrusive remark (to fill out the line),
"ne fu merveille" (961). And, of course, there is no other perspective on the moment to render it more subjective. This last
device is what makes the *Erec* description so important as a
testimony to the emerging sense of the autonomy and limited
nature of individual awareness and response.

In Chrétien's *Lancelot,* the scene in which Lancelot and
Guinevere first meet shows the same principle at work. Lancelot
has defeated the queen's abductor and is now led into her presence by King Bagdemagus. Instead of thanking Lancelot, as we
expect her to, Guinevere rebukes him, and, without explaining
the reason for her pique, leaves the room (3934-69). Both men
are dumbfounded. Lancelot's eyes follow Guinevere until she is
out of sight; but his heart,

> . . . qui plus est sire et mestre
> et de plus grant pooir asez
> s'an est oltre apres li passez,
> et li oil sont remes defors,
> plain de lermes, avoec li cors. . . .
> [3976-80]

The king, far from being caught up in such love-longing (expressed in conceits elsewhere in Chrétien, and common in
twelfth-century love literature), is indignant:

> Certes, fet li rois, ele a tort,
> que vos vos estes jusqu'a mort
> por li en avanture mis;
> [3997-99]

but he adds, without pause,

> or an venez, biax dolz amis,
> s'iroiz au seneschal parler.
> [4000–01]

Lancelot courteously agrees to visit Kay, Arthur's seneschal, also imprisoned in Gorre; but Chrétien has made it clear how differently the two observers have reacted to Guinevere's snub; Lancelot's grief, caused by love, is sharply distinguished from Bagdemagus's straightforward, but not deep, objection to ingratitude. The result of the juxtaposition of responses is to underscore the uniqueness of Lancelot's inner world of love-awareness.

We see, then, that multiple perspective is a technique rendering, and expressing the importance of, the individual's subjective experience of reality. The figures of the *vavasor* and King Bagdemagus, by their inability to share the intense experience of a moment with the protagonist, also suggest the necessary tension between the individual, in his quest for self-fulfillment, and the "world outside" which, not sharing his perspective, cannot or will not support him. When Erec goes off on his adventure quest with Enide, his father, King Lac, and later Arthur and his court, give him up as dead, and grieve at his departure on what Erec knows will be a necessary quest for self-fulfillment and *joie,* if he is to have them in marriage.[12] All the court can see is that Erec, in rejecting their prescriptions and expectations for him, has in effect destroyed the identity by which they knew him, and has, therefore, become "dead" to them. The two perspectives can only by resolved, in *Erec,* through the *joie de la cour* adventure; other romances arrive at a resolution by means of the chivalry topos (the tournament in *Partonopeu*) or its rejection (*Yvain, Ipomedon*); still others do not have a resolution (*Le Bel inconnu, Cligès*). In any case, differing social and personal perspectives on the protagonist's destiny are basic to the impact and mimesis of twelfth-century chivalric romance.

The technique of limited and multiple perspective can be applied to scenes as well as moments; one of the most interesting and extended examples in a courtly narrative is the middle section of Gautier d'Arras's tripartite *Eracle*. *Eracle* is not, properly speaking, a chivalric romance, but a mixture of saint's life, fabliau, and fictional history written for the same audience that was enjoying the first chivalric romances.[13] Eracle (a fictionalized version of Heraclius, seventh-century Byzantine emperor) rises from slavery to become the Roman emperor's special adviser, by virtue of his God-given power to judge the true worth of horses, precious stones, and women. The first section of *Eracle* demonstrates his infallibility in each of these areas of competence. Gautier's point is that the true worth of things and people lies hidden behind a mask of appearances and that a godlike gift is required to distinguish true goodness from illusion and hypocrisy. Part two states the case negatively by showing folly triumphant in a world of men and women not guided by God toward objective judgments of themselves and others.

Eracle in effect reveals the story of this episode before it happens. The emperor, Lais, has, through Eracle's powers, found and married Athanais, the most virtuous woman in the empire, whom he had discovered living in poverty. After seven years of wedded bliss, he must leave Rome to besiege another city. Practicality forbids his taking Athanais, but he is terrified to leave her behind lest he lose her. Eracle councils Lais that his best protection is Athanais's virtue and that to restrict her freedom in any way could bring about the very situation the emperor wishes to avoid. Despite this warning, Lais, rendered foolish by his love, places Athanais in a well-guarded tower when he leaves. What follows is expectable: rendered miserable by her undeserved dishonor, the empress sees and falls in love with a young nobleman, suggestively named Paridès, who is equally smitten with her. With the aid of a knowing, avaricious old lady, the lovers consummate the relationship at the go-between's hovel, in a small, concealed hole dug beneath the floor for this purpose. Eracle discovers what has happened and tells the emperor, who returns in a rage, ready to punish his wife and kill her lover. Athanais offers her life to save Paridès,

but Eracle, reminding Lais that the whole situation is the result
of his original *folie,* convinces the emperor to divorce his wife
so that she can live with her lover in modest circumstances. At
this point the work moves into its third part.

Thus summarized in bare outline, the episode stands as an
exemplary fabliau, offering a purely ironic view of the characters trapped in *folie,* playing out their parts in a serio-comic
drama predicted and then resolved by the morally and perceptually superior Eracle. But such a view is misleading, for the
story is also a study in how flawed and limited, but also clearly
distinguished, individual perspectives on reality create a complicated and disastrous situation. We can say of Gautier's art,
as E.H. Gombrich says in *Art and Illusion* of a Hellenistic battle
painting, that its separately realized figures "all draw us into the
scene . . . and in thus lingering on the situation we come to
share the experience of those involved"—to share, that is, the
experience of individuals, so defined by the disparateness of
their imperfect comprehension.[14]

The story of Lais, Athanais, and Paridès is a variant of a
fabliau plot that Charles Muscatine says has "almost an a priori
status," namely, "that triangle of the dull-witted or jealous
husband, the sensual wife, and the lecherous priest or clever
clerk." But where fabliaux are characterized by, in Muscatine's
words, "blunt economy of plan and procedure,"[15] Gautier stuffs
his with a complexity of motivation and with the conventions
of twelfth-century *fin amors,* in order to individualize his
characters and their *folie.* The emperor's attachment to his wife
is genuine love, quite unlike the foolish, impotent doting of a
fabliau husband, but it leads him to mistreat her by confining
her in a tower. When he learns the consequence of his misjudg-
ment, his reaction is a further error of perspective. He tells
Athanais that he considers her betrayal a compound of ingratitude to her benefactor and bad judgment in giving up her status
as empress for an obscure lover (4796–813). So great is her
folly, he adds, that she is sure to extend it by treating Paridès as
she has her husband, by becoming chronically unfaithful (4981–
87). To Lais, then, this is the case of an ungrateful, irrational
slut who betrays the man who has given her everything.

Of course this analysis is all wrong. Athanais has acted not from ingratitude but from a sense of injured innocence; her conscience tells her she has done nothing to deserve her husband's treatment, and, to her, such imprisonment, even with imperial status and riches, is dishonorable.[16] In loving Paridès she has sought to flee, not find, dishonor. As for abandoning her *ami,* that, she says, is unthinkable; *fin amors* has forced her to love and will continue to do so: "et cil qui aime finement/N'en puet partir legierement:/Ne s'en part mie quant il vueut/ Cil qui de fine amor se dueut" (4956-59).

On the other hand, Athanais no more understands her husband's motives than he hers. She sees only cruelty and injustice in his actions; in her first soliloquy (3240f.), which does not sound like one from a fabliau, she decides that the envy of evil men caused her persecution.[17] Given her predisposition, Athanais easily falls in love with Paridès. He, on the other hand, when he feels the force of her glance, at first resists the *folie* of love (again, in a fashion alien to the fabliau), for he is sure she would kill him if she discovered his presumption (3774). Such, he says, is the pride of women.[18] Given Athanais's simultaneous infatuation, Paridès's opinions are as wrong as everyone else's. Even the old lady, ancestress of Jean de Meun's duenna and Chaucer's Pandarus,[19] with all her experience and practical knowledge about love, advises Paridès not to let the lady see his pains lest, in her pride, she scorn him (4160f.; compare 4183-86). All the illustrative material *la vieille* draws from her own career is inapplicable in this situation, but it supplies the only love perspective she has.[20]

Eracle himself, for all his omniscience, chooses to interpret the catastrophe he has predicted in a curiously myopic fashion: he castigates the emperor for committing *folie* that will cause Eracle to be accused by posterity of having misled his lord into marrying a false woman (4765-73, 5026). From Eracle's perspective, the episode illustrates the *folie* of a lord's refusal to follow the advice of an honest councillor, although the events of part three, in which Eracle, far from being disgraced, becomes emperor and saves the Holy Cross, belie his concern with his reputation.

To the list of limited perspectives must finally be appended that of Paridès's mother, whose main concern about her son's love affair is that he has stopped eating (4149-50, 4223-25). Like Enide's father, she misses everything about the situation but what most narrowly concerns her; yet that concern is real, is uniquely hers, and, as an incomplete perspective, is different in degree but not in kind from those of the other characters.

The primacy of individual experience and the limits of the individual's perspective on reality mean that all the characters in the episode are, in effect, wrapped in a cocoon of personal formation, woven of self-interest and prior experience.[21] Repeated images of enclosures which hide or distort the truth, or which imprison people, objectify this central aspect of Gautier's vision. The emperor remarks early on that even Eracle cannot see his *courage* and thus understand his love for Athanais (3064-66). Athanias must hide her *courage* from her guardians (3442-51), while Paridès hides his until *la vieille* convinces him, "Folie . . . est del celer, et sens del dire" (4101-02). Athanais is enclosed in her tower (3144-71), and to free herself she must arrange to fall, as if by accident, into a water-filled ditch (4565f.), in order to carry out an assignation with Paridès—in a small, covered hole! (4605f.).

The single most suggestive image of this kind is the pie which Athanais sends to *la vieille* as part of her scheme to meet her lover (4410f.). She has warned the old lady to expect a present for herself, the *sourplus* of which is to go the youth. Athanais then orders a pie baked, slips a love note under its crust, and places it on a silver tray; pie and tray are then dispatched to the go-between. When *la vieille* receives the gift, she misunderstands its significance; being avaricious, and counting on being rewarded for her services, she is furious, for it seems that the pie is for her and the *sourplus,* the valuable tray, is for Paridès. She curses the empress and angrily smashes the pie, whereupon she discovers the note and understands that *it* is the *sourplus;* her curse turns to blessing, for now she sees the silver is for her (4440-74).

The old lady's misconception, prompted by her limited,

greedy perspective on the love affair, points up the appropriate-
ness of the pie, with its unperceived stuffing, as an image of the
gap between appearance and reality which Gautier has more
seriously explored in the first part of *Eracle;* the lady's accidental discovery of the truth by breaking the pastry in anger is,
in fact, a parodistic version of Eracle's feats of perception on behalf of the emperor. *La vieille* is much less interested at the moment in the effect of the discovery on Paridès than she is in the
fact that she has her reward. In other words, the truth is a by-
product of our pursuit of narrow interest; we are not changed
into something less ourselves by our discovery of it. In such
gloomy terms, yet within a courtly comedy of errors, does
Gautier force us to contemplate the inescapable, deflating fact
of our individuality. His moral, ironic judgment on limited perspective as an expression of our fallen nature goes far beyond
the more nuanced ironies about *folie* characteristic of most
chivalric romance. (Chrétien's *Cligès* is perhaps as cynical a romance as is *Eracle;* see chapter 3, above.) Yet he shares, in this
episode, the assumption of the romances about the fact of individual perspective and the method of constructing a model of
reality by juxtaposing personal views on an action, all of which
taken together define what the episode is about.

A less austere but almost equally problematic use of multiple
perspective occurs in my last example of this technique, the
tournament of Noauz in Chrétien's *Lancelot* (5359-6056). Here
Chrétien explores the relationship between perspective and
knowledge, or, more precisely, between personal viewpoint and
the illusion which prevents knowledge. The effect sought in this
episode is amusement through irony at the expense of the individual (here Lancelot) in love. Our perspectives, Chrétien is saying
in effect, are personal and limited, and we can easily be misled,
given our individual limits and the peculiarities inherent in the
behavior and circumstances of other individuals. In particular,
the private world and imperatives of the lover subvert accurate
perception of him by other observers, and therefore tend to
subvert as well any actions based on such perceptions.

The unmarried ladies of Logres proclaim a tournament, to

bring together the knights of Logres; those who acquit themselves well in battle will be chosen for husbands.[22] Guinevere
consents to be present, and this news reaches Lancelot, who has
been imprisoned in a tower by Meleagranz. Lancelot is desper-
ately anxious to attend the tournament—we later see that he is
prompted solely by his desire to distinguish himself before
Guinevere—and he wins temporary release from captivity, and
the loan of a suit of armor, from the wife of his jailer, who loves
him and aids him, though she knows he does not love her. He
arrives at the tournament unknown to all but a herald, who
recognizes him but promises not to reveal the identity of his
former benefactor. On the first day, Lancelot performs out-
standingly while Guinevere and the ladies look on. The queen,
guessing his identity from his prowess, sends him a command to
do poorly, a command he at once obeys.[23] That night, all the
spectators heap abuse on Lancelot, much to the discomfort of
the loyal herald; only the queen rejoices at this proof of Lancelot's identity and loyalty. The next day, after testing him once
more by telling him to do poorly, she rescinds the order and
urges him to excel, which of course he does—so well that, by
the time he leaves the field late in the day, all the damsels of
Logres have decided they must marry him alone, although they
do not know who he is. With Lancelot gone, the tournament
ends a fiasco, with none of the ladies willing to marry the
knights they had summoned to it.

Clearly Chrétien is here, as throughout *Lancelot,* exploring
the personal and social effects of the love relationship, imagined
within the conventions of chivalry, from a point of view which
emphasizes everything problematic, ironic, and negative about
the quest for personal fulfillment through love.[24] The basic
technique of the scene is to use the typical romance device of
concealed identity (further discussed in chapter 6, below) to
probe the chivalry topos and make it the focus for an ironic
statement about how illusion, the result of love's necessarily
private stratagems, contributes to the multiplicity of perspective
which marks our collective experience of the world.

The ladies hold a tournament based on an institutionalization of the chivalry topos: they will marry the knights who do best in the battle. The complication that mars this scheme (and thus mocks the neatness of the topos) springs from the fact that Lancelot's love for Guinevere prompts him not only to fight well, but to fight badly, if his lady so prefers. Thus a specific love relationship proves too idiosyncratic for the conventional assumptions to apply to it. As a result, Lancelot's behavior means different things to different people. The ladies (5714f.) and other knights (5736f.) heap scorn on "li chevaliers ver-mauz"; these observers are privy neither to Lancelot's identity nor his motives. The loyal herald knows who Lancelot is but not why he behaves as he does (why he fights as though he weren't Lancelot the unsurpassed knight), and he is "molt maz et molt desconfiz" (5769) at the first group's negative judg-ment.[25] Given what the various observers know—and don't know—both perspectives are legitimate. Finally, the queen, knowing Lancelot's identity more fully (being privy to the love which controls his inner life and thus his outer behavior), is fully satisfied at the brave-cowardly Lancelot whom she, like an artist, has "created."

From this situation issue the following perspectives on chival-ry: the herald's devotion to Lancelot (a relationship based on gratitude and service, like that of Lunete to Yvain) proves nobler than chivalric love, for it wishes only to exalt its object. But the "new" chivalry topos embodied by Lancelot—love in-spires prowess, but also, if necessary, cowardice—becomes an instrument whereby the tournament's other participants and spectators learn the dangers of hasty judgment and slander (5759-61); for them chivalry is an educational force.[26] But this in passing; Guinevere's perspective on chivalry is not that it is an educational force but a medium for her to exercise complete control over her lover while testing him. The ladies learn that a tournament that encourages prowess is no fool-proof way to get husbands, and, as we watch their disappoint-ment at the failure of the tournament in its stated aim ("l'anha-tine ensi departi/c'onques nule n'an prist mari," 6055-56), we learn that an individual relationship in which the lovers achieve

an identity defined by and for each other alone is potentially
both confusing in its subjectivity and socially disruptive. Finally,
Lancelot's "reward" for winning the tournament is, with
ironic symbolism, a return to captivity which he has temporarily escaped through the aid of his jailer's wife. The wife is thus a
parody of Guinevere, and her helpful (though unrequited) devotion provides a perspective from which we can criticize the
queen's behavior, as the behavior of the horse and lion in
Ardenne allow us a critical perspective on Partonopeu.

In addition to all the other perspectives that embody the concept of the individual within this scene by exhibiting the limits
of individual perception, Chrétien has found a way to present a
perspective recalling that of Enide's father in the scene from
Erec discussed earlier. Just as the words of the *vavasor* to his
daughter on the care and feeding of Erec's horse reveal that the
speaker is completely unaware of any but the least significant
dimension of the action, the conversation among the spectator-
knights viewing the tournament betrays analogous ignorance on
their part. While the queen and the sponsoring ladies see important things at stake for themselves in the field below, the knights
(5772f.) are absorbed in identifying the participants they can
recognize and in describing to each other, in tones of knowledgeable expertise, the origin and heraldry of the various shields.
The effect of these remarks is one of pompous, and therefore
humorous, irrelevance;[27] yet even such "professional" chivalric
comments are a contributing part of the scene's mimetic impact—another viewpoint on the human experience of the
tournament.

I suggested earlier that the question of perspective in chivalric
romances could be approached two ways; the bulk of this discussion has been concerned with simultaneous multiple perspective, but I want now to consider an instance of what might
be called consecutive or sequential multiple perspective, or
indeed the gradually changing perspective on reality. This
technique consists in emphasizing the relationship between
perception and physical placement in space; as we (and objects
in our environment) move in space and time, the appearance

and meaning of external reality changes, and our understanding and apprehension develop or change progressively as well. This type of multiple perspective is a mimesis of the individual's learning process as it results from his interaction with earthly experience. We have seen it operating with respect to Urraque in the Ardenne episode, and a similar, though less particularized process is going on in Enide as Guivret gallops toward Erec. Once again, this presentation of developing knowledge assumes the worth of earthly experience subjectively perceived rather than objectively revealed or symbolically interpreted. It validates the processes and context of individual perception, as the first type of multiple perspective validates the privateness, subjectiveness, and even the incompleteness of individual perception.

In *Erec,* the arrival at Arthur's court of Yder, the knight who insulted the queen and whom Erec has defeated in connection with the "custom of the sparrowhawk," gives Chrétien the opportunity to present an encounter between a knight errant and a courtly society in terms of an evolving perspective on reality. Yder has been sent ahead by Erec to announce the latter's triumph and imminent return. The court awaits Erec's return with double anxiety, both because they do not know if he is still alive and because the queen has persuaded Arthur to put off until Erec's return the awarding of a kiss to the most beautiful damsel at court, in accordance with the "custom of the white stag." Since every knight at court is convinced that his own *amie* is the most beautiful, and will fight to defend his belief, chaos threatens the court, and Erec's return may somehow, the queen hopes, head it off.[28]

The fact that Arthur's court is looking to the outside world for a solution to its problem explains why Chrétien presents Yder's arrival not from the knight's perspective but from that of the court. There are many instances in medieval romance where a knight arrives at a strange city or castle that will prove crucial to his attainment of his personal quest, and the poet underscores that fact by describing the edifice from the knight's single perspective, that is, from an external vantage point (sometimes one that shifts with the knight as he approaches the castle); often, such descriptions also suggest the mystery or danger within that await the lonely, determined protagonist (consider, for example, Partonopeu's arrival at Chef d'Oire, Guinglain's at Sinaudon in *Le Bel inconnu,* Gawain's at Bercilak's castle in *Sir Gawain and the Green Knight,* Sir Orfeo's at Pluto's castle). By reversing the vantage point Chrétien suggests society's need of, and challenge from, the sphere of personal experience.

The scene opens as Yder, leading his *pucele* and his dwarf, comes to Caradigan, where Arthur is holding court. At once (1085) Chrétien shifts his attention to the spectators within the walls:

> Es loiges de la sale hors
> estoit messire Gauvains lors
> et Kex li seneschax ansamble;
> des barons i ot, ce me samble,
> avoec ax grant masse venuz.
>   [1085-89]

Kay sees the approaching knight first and immediately guesses ("mes cuers devine," 1093) that this must be the knight who offended the queen the previous day since there seem ("ce m'est avis") to be three in the party (1097), and he makes out the *pucele* and the dwarf (1098). Gawain confirms these facts and adds that the knight is armed and his shield battered (1100–04); he tells Kay to summon the queen, who is in her chamber. The seneschal describes to Guinevere the approaching knight, adding that if his eyes do not deceive him (1119), there is a pucele with him and, it appears (1121), the dwarf holding the scourge which beat Erec as well. The queen agrees to go with Kay and they hasten back to the castle gallery, where she confirms the identification of Yder (1140), and fills in details on his embattled appearance:

> . . . molt a cos an son escu;
> ses haubers est coverz de sanc,

> del roge i a plus que del blanc
> [1146-48]

—which Gawain immediately confirms (1149-53).

It is now obvious to the observers that the approaching knight will have crucial information about Erec's condition. Gawain states the alternatives: either Erec has conquered the newcomer, or vice versa (1159-64). The queen agrees (1165), and a chorus of other courtiers, present but hitherto silent, concurs (1166). Finally (1167), Yder enters the gate, "qui la novele lor aporte" (1168). The scene now dissolves into a bustle of welcome for Yder. He gives his news of Erec, reveals his identity to the queen, and is taken by her to Arthur, who receives him pompously and offers him a place at the court. At this point, Chrétien abruptly abandons the scene ("or redevons d'Erec parler," 1238).

Chrétien has here portrayed with accuracy and attention to detail the manner in which an approaching figure in our field of vision becomes progressively clearer and larger, so that we can perceive more and more details about him. These sensory impressions allow us to make conclusions about their significance based on our prior knowledge; finally, when the movement leads to an actual encounter, speech confirms or denies assumptions based on sight and on particular knowledge. (Here again subjectivity enters in, though on a group level: Yder's arrival means more to Arthur's courtiers than anyone else because they know Erec's history, and can thus interpret the sight of Yder's companions and battle marks in a specific way unknown to hypothetical casual observers relying only upon their present sensory impressions of Yder.) Chrétien keeps before us various forms of the verb *to see* ("voir"), in Kay's description of Yder to Guinevere (five instances in sixteen lines plus the qualification, "se mi oel ne m'ont manti"), and also salts the dialogue with subjective qualifying phrases ("ce m'est avis," etc.) as the courtiers describe Yder's appearance and confirm each other's observations. Thus the importance of sensory perception cannot be forgotten, nor that of personal memory (as when Kay says to Guinevere, "Dame, . . . s'il vous remanbre/del nain qui hier vos correca," etc.). The building up of tension among the observers, to be resolved only by the arrival of Yder and his message of either victory or defeat, also reminds us of the limits of perception: Yder's scars can be interpreted in two opposite ways. In short, the scene is a fine, even loving portrayal of how real people really perceive experience, progressively, personally, and within the limits imposed by the actual human condition. Altogether, the scene, so unimportant within the plot of the romance, stands out as quite an important testimony to the grounding of the chivalric romance poet's art in the personal, individual perception of reality.

I cannot leave this section without raising a question about the possible relationship between the techniques of multiple perspective (and especially the limits of personal perception thereby implied) and the technique of creating unsolved mysteries which various chivalric poets, especially Chrétien, exploit from time to time. R. Guiette, in an extremely compelling essay which can now be seen as the beginning, practically, of a school of romance criticism, discusses the "symboles sans senefiance" of chivalric romance: the artifacts or incidents which should (or seem to) refer to some larger sphere of meaning, theological or otherwise, but are not explained. Guiette relates these meaningless symbols to the poets' pleasure in making of their stories literary performances, deliberately free of symbolic meanings of a kind medieval man is often supposed to have lived with so easily.[29]

Guiette's thesis is attractive, but I wonder if it cannot be modified a bit by assuming that there is a parallel between the incompleteness of perception of reality by the individual and the audience's incomplète perception of the "world" created by the poet. In other words, the apparently outrageous mysteriousness of some romance episodes may not simply be fanciful and "gothick" or exotic—or the marks of the sublime freedom of the artist from the restraints imposed on us by reality in our lives[30]—but rather part of a strategy to present personal perspective as normative, in all its inconvenient, ridiculous, or comic limitedness. The poet presents a world which is too complicated for him, as an individual, to explain, or we, as individuals, to comprehend fully. There are no outside, objective perspectives to clarify all, just as there are no levels of meaning outside the hero's personal quest to objectify and universalize individual experience as part of a providential or historical scheme. The individual's limited vision is the mark of his individuality, and we are made to share in it.

There is an interesting possible parallel here between this technique of leaving certain things unexplained, in an attempt to make the poetic universe seem more like the world perceived by the unaided individual, and techniques used in the visual arts to approximate the limits of our limited visual perception of the world, to create the illusion of the way in which people "really" see their environment. Gombrich discusses this visual mimesis with reference to the conceptual breakthrough which allowed Greek illusionistic painters to present figures "missing" parts of their body, in order to reproduce the effect of seeing the world at "one moment of time" and from "one angle of view."[31] This technique reflects a desire to create the illusion of reality as we experience it: a partial reality given its peculiar shapes, dimensions, and abridgements by the perspective from which our two eyes see it at any given moment. Such an aesthetic (and the philosophy of the primacy of individual perception underlying it) runs counter to the canons of more primitive, ritual-related art in which the image, to be potent, must be complete and objective—free, that is, from the limits of mere mortal perception.[32]

It remains to be seen how far parallels between the visual arts and either the mysterious element in chivalric romance or perspectival mimesis in twelfth-century courtly texts can be extended. In any case, multiple perspective remains a central and fascinating aspect of the chivalric poets' art, one that contributes greatly to the complexity and attractiveness of the romances as statements about the problematic limitations of individuality.

6: THE ROMANCE PLOT AND THE CRISIS OF INNER AWARENESS

The last three chapters have explored all but one of the criteria I have used in determining the presence of a concern with individuality in twelfth-century chivalric romance. Only the representation of the inner life—that entirely personal sphere of experience—remains to be studied in greater detail. Rather than pile up analyses of inner dialogues such as those of Enide and Partonopeu that I examined in chapter 2, the present chapter undertakes to demonstrate how the chivalric poets made entire plots into metaphoric representations of the dimensions and crises of the individual's interior world.

The largest and most basic metaphor in chivalric romance was the chivalric one itself, with its central assumption or topos— love inspires prowess, prowess inspires love—which it delighted in testing and considering from an ever-increasing variety of perspectives. The scenes, motifs, and techniques so far considered in this study make it clear that no two chivalric romances approached their organizing topos in the same manner nor to the same end. In its individual-centered meditations on the nature and goals of secular experience, placed in subjectively perceived space and time, romance used its conventional, idealized canons of human behavior with variety and ingenuity. Thus *Yvain*, as we shall see in this chapter, crowns its chivalric vision with the subordination of prowess to love in its many forms (desire for the beloved, love of kin, loyalty to companion and benefactor, reciprocal hospitality and service), with the aid of quite outrageous *engin*; the result is to suggest that chivalry can only be made to work against great odds, by the skin of its teeth, and in a modified form. *Lancelot,* as we have seen, shows love subverting prowess, even prowess which, guided by desire, becomes a liberating force in personal and social life. *Lancelot* (albeit thanks to Godefroi) ends with a climactic battle and with love deemphasized; *Yvain* ends with inconclusive displays of prowess and reunions achieved by trickery. *Partonopeu* (in its original version) offers the spectacle of the chivalry topos working perfectly via a tournament in which the hero wins the heroine. In Hue de Rotelande's *Ipomedon,* the protagonist combines the career of Yvain and the skill of Lunete; Ipomedon's *engin,* as we have seen, educates others to the folly of dependence upon prowess, yet he too is a prisoner of prowess and can only be united with his beloved through the unexpected intervention of a half-brother. Fraternal love, not normally a factor in the chivalry topos, here becomes a symbol of the possibility for reconciliation within, and liberation from, a world dominated by impersonal violence.

To name but one other twelfth-century romance, Renaut de Beaujeu's *Le Bel inconnu* ingeniously opposes to the world of public success and honor gained by prowess a mysterious and private world of love where self-fulfillment depends upon complete obedience to the beloved's magic power. In this situation, clearly inspired by a similar juxtaposition of worlds in *Partonopeu,*[1] Renaut's hero makes the wrong choice, of honor over love; the poet seems to argue that the chivalry topos is irrelevant to, if not subversive of, the individual's quest for happiness. Yet even here there remains at least the possibility of a final resolution of the basic impulses toward public and private gratification, thanks to a trick ending that violates and complicates the fictional world Renaut has created, as we shall later see. *Le Bel inconnu* combines highly derivative adventures, a "gothick" taste for the mysterious and illusory, and a highly original treatment of its protagonist's delayed initiation into, and sudden loss of, love. Its effect, intended or not, is to present in exaggerated form the opposing tendencies in every twelfth-century chivalric romance toward symbolic statement about personal destiny, on the one hand, and self-conscious exercise of literary virtuosity through playful manipulation of fictional conventions, on the other.

The medium through which all these versions of chivalry were broached and tested was the plot structure of the romance genre, which allowed the chivalric poets to organize the narrative around their protagonist and his biography. In this chapter I will explain how the romance plot also, and more particularly, enabled Chrétien de Troyes and his contemporaries to place in special relief the idea that the development of self-consciousness is the keystone of the individual's quest for happiness and self-perfection. The generic form of chivalric romance is closely linked to its quasi-didactic interest in presenting to the courtly audience an image of life in which individual aspiration has pride of place—whether it succeeds or fails, is serious or comic— and in which recognition of its priority is the necessary precondition to truly rewarding human activity.

Twelfth-century chivalric poets did not invent the kind of plot critics nowadays call romance. (They did invent the term, but originally used it simply to distinguish works in the French vernacular from those in Latin.) Chivalric romance reflects the literary conventions of a specific society and cultural moment— twelfth-century courtly society—by placing the chivalry topos, fantastic episodes, and idealized protagonists drawn from a single social class within a narrative form present, more or less centrally, throughout the history of Western literature. As I have suggested at the beginning of chapter 2, and at various points since, the defining attribute of the romance form is its plot, which organizes incidents ranging widely in space and time around the life of the hero without any larger controlling narrative context, action, or system (such as fate, providence, or national destiny). The frequent lack of any overt logical sequence connecting one incident to another makes the plot *episodic* as well as *biographical*. (A consideration of the "adventure" section of most chivalric romances shows how often episodes could be interchanged without loss of comprehension, and how often coincidence, instead of inevitable consequence or providential intervention, determines turning points and *kairoi* in the hero's career.)

In categorizing romance plots, the easiest distinction to make is that between *active romance* (usually heroic, but also possibly ratiocinative, as in the contractual quest of a Sherlock Holmes type of literary detective), in which the hero's adventures—his experience of life in all its variety and its potential for dangers or surprises—are willed, and obstacles are overcome by force or skill, and *passive romance,* in which adventures are initiated by chance (or, put more abstractly, Fortune)—shipwrecks which separate families, gypsies who steal children from their cradles—and must simply be borne by weak or outnumbered protagonists. Greek romances like *Daphnis and Chloe* or Xenophon's *Ephesian Tale* are primarily passive romances.

In the basic structure of the episodic romance, a hero moves away from and then back toward a situation of stasis, through an intervening period of often arbitrary adventures involving loss, exile, hazard, or search. Romance is thus a fictional form which incorporates a circular, and by extension cyclic, perception of life, and to the extent that novels, epics, and other literary forms contain cyclical plot elements, they participate in the romance genre.[2] This characteristic romance perception is rooted in our recognition of the endless seasonal cycle of death and rebirth, or loss and recovery of fertility, in nature. Ritual commemoration of life's cycles is very ancient, as archaeological evidence shows. New year rituals commemorating the rebirth of nature were also rituals of political significance, in which the king assimilated his own life to the seasonal cycle to insure the revived fertility of the land and continued prosperity of his people.[3] As culture evolved, so did fictional forms which were an imaginative response to, and displacement from, these rituals and their underlying apprehension of life.[4]

The sequence of displacements here offered from cyclical myth or ritual toward romance is hypothetical, pragmatic, and not necessarily chronological; it reflects only my desire to place the romance plot in a context which best illustrates its peculiarities. The first fictional form to be displaced from cyclic

ritual was probably the hero's trip to the underworld to discover and bring back the departed god(dess) whose return to
earth was necessary for a revival of nature. G. Levy believes that
this quest narrative evolved from *rites de passage* marking the
attainment of manhood by youths in stone-age cultures—rites
in which the youth was isolated in a closed cave and later re-
leased with communal celebration. The successive stages of
evolution were (1) from the human ritual to the myth of the
(seasonal) journey of a god into and out of the underworld,
and (2) by further transference, "from the god who is sought
to the hero who seeks" him or her.[5] (One may here compare the myth of Proserpina with the quest of Gilgamesh for
Utnapishtim in the garden of immortality, although this latter
quest has been even further displaced toward human reality,
that is, the hero goes in search of information about immortality, rather than to bring back the immortal one.) The heroic
quest is presented as a single adventure but it clearly still refers
back to and explains the process of renewal in nature; its ultimate significance, the meaning given it by its audience, is
mythic and cyclical. The hero's experience is not a paradigm
of nor comment on the audience's own experience, but rather
inhabits the realm of mythic fantasy and wish-fulfillment
in which, like nature itself, we overcome death and achieve
immortality.

In a truly cyclical world, where all people would experience
the same endless round of death and rebirth, no progress or
turning points are possible; time as irreversible sequence is
ignored and concepts like personal identity (based on individual
experience or unique destiny, including the time, place, and
manner of death) or history (which is, in effect, group identity
evolving in time) are irrelevant. With the next fictional form in
my sequence, the myth of the golden age, the actual racial, historical, or moral experience of mankind, in however symbolic a
form, does replace the cycle of nature as the key to the fiction.[6]
The cyclical pattern of loss and recovery is "straightened out"
into a linear version of time in which there is one moment of
loss, not of nature's fertility, but of society's (and nature's)

harmony. The period before this loss is the golden age; that following, the iron age in which men now live unhappy and corrupt lives. (There are, in some versions of the myth, ages of silver and bronze through which mankind sinks gradually into depravity, but the beginning and end of the process are the same.[7]) The catastrophe which begins the decline or fall can be the discovery of gold or of some other awful contents of Pandora's box. As Levin says, the golden-age myth has no real plot, simply these two stages, to which is usually added a longing for the return to the golden age, the age of *Astraea redux,* the millennium, which recaptures the past in the future. It is this wish that transforms the myth from a form of universal nostalgia to a myth of eternal return, in time or space, and looks back to the circularity of the seasonal ritual.[8] Yet the rupture with a cyclical vision is real: there is no constant cycle of (winter-) loss and (spring-) recovery, only the awareness that mankind was once happy, then lost its happiness, and someday may regain the lost state for all time.

A variety of literary genres is related to the golden age myth: arcadian pastoral and certain types of etiological myth dwell on the golden age itself and recount the entrance of evil into paradise; the anatomy of the evils of the iron age is satire; and the portrayal of what may come after occupies the utopian tract and the apocalypse. The Christian story, embodied in a special reading of the Old Testament in the light of the New, is a complex version of the golden age myth with various stages marked on the path toward regaining at the end of time (the *eschaton*) the golden age lost at its beginning: chosen people, redemption, final resurrection, and universal judgment.[9] Human experience here is fundamentally linear—God entered history only once, and gave it irreversible meaning—yet the form of history is that of loss and recovery of intimacy with the Creator. Since this pattern is recapitulated in each life, according to patristic theology, the Christian version of the golden-age myth is both universal and personal and provides a logical point of transition to our next displacement in fiction away from the celebration of nature's cycle.

Just as the myth of the golden age, its loss, and its wished-for recovery is a social version of cyclical rhythms stretched out into history so as to happen only once (and thus to call history into being and give it form), so romance is an individual, biographical version of those rhythms, stretched out into personal history. In each case, the uniqueness of the cycle introduces an element of linearity (as opposed to periodic recurrence) into experience which exists in tension with the plot's inherent circularity.

The differences between the romance and the literary form derived from the golden-age myth are important. First of all, it includes all three parts of the possession-loss-recovery scheme, but stresses the period of loss, which is that of adventures between an opening stasis (preceding the calamity or change which sets adventures going) and a final, happy ending. (Most golden-age-related literature, as I have said, stresses one period or another with varying effect.) More important for my purposes is the fact that since cyclical or circular movement becomes anchored in personal history, it makes possible the further dominance of the element of linearity over that of circularity in the fiction recounted.

The potentiality for complexity and sophistication in a romance plot lies precisely in the fact that human life is a phenomenon extending into time, is biologically irreversible, and is cumulative in terms of memory and learning experiences. That is, man *grows* and *progresses* in various ways, and the exploitation of growth or progress can be an extra force for linearity. The circularity of the loss-recovery or exile-return plot can never be entirely effaced; its presence expresses the faith of the romance writer that reunion or reconciliation is possible in human life, or that personal decline or misfortune is reversible, or that our experience, however varied, does constantly drive us back to confronting and understanding the element of constancy in our identity, character, and situation while we live. But the romance hero can be presented as more or less the product of linear factors in his life. If the hero is agelessly and changelessly perfect (as comic book heroes tend to be), there is little linearity in romance, which instead becomes the endless repetition of the hero's quests for those who disturb the status quo of law and order in an ahistorical society. Or the author may simply ignore the fact of growth in recounting, for example, the adventures of a shipwrecked merchant who finally returns to his own city, or of a husband and wife separated by war and later reunited by chance. In these essentially atemporal versions of romance, the plot's great circle in space sets the work's tone.

To introduce the idea of growth in time into the world of the romance protagonist's adventures in space is to ensure that he never returns to "where he started" as quite the same person he was when he set out. If the romance is about a king's son deprived of his inheritance while still a child and exiled by the villain, then *physical* growth in time allows him to win back his land once he has grown into a mighty warrior (see, for example, the Middle English romances of *Horn* and *Havelock*). *Mental* growth makes "the brave man slowly wise" and capable of performing a task he earlier failed through folly. *Moral* growth is also possible. If the result of such growth is the ultimate arrival at a new, transcendent locale or experience which the hero has known about or been assigned to reach, we have quest romance proper (as in the *Queste del saint Graal* or Galahad/Perceval romances), an even more linear type of romance, in which the hero's adventures can be made to show his progressive attainment of the virtues necessary to complete the quest.

Any of the changes that occur as time passes—physical, mental, or moral growth—may render the romance hero at least temporarily unrecognizable, on his return, as the person who started out long ago. Indeed, his experiences may have so changed his outlook and behavior that the question of whether or not he is "the same person" can legitimately be raised. For these reasons, the complexity and precariousness of individual identity are often a major theme of romance. If all men did indeed partake of seasonal death and regeneration, the biographical landmarks that give them a personal history would be planed away; when a plot contains both a large circular movement back to its starting point, and constant human growth, paradoxes of identity occur. The hero remains the same person throughout the story, yet may also change his identity during his adventures through a change of personality (amnesia, moral reformation), disguise, or a stroke of misfortune (the king's son stolen and raised by gypsies). Making our various identities (and the destinies they imply) fall together in and through time is one of the goals of romance, as shown by the frequency of climactic scenes in which "true identities" are revealed, resulting in reunions, attainment of rightful worldly power, etc. The implication of the synthesis of those identities which adventure has foisted upon the hero is that man can, in and of himself, give meaning to the disparateness of experience by his own attainment of happiness, that individual experience is important, with its unifying focus located within rather than outside the individual. We are more than what someone else thinks we are, what we may temporarily pretend to be, or what fortune makes us; our many identities cannot defeat, though they may long deny, the personal destiny that is ours alone. (By contrast, disguise and mistaken identity rarely occur in early medieval narratives. The hero and his opponents are all too clearly known to themselves, each other, and everyone else, even if—as in the case of Grendel—not much is known of their background.)

The diverse identities used by romance to explore the nature of personhood include natal (identity by parent and inherited title or situation), qualitative (identity by the intermingling of virtues and vices), circumstantial (who the world judges us to be in a given situation), assumed (strategic disguises), and desired or destined (whom we want to be or become again). In a romance world of change and adventure, where there may be immature stages in a process of growth, the hero cannot always control his identity; yet the unstated principle of the genre is that *in time* his qualitative identity will enable him to regain his natal, or gain his desired, identity, passing in the course of his quest through various circumstantial (and sometimes assumed) identities. In other words, identity in romance is at once a *given,* a *process,* and a *goal*—a past, a present, and a future.

The most sophisticated version of romance is that in which human growth in time subordinates the circularities of experience to the point where they become milestones on the road of progress toward the perfection of personality. In such a fictional model, the fruitful, progressively more successful interaction of a hero's qualities with his experiences can be measured by comparing his behavior on successive occasions of "return" to a place or situation already encountered. Since the hero becomes a more complex figure if his deeds proceed from awareness as well as competence, his linear growth, with its refining effect on his motives and its ever more nearly complete control over repeated circumstances, will in sophisticated romance be a conscious, rather than an accidental, process. The two main types of conscious linear growth are spiritual and moral, and for both the necessary prerequisite and catalyst is self-awareness, that mysterious epiphany of inner identity by which an individual differentiates himself from his outer circumstances and locates himself within the continuum of his life and the context of his character. Such an epiphany, or shock or recognition, is *dynamic,* for through it the hero arrives for the first time at a comprehension of where the concatenation of his virtues (or vices) and his circumstances is leading him in life. That is, to know what (and therefore who) one is, qualitatively, is to know what one will be or can become.

It follows that in the most sophisticated romances the hero's sudden or progressive arrival at self-awareness, rather than some external catastrophe (shipwreck, separation) or a willed quest undertaken for socially approved motives (honor, wealth), initiates and propels forward his climactic adventures. These adventures (which frequently involve deliberate changes of identity—disguises—instead of imposed ones) eventually culminate in a "return" which, even if it completes a spatial circle (or several, as in *Yvain,* where the action repeatedly returns to the magic spring), in fact marks the attainment of a long-sought, fulfilled,

perfected self. Whatever the social repercussions or ironic com-
plications of such a happy return in a given romance, its basic
significance lies in its bringing the hero to a unique, private
destiny which self-awareness has taught him is to be his alone.
The prospect of self-fulfillment, which has constantly guided
his use of his virtues and his control of his environment, here
becomes fact.[10]

Love plays a special role in the attainment of self-awareness
(and thus the initiation and conduct of adventures) in sophisticated romance. It fills the hero with yearning for the lost or not
yet won beloved, and it simultaneously prompts him to act to
bridge the gap across which desire reaches out toward its object.
Since the end of love is to make a new, inviolable relationship, a
new "person" out of two previously separated selves, the outer
adventures of the love quest function concurrently as a metaphor for the self's great inner adventure: its quest to become
the image it has generated of its own triumphant perfection.

The two forms of romance which most clearly concern themselves with the growth of the hero in the terms just outlined are
religious romance and twelfth-century chivalric romance. In
both cases the outer adventures of the protagonist have their
ultimate reference in the inner life, in the struggle for the perfection and harmony of the self's desires, once these have become manifest to the hero, usually as the result of a crisis of
self-awareness. (It is worth noting that in the heyday of chivalric literature, the twelfth and thirteenth centuries, courtly poets
were also producing religious romances written in the same
verse form and style as secular ones; and some narratives—notably the Anglo-Norman *Saint Brendan* and *Guillaume d'Angle-
terre,* probably by Chrétien de Troyes—could in some respects
as easily be called secular as religious romances.[11])

The love-object in religious romance is God, and union with
the object is salvation, fully obtained only in the next life. The
"return" of the soul—the inner spirit, unique to each Christian—
is to heaven at death, to the Maker from whom the soul came
into earthly life. The progress of the religious romance hero (the
saint) toward God and fulfillment is initiated by the hero's

humble recognition of his sinfulness, of God's desirability, and
of the gap between these two facts. The link between humility
and self-awareness in the sinner's personal confrontation of God
is clearly stated in the late-fourteenth-century English mystical
treatise *The Cloud of Unknowing:* "Meeknes [humility] in itself
is not ellis bot a trewe knowyng and felyng of a mans self as he
is"; it results from two kinds of knowledge—"the filthe, the
wrecchidnes, and the freelte of man . . . " and "the overaboun-
daunt love and the worthiness of God in him-self."[12] The awareness of his distance from God triggers the protagonist's rebirth
in grace, the spiritual *kairos* of his career, which may be conversion, baptism, or, like Dante, a refinding of himself in the middle
of his life. At this point, he revolutionizes his life, leaves behind
worldly pleasure (or the *selva oscura* of sin), and, physically or
mentally, sets off "on adventure" to find the full union with
God which he has now perceived as the goal of his fulfilled self.
The path may lead to Anthony's desert, Alexis's self-banishment
in Syria (and later, to his long residence, "disguised" by holiness,
under his parents' staircase), or Dante's cosmic vision.[13]

The treatise describing the discipline of the mystic can be said,
in a sense, to be the furthest displacement possible of a narrative away from a cyclical ritual. Here the quest is entirely within, and the moment of return to God, after the trials of mental
and spiritual testing, takes the form of self-fulfillment that is
also, in a sense, self-annihilation. As Bernard puts it in *On the
Love of God,* speaking of the fourth and highest degree of love
for God, "Blessed and holy should I call one to whom it has
been granted to experience [union with God] in this mortal life
at rare intervals, or even once, and this suddenly, and for the
space of hardly a moment. For in a certain manner to lose thyself, as though thou wert not, and to be utterly unconscious of
thyself, and to be emptied of thyself, and, as it were, brought
to nothing, pertains to celestial conversation, not to human
affection. . . . O pure and perfect intention of the will! surely so
much more perfect and more pure as there is in it nothing now
mixed of its own; the more sweet and tender, as all is divine
that is felt. To be thus touched is to become godlike *(Sic affici,*

deificari est)."[14] As Colin Morris has pointed out, at other points
in his mystical writings Bernard stresses the self-confirmation
that results from the soul's momentary attainment of union
with God.[15] These two outcomes—complete self-effacement
and heightened self-awareness—are paradoxically related, because both follow from the attainment of that humility which
the *Cloud* author identifies with the "trewe knowyng and
felyng of a mans self as he is." Norman Cohn puts it well in
saying that the mystic emerges from his inner quest "as a more
integrated personality, with a widened range of sympathy and
freer from illusions about himself and his fellow human beings,"
that is, as a stable individual.[16]

For the mystic the *kairos* becomes the split second in which,
with proper control of the will, he can attain the vision of God.
As *The Cloud of Unknowing* puts it, speaking of the subjectivity
of time, "and therefore take good keep into tyme, how that
thou dispendist it. For nothing is more precious than tyme. In
oo litel tyme, as litel as it is, may heven be wonne and lost" (p.
20). The soul's quest for the self-knowledge and self-control
that must precede its "oo litel tyme" with (and in) the beloved,
though completely internalized and completely intentional, is
nonetheless analogous to the accidental adventures of a Greek
romance protagonist, or the fortuitous but sought encounters
of a knight errant in the perilous forest. It is no mere rhetorical
affectation but rather perceived generic similarities that leads
the author of another late medieval English mystical treatise, *A
Pistle of the Discrecioun of Stirings,* to describe the soul's
journey toward inner harmony as a type of metaphorical romance plot:

> And parauenture thou knowest not yit thin owne
> inward disposicioun thiself so fully as thou schalt
> do herafter, when God wole late thee fele it bi
> the profe amonge many fallynges and risinges.
> For I knewe neuer yit no synner that myht come
> to the parfite knowing of himself and of his in-
> ward disposicioun, bot if he were lernid of it

before in the scole of God, by experience of
many temptaciouns [and by many fallynges and
risinges]. For riht as amonge the wawes and
the flodes and the stormes of the see on the to
partye, the pesible winde and the calmes and
the softe weders of the ayre on the tother partye,
the sely schip at the last atteineth to the londe
and the hauen: riht so amonge the diuersite of
temptaciouns and tribulaciouns that fallen to a
soule in this ebbing and flowing liif (the which
ben ensaumpled bi the stormes and the flodes of
the see on the to partye) and amonges the grace
and the goodnes of the Holy Goost, the manyfold
visitacioun, swetnes and coumforte of spirite
(the whiche ben ensaumplid bi the pesible winde
and the softe weders of the eire on the tother
partye) the sely soule, at the licnes of the schip,
atteineth at the last to the londe of stabelnes
and the hauen of helthe, the whiche is the clere
and the sothefast knowing of himself and of alle
his inward disposiciouns; thorow the whiche
knowing he sitteth quietly in hymself, as a king
crouned in his rewme, mihtly, wisely, and
goodly gouerning himself and alle his thouhtes
and steringes, bothe in body and in soule.[17]

As opposed to religious romance and mystical treatise, chivalric romance makes the goal of the hero's quest the winning of,
or reconciliation with, an earthly beloved. The progress toward
that goal is instigated by a crisis of self-awareness; then come
the romance adventures through which the hero seeks to overcome the gap he now perceives between present (imperfect) and
future (perfect) selves. By placing this crisis of awareness and its
consequences within the literary frame of the chivalry topos,
the twelfth-century poet gained a double narrative and thematic
advantage: he could use the crisis to probe the limitations of the
topos, and the topos to give literary shape to the crisis. Self-

awareness (and therefore the fact of individual destiny) becomes the central issue of the chivalric romance world when the
smooth interaction of love and prowess breaks down because of
tensions between love's demands on a knight and demands of
honor, valor, or obligations related to the knight's social status,
that is, his natal and circumstantial identities. Tension leads to
crisis, crisis to self-awareness, self-awareness often to self-hatred
or self-alienation. This stage is frequently represented by a
change of identity, either willed (as when Yvain chooses the
name Knight of the Lion to hide his "true" identity until
Laudine forgives him) or unwilled (as when Partonopeu is so
changed by his melancholy as to be practically unrecognizable).
In *Ipomedon,* as we have seen, the protagonist adopts two
different disguises simultaneously, to represent both the depersonalizing effect of prowess in a rigidly applied chivalry
topos and the difficulty of judging inner worth, and therefore
identity, from outward appearances.

The heroic adventures which follow the attainment of self-
awareness in chivalric romance function metaphorically, as we
have seen in the Guivret and Ardenne episodes. The protagonists,
and other sympathetic characters like Urraque, show us how
awareness leads to control of self and environment in the service
of final self-fulfillment, the attainment of the previously imagined state of union with another that brings truly personal
happiness and establishes purely personal destiny.

The romance plot as used by the chivalric poets not only sets
the hero free from social or doctrinal systems larger than his
own experience, such as define early medieval religious and epic
heroes; it also exalts inner experience—the perception of one's
individuality and private destiny—to a central position in determining the shape of the hero's career and allows adventures in
the outside world to illustrate the hero's control over and focusing of his private impulses so that they serve his unique vision of his "happy ending." Of course, the version of the sophisticated, awareness-centered romance which I have given is too
schematic; romances, like their heroes, are individual, and each
chivalric poet, as I observed at the beginning of this chapter,

created variations on the chivalry topos which involved variations as well on the form and manifestations of self-awareness.
Chrétien's *Erec* and *Yvain* are the classic examples of the
chivalry topos extended into a romance plot the major turning
point of which is the accession of awareness to the hero, an
accession that determines the direction of the rest of the plot.[18]
Partonopeu de Blois is very similar in structure and significance,
while *Le Bel inconnu,* despite its structural and thematic
originality, makes the crisis of awareness central to the hero's
transfer of allegiance from the world of public martial service to
the world of the private love quest.

In *Erec* and *Yvain* the first movement of the plot is through a
preliminary adventure toward a deceptive stasis, in which the
impulse toward private aggrandizement through love and marriage seems to be capable of harmonization with the social
aggrandizement (honor) the knight achieves, and with the
communal happiness, or *joie,* of the entire court. Then comes
the personal crisis (the equivalent of external catastrophe in less
sophisticated romance) where the hero realizes the implications
of his behavior (he becomes self-conscious) and resubmits himself to the world of unforeseeable experience (adventure) as an
external symbol of his taking on the task of controlling and
shaping the newly understood world of contrary impulses within himself by means of a new understanding of his desired
destiny. In *Erec,* the hero chooses a life of love at the expense
of prowess, loses his honor, and is "awakened" by Enide to the
necessity both of proving his own prowess and of showing
Enide the role her awareness must play in their quest for the
shared destiny of a happy marriage.[19] In *Yvain,* the situation is
reversed; the hero chooses honor earned by prowess—public
identity, in short—over the private satisfactions of love, with the
outcome that he loses his love and, as a result of realizing that
melancholy fact, his sanity as well. Since the larger scope of this
study forbids my analyzing the role of self-awareness in both
these romance plots, I shall here confine my attention to *Yvain.*

In the first section of *Yvain,* the hero, with flimsy provoca-
tion, kills the defender of the magic spring, and then, while

imprisoned in the dead man's castle, falls in love with his grief-stricken wife. (I will discuss the metaphoric implications of Yvain's captivity, and his liberation from it by the wit of the damsel Lunete, later in this chapter.[20]) When Yvain has won Laudine and successfully defended the magic spring against Kay, the representative of Arthur's court who has come to see the marvellous place, he is honored by Arthur and seems thus to have attained public and private felicity. But now his friend Gawain convinces him, by arguing the danger marriage poses to the life of honor, to go off for a year to joust in tournaments—a form of prowess as amoral as the usage of the magic spring, though less lethal and more conducive to instant social acclaim. Yvain agrees to follow his friend's advice and example, promises to return to Laudine after a year's absence, leaves her, and, of course, forgets his deadline.[21]

The shock of awareness comes to Yvain at the height of his glory, when his triumphant prowess has made him the center of a world preoccupied by honor (2681-95); his fame is so great that Arthur comes to his "court"—his tent set up outside the city walls—instead of vice versa. Suddenly, he remembers his promise, and almost immediately thereafter Laudine's damsel appears to reveal publicly his disloyalty and to demand that he return her mistress's ring, symbolizing the end of their love (2696-782). Yvain's grief quickly turns to self-hatred (2792), thoughts of self-destruction (2793-97), and finally the inner storm of madness (2806-07).[22] He strips himself and flees to the forest to live the life of a game-hunting wildman.

In the scene just described, Chrétien makes it clear that Yvain realizes his fault (2701-03: ". . . Car bien savoit/que covant manti li avoit/et trespassez estoit li termes"), before he is accused of it by the messenger from Laudine (2720f.). His subsequent deranged behavior is both an outer mimesis of the implications of his previous behavior—he has been "mad" and "subhuman" to forget his wife—and a response of alienation and despair to the realization of whom he has become (a brave and honored knight, "Yvain the hero," but also "Yvain the traitor" to Laudine) and what it has cost him. Yvain's madness and subhumanity are incisively defined by an ironic comment (2861–63) explaining his return, even in his distraction, to the hut of a hermit who gives him water: "mes n'est nus, tant po de san ait,/qui el leu ou l'en bien li fait,/ne revaigne molt volentiers." In overstaying his leave from Laudine, Yvain has precisely *not* come back to the place where he had been treated well. This comment condemns the hero's earlier behavior and establishes a perspective on his *folie* in the same way that the battling horse and lion define through contrast Partonopeu's loss of will to survive and struggle in the episode discussed in chapter 2. (See also line 6774, where Yvain tells Laudine, "folie me fist demorer," that is, caused him not to return to her within a year.) By becoming aware of the tremendous gap between what he has accomplished and what he really wants (Laudine's love), Yvain is redefining himself in terms of desired happiness rather than possessed honor, in terms of an identity perceived but not attained, whose ultimate referent is personal and private. The "inner distance" between his new state of realization and its desired goal is so insurmountable to Yvain as to call forth a negative response of madness and escape to the woods— an inner and outer escape from the hated self whose hideous distortion stands revealed in the light of awareness cast by remembered love.[23]

Yvain's inner crisis is a negative version of religious conversion as it might be found in a religious romance—a horrified turning away from the old self owing to sudden illumination by grace. In the absence of any such illumination to overcome the awareness and memory of the evil past and to metamorphose character instantaneously from outside, the hero can only act out (in "mad" behavior) his awareness of the past, as a gesture of simultaneous self-knowledge and self-condemnation.[24]

All of Yvain's responses in madness have inner significance: in running away, stripping himself, and taking bow and arrows, he abandons his social identity and the hateful meaning or form it has given to his martial impulses. He will now hunt for survival with unchivalric weapons instead of jousting in armor to gain (self-betraying) honor. His repudiation of his old self involves the repudiation of society and civilization as he has experienced them until now, shaping his behavior by their values; hence he eats his meat raw, an act symbolic of a precivilized state, and lives alone in a presocial existence.

Yvain's crisis of self-awareness, and the change of situation which it prompts, thus set up the *form* his adventures will take in the remainder of the romance, and give them their *goal* and underlying *significance*. His adventures will involve regaining a state of existence which is again civilized and socialized, but based on new, non-self-betraying values.[25] We see the stages of this in Yvain's successive relationship with the hermit, the lion, and various humans, in all of which the reciprocal offering of service through prowess and service through hospitality or other aid is central, not the quest for honor and dominance. (He brings meat to the hermit in return for water; he rescues the lion and gets obedience and a loyal helper in battle; he saves Lunete and she finally saves his love.[26]) The goal of his adventures is now clear and personal: reunion with Laudine. And the significance of his adventures as Knight of the Lion also proceeds from and illustrates his new self-awareness: he must now rescue women whose situation in some way recalls or represents his treatment of Laudine, and, as we have seen, he must sometimes act within a rigorously limited time period, in effect illustrating his awareness of and self-chastisement for having forgotten to return on time to his wife.

These adventures are all organized by and consequent on the inner-generated crisis and turning point which Chrétien has built into his sophisticated romance structure. Furthermore, by means of the episodic romance plot, Chrétien could choose and arrange Yvain's adventures to fulfill several functions at once. The lion, while no simple allegorical beast,[27] does serve in part to represent the accession of loyalty to Yvain, as, for example, when he controls his "prowess" instinct ("Si le semont feins et nature/d'aler en proie et de chacier . . .") and refuses to kill a deer until the man who has saved him, and to whom he therefore owes loyalty, gives him permission. (See 3412–44; once again the ironic contrast to Yvain's disloyal surrender to the voice of prowess in leaving Laudine is clear.) The lion's adventures, therefore, reflect Yvain's progress in facing himself, and controlling his martial prowess by means of other, private imperatives. Meanwhile the adventures are creating a pattern of moral service through prowess, a pattern that charts Yvain's discovery of a new mode of relationship with society that will allow him to pursue his happiness and fulfillment in other than complete isolation. Finally, as Yvain's awareness leads to these consequences, the audience's awareness is being raised by its repeated exposure to metaphoric adventure situations, so that its progress through the romance quite literally duplicates the protagonist's.

In short, the combination of biographical form, inner crisis of self-awareness as turning point, and metaphoric adventures chosen to reflect the state and effects of self-awareness enables Chrétien to offer in *Yvain* (and in *Erec*) an experiential, nondogmatic, nontheoretical exploration of the nature of individuality—its defining relationships and its personal destiny—unmatched by any previous medieval literary form.

The Ardenne episode of *Partonopeu de Blois,* which I have already discussed, forms the latter part of a narrative sequence that provides another instance of the use of the romance plot to focus on inner loss and recovery (or exile from and return to the vision of self-fulfillment), and thus an indisputably individual experience. At the beginning of the romance, Partonopeu, count of Blois and nephew of the king of France, is a brave and handsome boy of thirteen. Transported in an unmanned boat to a mysterious city of beautiful but empty palaces, Partonopeu goes to bed in the most beautiful one, and in the dark is visited by a woman he cannot see. He rapes her, or so it seems; after the deed is done, she identifies herself as the young empress of Byzantium, Mélior, who, pressed by her vassals to choose a husband, has selected the young count and magically transported him to her, with the intent of enticing him to her bed. The apparent emptiness of the city is also effected by her magic, and she now tells him that if he wishes to marry her he must stay in the city alone for two and one-half years (until he is old enough to be dubbed knight by her), during which time he can enjoy her at night but must not try to see her face. These conditions are necessary in order to prevent her vassals discovering that she has, out of love, chosen a mere boy as her husband and has granted him her favors before she has either knighted or married him. Discovery would bring disgrace and death to both of them.

Partonopeu, smitten with love, agrees to Mélior's scheme, but after a year he asks her permission to return to his home in France. She agrees, saying that he will there be able to win great glory through saving the Franks from invasion by their enemies. Her prediction is borne out, but in France Partonopeu is also subjected to a new danger: his mother and his royal uncle become convinced that his beloved is an evil spirit and insist that he not return to her. With the aid of a love potion they almost force him to marry the king's beautiful, rich niece, but his love for Mélior saves him at the last moment, and he returns, shaken and repentant, to Chef d'Oire, Mélior's city. When, some months later, he requests leave to return to France again, Mélior warns him that this time he will succumb to the wiles of his kin and betray her. Disregarding this prophecy, the young man goes home, where he is soon convinced by his mother and the bishop of Paris that Mélior is an ugly demon who seeks his damnation. They give him a marvellous inextinguishable lantern with which to see her when next he goes to bed with her, and Partonopeu, once back at Chef d'Oire, uses it—only to discover that Mélior is young and beautiful, and to realize that he has broken his promise and betrayed her. His self-hatred is matched by Mèlior's rage and despair; her magic has been impaired by the betrayal, and the lovers suddenly find themselves surrounded by the court ladies of Chef d'Oire. While Mélior expects her vassals to arrive momentarily and put an end to them both, her beautiful and witty sister, Urraque, appears instead and urges that she curtail her grief, forgive Partonopeu for his folly, and make hasty plans to deceive her vassals into accepting Partonopeu as her husband.

Neither Partonopeu nor Mélior will be comforted by Urraque's

Lunete-like advice; the empress rejects her lover, and he leaves Chef d'Oire for France in a state of extreme self-torment and depression. At this point the Ardenne episode begins, culminating, we recall, in Partonopeu regaining the will to live and repairing to Urraque's island, whence, after more intrigue, he will issue to win Mélior in the tournament she has ordained.

Partonopeu is a romance of a young man's coming of age. At the beginning of the story the hero is an adolescent, full of promise but untested in love or war. The first episode is a superb evocation of his introduction to the mysteries of love, an initiation into passion which creates a private world entirely divorced from the life of relationships and activities he has thus far experienced. Mélior has structured the world of love as one which must remain a secret from the world of honor (her vassals) until it can be presented to this public world on the latter's terms and receive its blessing. The antagonism and disjunction between a world of love, full of pleasure but hedged round with prohibitions and permitting only limited perception of reality, and a threatening world of honor and public responsibility provides the audience with an anti-chivalric paradigm which must obviously be modified as the hero grows toward physical maturity.

The sensually pleasing but impercipient world of young love in which Partonopeu finds himself reflects both his and Mélior's immaturity in its taboos and its fearful avoidance of antagonistic external reality. His noble nature, which has led Mélior to choose him as lover and husband, and which has cooperated with her magic in bringing him to a relationship with her,[28] now initiates the crucial phase of interaction between his private world of love and the public world of responsibilities in which a courtly young hero is led by his will to participate. When Partonopeu returns to France after a year with his beloved, he wins honor through prowess prompted by love.[29] But he also discovers that the people whose values controlled him before his discovery, in love, of a private destiny challenge his love vision and thereby test his ability to perceive the true nature and goal of his desire—to understand himself. His mother and his feudal "father" the king set themselves against his private identity and propose a pseudo-love identity instead, in the form of a socially sanctioned and apparently desirable marriage. The attractions, symbolized by the love potion,[30] through which society in fact seeks to control the destiny of the young courtier are seductive and perilous. Love, however, has given Partonopeu sufficient self-awareness to perceive that this is not the end he desires, and by thinking of Mélior he resists the workings of the potion.[31]

Partonopeu's love cannot counter his fear of damnation, however, and where his blood and feudal relations have failed to trap him, his spiritual father, the bishop of Paris, succeeds. Respecting the bishop's insight into his love more than his own, Partonopeu surrenders his autonomous judgment and accepts as a guide to perception the lantern which will ironically allow him only to perceive that the impulse of his love was correct and that his willingness to be swayed by another code of values toward another goal was an act of hideous self-betrayal.[32]

The moment of crisis in *Partonopeu,* like that in *Yvain,* creates negative self-awareness; the hero's conversion to self-hatred and despair[33] results in both romances from a broken promise to the beloved. Partonopeu, like Yvain, flees his own *folie;* his flight from Chef d'Oire to France, and from France to the wilderness, functions again as an external metaphor of the flight from the self, perceived as the hopelessly imperfect subverter of its own real desires. (Yvain's active, wild madness as a hunter of beasts grotesquely parodies the prowess he had earlier set above love, while Partonopeu's passive, melancholy madness and desire to be eaten by beasts recalls his passiveness before, and manipulation by, the figures who embody the restraints and values of his public world.)

This is not to say that the moment of crisis in *Partonopeu* lacks originality. The poet links Partonopeu's betrayal to the sudden, full visibility of Mélior's own public world and to the appearance on the scene of Urraque, whose virtues will be so important in bringing the romance to a happy and harmonious conclusion. In other words, he suggests that this is a *felix culpa,* a fortunate fall through which the lovers face the full complexity of their relationship to the external world and its values; from this perception, however painful, they can ultimately move to accepting their own imperfections and the hostility of society to their private love, a hostility neither as terrible nor as insurmountable as ignorance and innocence have led them to believe. The magic of love has been irrevocably destroyed by the fall, but so have its illusions, and the way is clear to discover how to outwit and manipulate society for the sake of love while apparently observing its behests in order to gain honor.[34] The ambiguity of this turning point is focused for us by means of an important word-play in lines 4821-22. As Partonopeu pleads with Mélior to forgive him for his *folie,* "A ces paroles vint li jors,/ Qui lor *devise* lor amors" (italics mine). Old French *deviser* means to separate or divide, but also to observe, to (make to) understand, to place in order. That is, this moment is an ending and a sundering for the lovers, but also the beginning of a difficult but necessary period of learning that will finally enable them to order their lives and social environment for personal fulfillment.[35]

All the positive possibilities of Partonopeu's crisis of self-awareness are summed up in Urraque, who now enters the narrative with counsels of moderation (4963-78), an understanding of Partonopeu's human weakness (4943-50), and schemes which will compensate for his *folie* and counteract the opposition of Mélior's vassals to her quest for private fulfillment (5001-38). Through Urraque's eyes we see Mélior not as a fairy-mistress but as a petulant young girl who has not learned the necessity for tolerance in love; we also realize that heroic rage or self-laceration cannot be final responses to love gone wrong any more than secrecy and isolation can be to its birth. The two protagonists are equally culpable in the dislocation of their love. Both have been guilty of too great respect for the norms and pressures of society: Mélior has been led by her fear of her vassals to create the spell of isolation for her love affair and to impose on her lover the promise that he will not try to perceive who she is, while he has been led by his respect for the advice of his sponsors to break the promise. The lovers' crisis of aware-

ness makes the audience aware, as well, of how limited and immature their earlier felicity had been, and the presence of
Urraque assures us that good can come of the end of innocence.

Partonopeu's self-hatred, melancholy madness, and quest for
self-destruction in Ardenne show the negative results of self-
awareness based on his deed of commission (Yvain's, we recall,
was one of omission toward his beloved). Urraque's *engin* overcomes the hero's negative self-awareness; it also manipulates
Mélior into admitting that she still loves Partonopeu. The stage
is then set for a rescuing of the love affair through the operation
of the chivalry topos in the conventional form of the tournament for Mélior's hand. The structure of *Partonopeu* is much
tighter than that of *Erec* or *Yvain,* which simplifies the task of
interpreting each episode. On the other hand, the *Partonopeu*
poet, by borrowing and adapting the fairy-mistress motif used
by Marie de France in several of her *lais,*[36] as well as a version
of the Cupid and Psyche myth,[37] and by his use of Urraque,
makes Partonopeu's development less autonomous than that of
Chrétien's heroes. But clearly the central assumptions are the
same: sooner or later the individual arrives at a moment of crisis
in which he realizes the nature and effect of his actions; he confronts his identity and the destiny to which it is leading him.
The clash between this realization and the hero's equally intense,
equally private desire to obtain the vision of happiness that love
has created within him shakes his being to its foundation. But
out of this cataclysm are generated the inner and outer paths
that the hero must travel if he is to reconcile awareness and desire. In the course of this process of harmonizing present and
(hoped-for) future states, the hero—and the poet—test the
assumptions of chivalry and, as we have seen, either approve,
reorganize, or reject them.

In *Ipomedon,* the hero's crisis of awareness comes early in the
work and is evenly matched with an analogous crisis on the part
of the heroine; both realize that the assumptions on which their
behavior has rested—Ipomedon, that he can win La Fière without a struggle, and she that she can force love into the mold of
the chivalry topos by proclaiming she will marry only the best

of knights—cannot satisfy the demands which their new love is making within them. (See 945-1112, for La Fière's speech of realization and regret after Ipomedon leaves her court at her urging; and 1113-234, for Ipomedon's symmetrical complaint that he has lost La Fière through his foolish pride in hiding his royal identity from her.) The romance proceeds to test two standard narrative devices of chivalric romance—the tournament and the quest undertaken to rescue the beautiful lady threatened by a tyrannical knight (as Guinevere is by Meleagranz in *Lancelot*)—and finds each insufficient to bring the lovers together. Instead, Ipomedon's awareness of the shortcomings of prowess as an instrument of self-fulfillment and his ingenuity in manipulating his environment turn both episodes into lessons for the court and La Fière in the inadequacies of chivalry. That is, Ipomedon treats his experiences like a chivalric poet, instead of a chivalric hero: he structures them to provide epiphanies, and resultant increased awareness, for other characters in the romance. Despite this cynical and artful manipulation of chivalric conventions in *Ipomedon,* Hue de Roteland still begins with the same assumptions about the centrality of the hero's self-awareness to the structure of the romance as those of Chrétien and the *Partonopeu* poet. Ipomedon is impelled by his awareness of his desire for La Fière; his uniqueness lies in the fact that his creator has placed in his hands the ability to organize the plot to teach himself and his beloved necessary lessons.

But Ipomedon, for all his *engin,* is imprisoned, like the oversized Mabonograin in Chrétien's *Erec,* in his attempt to show his lady by his prowess that he is a knight worthy to be loved.[38] Although he is aware of the hopelessness of his situation, he is helpless against it until kin-love, a force outside the chivalry topos, liberates him in a last, sudden twist of the already tortuous plot. The parallel between Hue's use of fraternal love as a catalyst to the union of his protagonists and Chrétien's use, in *Yvain,* of Lunete's *engin,* inspired by her gratitude to Yvain and loyalty to her mistress, is no accident. In these cases, and many others in chivalric romance, relationships of love and service based on the recognition of personal uniqueness in another human being—one's brother, one's benefactor—replace strict application of the chivalry topos as the key to individual happiness.[39] In such versions of the romance plot, final reunion or recovery affirms the cruciality of individuality not only by crowning self-awareness with success (through attainment of the personal goal which the protagonist has learned he really needs for self-fulfillment), but also by linking it to other ways of celebrating personal identity in a world of variety and confusion: confirming intimate family ties, rendering service owed specifically to the hero, and so forth.

In the last version of the romance plot I will discuss, that of Renaut de Beaujeu's *Le Bel inconnu,* the hero, Guinglain, undertakes a rescue quest as the representative of Arthur's court (albeit against the will of the court and of the damsel to be rescued) and undergoes miscellaneous adventures before surviving the climactic adventure of the perilous kiss in the enchanted city of Sinaudon. In these first, pre-crisis adventures, Renaut is not interested in showing his protagonist's inner growth, but rather how the young knight—who does not yet know his name—must overcome the hostility and imperfections of chivalric society (including Arthurian society) in the process of discovering his qualitative and natal identities, that is, his individuality as it is to be defined before awareness of love metamorphoses it.[40]

After proving his mettle in this way, the Bel inconnu comes to the deserted city of Sinaudon, resists its spells and menaces, rescues the lady of the city, and thereby wins the right to marry her. As a bonus, he learns his identity: he is Guinglain, the son of Gawain (3216–42). Again we come, in a chivalric romance, to a moment of stasis and apparent triumph for the protagonist, whose prowess of service has defined him as a person of particular gifts and social worth. (It is symbolically fitting that he is the son of Gawain, the quintessential upholder of court values, and foil to the hero, in all of Chrétien's romances.) He has saved a city and its queen from a calamitous web of illusion which seems metaphorically to represent the fact and consequences of society's deluded denial of the importance of the young knight's quest for recognition. (Such a denial characterizes the relationship between Guinglain and Arthur's court at the beginning of the romance, when the king begrudges him the perilous quest; it also recalls Yvain's need to leave court secretly to gain for himself the honor of fighting at the magic spring, since Arthur would never award him the adventure.) Esmaree, queen of Sinaudon, has been changed into a serpent by evil jongleurs who wish to marry her and who convince the citizens of Sinaudon that the city is about to be destroyed, causing them to flee it. Behind the facade of social beauty—the empty, fair city— Guinglain finds threats and illusions. Everything points to a falsely negative picture, an apocalyptic vision of social disaster linked to a presentation of society as dangerous to those who come to it alone. The evil jongleurs, in this reading, represent society's soured imagination of its own future, its ruler, and its would-be rescuers.[41] Guinglain's commitment to his ideals and lonely quest breaks this pattern of fear-induced social hostility and liberates the forces of beauty and beneficence, represented by Esmaree, that society should offer the individual who seeks to serve it and himself. But just when all seems well, Guinglain comes to a new level of awareness: he does not want the identity and destiny he has earned for himself; instead, he wishes to possess the "Pucele as blanches mains" whom he had encountered during his adventures en route to Sinaudon but had fled from because of his commitment to see his quest through.

Impelled by his new insight into his desires,[42] he returns to the Pucele and, after another set of tests which he fails comically because he cannot control his desire, he finally wins her person. Hearing, however, of a tournament which Arthur has called in order to lure him back to Esmaree of Sinaudon (the prize of the tournament), Guinglain asks leave to fight in it. He discovers the next day that he has chosen wrongly between love and honor: the Pucele has disappeared. (Renaut's debt to Chrétien's *Yvain* should be evident.) He fights in the tournament, wins, and marries the woman he earlier abandoned for love, while the narrator promises to let him win back his *amie* if only his (the narrator's) mistress will say the word!

There are, then, two turning points in *Le Bel inconnu*'s plot. The first opposes inner awareness of one's preferred, private destiny, not yet gained, to the public success and destiny already achieved by a self-imposed task of martial service on behalf of an unknown but, as it happens, very well-connected lady. Guinglain's suspension between claims of love and honor is resolved on this occasion in love's favor, but only after the lovesick knight overcomes his despair at having made the wrong choice (by continuing to Sinaudon) and, urged on by his squire (a figure similar to Lunete but lacking her wit), leaves his bride-to-be and returns to Isle d'Or and his beloved. He cannot win the Pucele through prowess, as he did Esmaree; in fact, his attempts to reach her bed (a parodic love-quest) end in comic disaster.[43] As soon as he stops trying, and obeys her order that he not enter her bedroom, she accepts him. Renaut's depiction of love's personal fulfillment as the reward of passivity and subservience, in a magic world removed from the sphere of adventure (a world patterned on Mélior's Chef D'Oire in *Partonopeu*), undermines the chivalry topos.[44] But then, in a second reversal, Guinglain, like Partonopeu and Yvain before him, makes the wrong choice (of honor over love) and finds himself thrust back into the world where the chivalry topos, at least in outward form, has been coopted by the court as a means to control his identity and destiny. Only an act of *franchise* outside the story altogether can save Guinglain as an individual, seeking and finding private self-fulfillment.[45]

By building his romance around two similar but opposed moments of realization, Renaut de Beaujeu is arguing that self-awareness is not a one-time crisis; its effect must be constant if the hero is to fulfill his private destiny. Renaut deliberately violates the conclusions of the chivalric romance plot as developed (probably) by Chrétien, but not its premises; the motivation for the turning point in *Le Bel inconnu* still comes from within the hero, who can, however, choose correctly and *then* incorrectly in Renaut's world. The poet is, of course, engaging in another kind of conceit at the end of the work: love does not find a proper outlet in prowess (Guinglain's prowess and chivalric service are his enemies in his love-quest),[46] but it does inspire the poet's "prowess," and it will inspire the narrator to give his anti-climactic romance a happy ending if love's rewards are forth-coming. To arrive at this conceit, Renaut constructs a romance in which the hero wins a lady, abandons her in a moment of awareness, and then wins her back in a tournament—the only problem being that she is not the lady he loves! This kind of play with the romance form and the concept of self-awareness springs from a knowledge that the audience share expectations about the form and the concept, but that they also are aware of, and enjoy demonstrations of, the problematic nature of an individual-centered vision of the world. At any stage of aware-ness the individual can still make the wrong choice in terms of his ultimate happiness, as a result of not understanding his personal priorities. The price of individuality is the constant possibility for self-betrayal, through lack of self-knowledge or self-control. This is the message Renaut propagates by his version, or rather subversion, of romance.

One other common plot constituent deserves attention in this consideration of the romance plot as the metaphoric repre-sentation of the role played by personal awareness in organizing human action and determining human happiness (or its absence): situations of forcible imprisonment. Imprisonment is especially inimical to the human condition considered as a personal quest, for it denies the hero the possibility of seeking the goals that proceed from his private awareness of his current situation and of its distance from his equally personal vision of eventual self-perfection, the final attainment of his greatest desires. Im-prisonment creates (and therefore represents) the unwilled gap between inner vision and outer behavior guided by it. It pre-vents the complete expression of perceived individuality and be-comes not simply a source of dishonor (as it is in the epic vision) but of despair. For despair, as we have seen with reference to Partonopeu in Ardenne, stems from and expresses a sense of absolute gap between the perfection of self, imagined in the sphere of uniquely personal experience within each of us, and the possibility of obtaining that perfection, and thus happiness, by any external action. This, incidentally, is the key distinction between the inner vision of the romance hero and that of mystical or devotional experience in the twelfth century: the latter need not find fulfillment in the world outside, indeed cannot. Thus the sense of enclosure as self-destroying and anti-individual in chivalric romance is not only opposed to the sense of enclosure as security in early medieval literature, it is equally opposed to the role played by enclosure in the second part of the *Life of Christina of Markyate* or in the great spiritual-devotional guide for women who have chosen imprisonment from the world, the *Ancrene Wisse*.[47]

The use of the image or situation of imprisonment in chivalric romance, then, can serve as a metaphor for any aspect of experience that hinders individual fulfillment. One need only think of the adventures of Odysseus and the various attempts made to imprison or restrain him (by Circe, Calypso, the Cyclops, and others) to realize the intimate connection between this metaphor and the romance vision.[48] The appeal of the image of imprisonment as an ordering force in chivalric romance may also be a suggestive, albeit entirely subconscious, comment on how the new sense of unique, individual experience in twelfth-century culture responded to the inherited theological, imaginative, and political structures of early medieval culture, as well as to the new structures of the ecclesiastical and intellectual Establishment of the day. (As we have seen, Abelard and Christina spend a good deal of their lives escaping from real or metaphorical imprisonment in order to pursue the personal life and destiny they have come to feel particularly theirs.[49])

Two of Chrétien's romances, *Lancelot* and *Yvain*, are particularly rich in imprisonment situations. *Lancelot*, and to a lesser extent *Cligès*, play ironically with the relationship between love and imprisonment in various ways, exploring a paradox frequently confronted in lyrics and also romance: that love, ostensibly the force making for the vision and attainment of self-perfection, and therefore a liberating force, can itself be a cruel tyranny of lady over knight, and thus a form of imprisonment of the lover's destiny in the beloved's whim. Some of this, in the lyric, at least, is merely the artful revelling in paradox or the erotic enjoyment of *suasoria* (persuasions to sexual love) presented under the guise of warning the lady against the detrimental effects on both parties of the poet-lover's passion becoming his prison.[50] In the romances, imprisonment has a more analytic function, as it is a narrative situation into (and out of) which the hero passes, not simply a timeless, symbolic state. In *Yvain,* imprisonment serves primarily as a more-than-erotic metaphor, while in *Lancelot* its use is primarily erotic.

In *Yvain,* Chrétien organizes his plot in almost Aristotelian fashion, juxtaposing scenes which exemplify the excess, mean, and deficiency of control in the life of the characters, especially the protagonist. The deficiency is represented by, among other images, the social chaos at Arthur's court (at the romance's beginning), the storm-causing fountain and its related ritual of amoral, destructive prowess, Laudine's nearly insane grief for her husband, and Yvain's madness in the forest.[51] At the opposite extreme, images of excessive control, or imprisonment, abound: Yvain trapped between gates at Laudine's castle (958f.), Lunete in her cell awaiting death for treason (3557f.), the three hundred damsels imprisoned within a stockade in the castle of Pesme Avanture (5182f.), the lion closed in a room to prevent him from aiding his master (5560f.). Both extremes represent a loss of that ability to control a situation and turn it to constructive use in seeking self-fulfillment which is the mark of the successful individual in chivalric romance. Using prowess, loyalty, and *engin,* characters in *Yvain,* as we have seen, obtain freedom of movement for themselves and others and then subdue forces which, in their uncontrolled state, threaten the disruption of personal relationships (whether the kin-relationship of the sisters of Noire Espine or the love-relationship of Yvain and the admittedly remote Laudine) and of whole social orders.

The integration of the motif of imprisonment (and its opposite, excessive, uncontrolled behavior) into a metaphorical scheme designed to illustrate the poet's central concern with individual destiny is particularly evident at moments in *Yvain* where images of constraint and excess exist side by side, as it were emblematically. When Yvain is trapped at Laudine's castle, he cowers invisible in his "cell" (the curiously shifting gateway-room in which he has been trapped by the falling portcullises) while the wife of the man he has killed nearly goes mad with grief (1150f.). She has lost all control over her responses, while he has become doubly imprisoned: physically, as a result of his prowess and desire for honor (he chased the dying knight to the latter's castle to get evidence of his victory to take back to Arthur's court and refute Kay's insults; see 890–99), and symbolically, by his nascent love of the lady. (As Chrétien puts it, Yvain is detained by Love and Shame.[52]) This apparently insoluble situation—Yvain loves the woman who most hates him as her husband's slayer—is then resolved by Lunete's formidable wit, or *engin,* which is activated by double loyalty: her desire to serve her lady, Laudine, and also to repay Yvain for past favors he has done her. The whole episode functions as a gracefully ironic, and problematic, psychomachia, the result of which is to demonstrate, like the Ardenne episode in *Partonopeu,* how individual happiness depends on the establishment of meaningful contact between sharply differentiated persons. In addition, a measure of control over the exercise of prowess accompanies the end of the protagonist's literal and metaphorical imprisonment: as Laudine's consort, Yvain becomes guardian of the magic fountain, and in this role he justifiably avenges his honor on Kay (when the latter activates the fountain), while now restraining his prowess to avoid injuring his rival.[53]

Of course, Lunete's arranged conciliation comes unstuck, and Yvain goes mad when he realizes he has betrayed Laudine and his own desire for self-fulfillment in love. Cured of his madness, he begins a series of adventures and forms a partnership with a loyal lion, with whom he leads for some days a half-civilized existence. Coming by chance upon the storm-causing spring, his grief at the memory of what he has lost nearly drives him mad again (3486f.: "par po ne reforsena/mes sire Yvains . . ."). The lion, thinking his master has killed himself, tries to commit suicide, and Yvain, seeing his loyalty, doubles his own self-condemnation and ponders suicide.[54] His soliloquy is interrupted by the comments of a damsel imprisoned in a nearby chapel, who tells him her grief is greater than his. His inquiries establish that it is Lunete, doomed to die the next day as a traitor because of his dereliction of duty to Laudine. Yvain identifies himself and promises to defend her in battle against her accusers.

In this scene, for all its comic and burlesque vein, Chrétien describes a meeting which is absolutely crucial for his hero. His self-hatred and despair, on the verge of passing out of control again at the sight of the memory-prompting spring, are metamorphosed into the desire to serve Lunete, the other person, he now discovers, he has betrayed. The service will involve converting the energy he has expended on grief into disciplined prowess, aimed at ending another's imprisonment, repaying a debt, and defending justice, in a case where he himself has been the instrument of injustice. The situation has all the main ingredients of a chivalric romance crisis or *kairos;* negative self-awareness is transmuted into the possibility of controlling one's situation through prowess ennobled by a moral motive (service, justice); the moment depends on the participants being Yvain and Lunete and no one else, for Yvain is stimulated by the knowledge that he is to blame for Lunete's predicament, and the meeting between the two has unique meaning for them as individuals with personal histories; finally, by setting a deadline before which Yvain must act if his prowess and intention are to be of use, Chrétien, as we have seen, underscores the importance of the earthly environment of time and space within which men act.

Yvain's experience of that environment and its imposed limits is complicated by the second adventure, with its demands for service based on loyalty to Gawain, which Yvain encounters later in the day. He must complete his battle against Harpin of the Mountain in time to return to fight for Lunete; here again, his deeds are shaped by personal factors applicable to him alone (his relationship with Gawain) and result in the liberation of a woman from male tyranny (Harpin wants the daughter of the castle as his wife, despite her revulsion). In other words, the imprisonments and constraints against which Yvain battles are either the result of or analogous to his treatment of Laudine, whom he abandoned because he lacked control over his impulses toward prowess and honor (when these were stimulated by Gawain.) The lack of control, in its turn, resulted from a lack of awareness of how basic to his happiness was his inner and personal desire for self-fulfillment through love. The image of Lunete imprisoned is thus the tip of the thematic iceberg, referring back, through a complex interaction of motifs of constraint and lack of control, to the protagonist's inability to perceive and pursue his personal destiny, that is, to establish himself as an individual in a world of social, courtly, and martial norms.[55]

In *Lancelot,* Chrétien uses the motif of constraint/imprisonment in a different fashion, but makes it central to the erotic world of his protagonist. The basic situation of the romance, a quasi-allegorical, comic adaptation of the Christian tradition of the harrowing of hell by Christ, involves the imprisonment of many of Arthur's courtiers in the land of Gorre, and the abduction of Guinevere by Meleagranz, son of the king of Gorre, from Arthur's court to his father's kingdom.[56] Lancelot, madly in love with the queen, goes after her and her abductor, and when he arrives in Gorre and defeats Meleagranz, he thereby liberates all other captives there, in accordance with Meleagranz's challenge to Arthur's court at the beginning of the romance (see 70–79). Chrétien emphasizes the social, and strongly suggests the allegorical, significance of Lancelot's action by an episode in which Lancelot enacts his role as savior by lifting the lid from a beautiful tomb (!), a task destined for the one who will free all

the prisoners in the land from which no one returns (1837-980).
Since the tomb is to hold the liberator himself, the parallel
between Lancelot and Christ is suggested with a forcefulness
that has smacked of blasphemy to some critics.

But there is a complicating element in all this, since the savior
has taken on his redemptive, liberating mission only because his
intense, private love for the queen prompts him to rescue her.
Chrétien uses the fanciful episode of the cart (321-444) to
comment on Lancelot's passion: while searching for the queen
on foot—he has lost his horse in battle—the knight meets a
dwarf riding in a cart normally used for the public exhibit and
disgrace of criminals. After brief hesitation, Lancelot accepts
the dwarf's invitation to continue his quest in the cart. His self-
abasement and forfeit of honor—he is derided by all who see
him or hear of his ride—earn him the title, Knight of the Cart
(*Chevalier de la charrete*), by which title alone we know him
until he is named as Lancelot by Guinevere in Gorre (3660).

Chrétien seems to be claiming that passionate love begets
deeds that give the lover his identity and destiny; in the process,
love becomes a tremendous force for universal liberation, and
challenges, in its transcendence, the very imprisonment of men
in their mortality—but only, as it were, accidentally. The social
consequences of seeking personal fulfillment are enormous, and,
since Lancelot will have to win Guinevere's freedom by a martial
encounter with her abductor, Chrétien is in effect making the
largest possible claim for the chivalry topos at this point, by
adding a term to its equation: love begets prowess, prowess in
the service of love overcomes the obstacles which alienate man
from his native freedom (here represented as imprisonment in a
foreign country). It seems at this point as though Chrétien is
tallying social dividends of successful love even greater than
those embodied in the *joie de la cour* episode of *Erec*.

Chrétien further supports the theme of love overcoming imprisoning constraints by the ingenious use of the motif of verbal
imprisonment or constraint (promises or other agreements
which bind men and women in disadvantageous situations). The
romance opens with Meleagranz challenging Arthur's court to let

any knight bring the queen into the forest and defend her against the intruder, with the queen's liberty and that of all the other courtiers imprisoned in Gorre as the prize. Kay, who is never an effective fighter in Chrétien's romances, undertakes the challenge, but only by tricking Arthur into promising to grant any request the seneschal should make. Having made his rash promise, Arthur now finds himself constrained to allow Kay to take Guinevere out of the court, to certain captivity; Arthur himself is already a captive of his own agreement.[57]

Later in the romance, Lancelot frequently finds himself acting on the basis of promises made by himself or others. One example must suffice: Lancelot meets a beautiful damsel who offers him needed hospitality for the night, but only on condition he will lie with her.[58] Most unwillingly, Lancelot accepts the condition and follows her to her castle. That night, he hears a commotion and finds her in her room, naked on her bed and about to be raped by a strange knight. She chides Lancelot, saying he has promised to lie with her and must prevent anyone from taking his place. Lancelot, in a soliloquy, declares that his quest for the queen should free him from any shameful hesitation to aid the lady in distress, and that the restraint offered him now by other armed knights in the room makes the rescue more honorable; his promise to the lady must also be considered. So he fights, only to discover that the lady of the castle has staged the whole melee. He goes to bed with her, constrained by his promise, but also constrained *from* making love to her by the fact that Love has constrained his heart and given it to another. The lady perceives his unwillingness and absolves him of further service (931–1261).

This richly ambiguous and illusion-ridden episode works out the implications of the fact that Lancelot must operate as a chivalric hero under several constraints at once, of which the chief is love—"Amors, qui toz les cuers justise" (1233)—which in its very constraining power frees him from other restraints (fear, lust) and enables him to free others from imprisonment by (or in) selfish force. Working within the inner world of awareness and aspiration—the world of individual rather than social norms and compulsions—love summons the quest-hero to freedom from imprisonment within the conflicting obligations and restraints of experience freely confronted. This is surely the point of the parallel between Lancelot's overcoming hesitation instilled by fear or confusion at the door of the lady's bedroom and his earlier overcoming of the voice of *Reisons* that made him hesitate for shame before leaping onto the cart (360–69). As Chrétien puts it,

> . . . Amors . . .
> . . . li comande et semont
> que tost en la charrete mont.
> Amors le vialt et il i saut,
> que de la honte ne li chaut
> puis qu'Amors le comande et vialt.
>   [372–77]

When Lancelot has entered Gorre like a wounded Messiah (having cut his hands and feet on the sword bridge connecting Gorre and Logres: 3094–117)[59] and "harrowed" it by defeating Meleagranz, there is a sudden *peripeteia;* Guinevere, instead of thanking him, scorns him because he hesitated two steps before jumping on the cart for her sake. Lancelot, not knowing the reason for her rejection, is grief-stricken. Soon he is captured by inhabitants of Gorre (another imprisonment), and Guinevere mourns for him. Rumor spreads that she has died and Lancelot tries to commit suicide. Eventually the knight and the queen are reunited, the queen forgives his lapse and arranges to speak to him alone, at night, at the barred window of her quarters; the presence of the wounded Kay in her chamber, as well as its locked door, prevent the lovers from being closer together (4506–25). But Lancelot, inspired by love at the night rendezvous, wrenches loose the bars, wounding himself in the process, sleeps with the queen, and leaves in the morning. His blood stains the queen's bed, and when Meleagranz comes to her room that day he concludes that Kay (whose wounds are still bleeding)

has slept with Guinevere; he thereupon declares that it is useless
to try to confine a woman:

> Bien est voirs que molt se foloie
> qui de fame garder se painne,
> son travail i pert et sa painne. . . .
> [4758-60]

By the end of this section of the romance, our understanding
of love has completely changed. It has led the deluded Lancelot
to attempted suicide, to self-laceration, and to behavior which
endangers Kay's life by making him appear an adulterer. The
self-destructive and socially disruptive effects of love (which, as
we have already seen, come up again later in the romance in the
tournament at Noauz) now dominate, and are summed up by
Lancelot's breaking the bars and climbing into prison, as it
were, to indulge his passion. In short, love has now become (or
can now be perceived as) just another imprisoning, constraining
factor in man's quest for individual fulfillment.[60] The fact that
Chrétien's portion of the romance ends with the hero imprisoned
in a tower by Meleagranz, and that he did not finish the work
himself, suggests that Chrétien had written himself into a corner;
by including passionate love among the other forces and circumstances which imprison and constrain the chivalric hero, both
publicly and privately, the chivalric poet renders self-fulfillment impossible and undercuts the romance paradigm whereby
the individual only fully defines and identifies himself by the
dynamic process of attaining a purely personal happiness (self-
perfection through union with the beloved).[61] Godefroi de
Leigni's ending is consistent with Chrétien's theme of constraint when it says that Meleagranz dies because he will not ask
Lancelot for mercy, "Car ses fos cuers li desansaingne,/qui trop
l'enprisone et anlace" (7084-85; italics mine). But Godefroi
simply ignores Lancelot's private world and concentrates exclusively on the social joy of Arthur's court at their champion's
victory (7093-97). Guinevere is mentioned in the last scene
only in another image of constraint: reason so binds up her
heart when she sees Lancelot come to court that she does not

rush to kiss him in front of the king and court (6820–53). This allusion to the adulterous nature of Lancelot's love reminds us that in *Lancelot,* as in *Cligès,* Chrétien has added a major ingredient to the problematic content of the individual's quest for fulfillment: the legal (and moral) unobtainability of the beloved. Godefroi's alternatives were to show the final impossibility of self-fulfillment in such a love, thus making the romance into its generic mirror-image and converse, the love tragedy in the manner of *Tristan and Isolde;* to opt for an ironically and transparently manipulated happy ending, as in *Cligès;* or to ignore the difficulty by treating Lancelot's battle with Meleagranz solely as a prowess encounter based on antipathy and vengeance, like a walk-down in a western novel or movie, and avoid commenting further on the love relationship, but leave it unsatisfactorily suspended in air, implicitly promising further unfulfilled yearning and constraint that moves the individual to self-negation rather than self-fulfillment. (That is, love will presumably constrain the protagonist in a cycle of pleasure, loss, grief, and renewed anticipation without allowing progress toward achieving the imagined, perfected self.) Godefroi has chosen this third course.

Outside Chrétien's canon, the motif of imprisonment is used in a variety of less central ways; in *Partonopeu,* for example, the hero is "imprisoned" in a love relationship of secrecy and absolute limitations in the first part of the romance, while in the latter part he is literally (but uninterestingly) imprisoned by a knight patterned on Chrétien's Meleagranz.[62] I have explored this motif sufficiently, I believe, to indicate its usefulness as a metaphor of the inner and outer obstacles which impede the individual's full encounter with experience in his pursuit of self-fulfillment. I trust I have also demonstrated in this chapter how I believe the chivalric poet used the romance plot—episodic, biographical, metaphoric—to measure the dimensions, sound the depths, and expose the dilemmas of that pursuit, creating in the process the most complex and most self-conscious narrative literature medieval Europe had yet known.

The argument I have developed throughout this study assumes a close relationship between twelfth-century chivalric romance and the larger cultural patterns and innovations of the period. One other, unspoken assumption has also been present: that the twelfth-century romances were as different from what came after as what went before, thus warranting the cultural significance I have attached to them as relevant documents in tracing the emergence of the individual during a specific period. It would require another book as long as this one (and one I am not qualified to write) to analyze the late twelfth- and early thirteenth-century developments that resulted in a new type of chivalric narrative and marked the end of the genre's commitment to the centrality of the individual's quest for fulfillment. The period I have here described was a brief one, stretching only from 1165 or 1170 to 1190 or 1195. This "first generation" of chivalric romance then evolved into something new and different—the great prose cycles of romance which took shape during the first twenty to thirty years of the new century. The matter of chivalric romance remained popular—and indeed, poets like Jean Renart and many others kept alive the form, though not the twelfth-century content, of the adventure romance[1]—but the Arthurian world found new cultural significance (as opposed to generic continuity) in a literary form that embodies a reaction against the individual-centered world view of twelfth-century courtly literature and against many of its artistic strategies as well.

If one were to seek to isolate those aspects of evolving European culture which made the thirteenth century inhospitable to the "adolescent" excitement, rebellions, and discoveries of the twelfth, he would need to take the following developments into account: institutional and intellectual life became more highly organized and systematized, with less room for the exercise of untrammeled, improvisatory *ingenium*.[2] Ecclesiastical justice became a smoothly functioning system, while the Lateran Council of 1215 imposed new, binding order on a range of theological concepts and disciplinary practices—order which the papacy and curia now had the authority and power to enforce. The codification of confessional practice, and especially the priest's role in interrogating the penitent systematically concerning the latter's sins, tipped the balance of Christian repentance away from the contritionism of the twelfth century, which had laid stress on the moment of inner openness to God's love that individualized the penitent's experience. In art, a mimetic interest in the human figure and its placement in earthly time and space (characterized by art historians as "the 1200 style," with its heyday during the period 1180–1220) gave way to more mannered techniques.[3] Finally, in liturgical observance the allegorization of all parts of the Mass and the increasing emphasis on the dramatic elevation of the Host testified equally, though in opposite ways, to tendencies subversive of accepting the individual experience of sensory reality as a normative one.[4]

The fascination (one might almost say obsession) with the elevation of the Host at the consecration, that is, at precisely the moment it ceased to be what it appeared to be, is especially interesting; its suggestion that there is a dramatic epiphany built into Christian ritual, available to the eye of faith but not the eye of experience, supports the idea that outward reality—bread and wine—masks a higher inward reality—the body and blood of Christ—for God's chosen ones.[5] The celestial truth revealed to the elect gives to the phenomena of the perceivable world a higher meaning (the Old French term for it is *senefiance*); *kairos*, in this scheme, becomes the moment of divine revelation, not, as in twelfth-century romance, the moment of heightened inner awareness of one's one desires via-à-vis other human values or experiences. In short, the autonomy of experience is denied, and the concept of the individual becomes the handmaiden of an epiphanic, "elitist" view of the Truth.

How, then, do we see these cultural developments affecting the imagined world of chivalry and adventure? First of all, what I shall call *the canonic impulse* came into play. This is the impulse to gather together and impose an order on a wealth of imaginative material which has previously come into existence, ostensibly about the same event but clearly with no order or relation between the various versions. A nonmedieval example would be the Greek traditions and oral poetry of the Trojan War; another would be the various gospel narratives and continuations of the first Christian communities. And the Arthurian romances of the twelfth century are the example that concerns us. In every case, the age which begets this literature is operating at white heat, as it were, producing from its collective imagination (which has been stimulated by specific events or developments having national, mythic, or cultural significance) a wealth of stories hung on a central, situational peg, but each manipulating and developing that situation to make the points that reflect the author's interests. Then, after the first enthusiasm for the situation and its metaphoric or cultural significance cools, and after the situation has become standard literary fare, the next generation sets out to order and codify the stories it has grown up with or inherited, as a way of seeking to make total sense out of an interesting but no longer quite comprehensible (viscerally, at least) literary tradition whose cultural moment has passed. So the extant stories are sorted out and placed in an order which its creators never foresaw; the results are a post-Homeric epic cycle of Troy, the biblical canon, or the early thirteenth-century Arthurian prose cycles. It is in the very nature of literary evolution that this urge to tidy up the material is the result of a later cultural moment than the one that invented it.[6]

As such it also represents a different view of reality—or at least the reality behind the literary material in question. There is now a desire to see the moment as an ordered whole, a completed story making a point about human reality from a historical (rather than an epic or romance) point of view. There must be a single plot, stretched out in a precise time period, which accounts for all the actors and subordinates them to a *social* moment playing itself out. Not the anger of Achilles but the fall of Troy; not the fulfillment of the single knight in love and adventure, but the rise and fall of Arthur's court, the Round Table. This is no longer an individual-centered literary vision; it sees humanity sharing a group fate, culminating in a common end (an *apocalypse*).[7] By recounting this end, the canonic cycle is able fully to conceive, and thus to understand, its inherited stories as a metaphor of social reality. In short, literary form and cultural vision intermingle, and the triumph of the canonic impulse with regard to Arthurian romance meant a turning away from the individual-centered art of Chrétien and his followers toward the society- and history-centered fatalism of the *Mort Artu*.[8] For, as Kermode points out, history imposes a plot on reality, as perceived *in time,* and thus sets up a movement toward a common end in time (an apocalypse), beyond which we project ourselves in reading the work, in order fully to understand what the work means (and therefore, by extension, what reality means).[9]

For Arthurian romances to be placed into a canon of stories held in place, as it were, by subordination to a single historical sweep it was necessary to combine the two Arthurian streams whose existence is traceable back to the early Middle Ages: one, the legendary, mythic Arthur, "the once and future king"; the other, the Arthur of history, the *dux bellorum,* the leader of the Britons against the Saxons at a moment of crisis in British history.[10] This latter Arthur had been given international stature by Geoffrey of Monmouth and a courtly veneer by Wace in his translation-adaptation of Geoffrey's *Historia regum Britanniae.* The Arthur of the chivalric romances, however, was a deheroicized monarch, a *roi faineant* and a focus of irony. In the cycles an Arthur emerges who is both the ruler of the great court of chivalric heroes and the effective fighter. Moreover, he is now the destined one: the king who shows himself divinely chosen to create a society and an ideal by pulling the sword out of the stone. He is, in short, a man with a mission, a man about and to whom Divinity makes epiphanic pronouncements by means of heavenly voices, or through the prophet Merlin.

Merlin entered the Arthurian world as a wonder-working *magus* and adviser in Geoffrey's *Historia,* probably on the model of William of Malmesbury's Saint Dunstan.[11] But in the second generation of romances he becomes the bearer of the divine message, the mysterious and awesome character in close touch with the higher reality. His demeanor and central role in the prose cycle of romances mark the replacement of the marvellous element in chivalric romance (the self-conscious device, as we have seen, by which the chivalric poet calls attention to his own ingenuity) by a new, analogous, but very different element, that of awe and epiphany—of what I call the "gothick" element of thirteenth-century romance.[12]

Merlin represents the reentrance of the supernatural into the secular world of twelfth-century romance, but this component of the new romance vision takes its most anti-individual form in the theme and plot of the Grail. (Already, Robert de Boron, writing after 1191 [?], linked his *Estoire dou Graal* to a story of Merlin.[13]) This is not the place to contribute to the enormous critical and polemical literature on the Grail and its sources; I wish only to point out that there are two Grail-impulses, each of which transforms the quest for self-fulfillment of earlier romances into something significantly different. The first, popularized if not originated by Robert de Boron, fabricates a pseudo-salvation-historical progress of the Grail (the chalice of the Last Supper) into the possession of Joseph of Arimathea, who also receives a secret message or doctrine from Jesus after His resurrection and then travels west with an elect group to find a new, destined homeland. Jesus also gives Joseph the promise of a knight who will complete Joseph's holy assignment as guardian of the secret, in the distant future and far away from the Holy Land.

The purpose of Robert's tale seems to be to create a pseudo-gnostic historical framework into which could be placed the story of Perceval's Grail quest, as recounted by Chrétien de Troyes, in his last, unfinished romance, *Le Conte del Graal*.[14] Chrétien's work, whatever its sources, originality, and intent—and I confess to being puzzled by all these aspects of it—seems to be turning toward a new imaginative paradigm of the quest for individual fulfillment, involving service to a Christian social and personal ideal rather than the pursuit of a perfection best represented by the purely private experience of love. Whatever the import of the antecedent stages, and there were several, when the Grail material becomes absorbed (as the *Queste del saint Graal*) into the new canonic cycle of Arthurian romances known as the Vulgate cycle it establishes a conflict between Arthurian society, a pseudo-historical society committed to chivalric adventure but also to an ideal of service through prowess, and the Grail experience—the intensely personal, anti-social, and self-annihilating quasi-mystical vision of God-made-man in the sacrifice of the Mass, available only to the purest and holiest of knights. The irreconcilable nature of this conflict endows the narrative with a nostalgic sadness, rather like Vergil's *lacrimae rerum,* which is completely foreign to twelfth-century chivalric romance because it reflects a fatalistic knowledge that history rules man, that time rules history, and that divine providence, by imposing a high duty on the Christian, makes his pursuit of pleasure or self-fulfillment on earth transitory and ultimately delusory.[15] (The *Queste* is uncompromising in its contention that Arthurian society is in fact stained by sin.) When Arthur, faced with the prospect of his knights undertaking en masse the quest for the Grail, laments the passing of his fellowship, we realize that he inhabits a literary world in which the lonely knight's openness to the adventures of personal experience no longer marks the first stage on an arduous and dangerous journey through self-awareness toward control of the environment and of his own inner impulses as well. Instead, the quest has become a corporate act, and a subversive one as well, when seen through the eyes of the king who stays behind.[16] Furthermore, the success of the quest, for the very few

who do succeed,[17] will mean a momentary epiphany precisely
analogous to the dramatic center of the Mass, when the Host is
elevated: the knight will see God and his vision will confirm the
irrelevance of all other earthly experience, except as it points
toward this one. (It is no accident that the adventures undergone by knights in the *Queste del saint Graal* usually don't
mean what they seem to; their *senefiance,* or spiritual and allegorical meaning, is made clear to the participants *ex post facto,*
by a nearby hermit or a heavenly voice.[18])

By moving toward a plot governed by social and historical,
rather than personal, norms, and by including within its com-
pass a Grail myth that exalts a private quest in which a pre-
destined hero (Galahad) attains a vision subversive of sensory
experience, the Arthurian cycle of the thirteenth century shows
its basic hostility to the individual-centered vision of twelfth-
century chivalric romance. Indeed, when the desire to perfect
the Arthurian story by giving it a beginning, middle, and end—
what I have called the canonic impulse—came inevitably to entail the need to destroy the society (to imagine its apocalypse),
the literary tradition of Arthur's death at the hands of his trai-
torous nephew Modred (largely the creation of Geoffrey of
Monmouth) was modified in an unmistakably anti-individualistic
manner. The vulgate *Mort le roi Artu* makes the Lancelot-
Guinevere liaison invented by Chrétien (but never used by him
to suggest the downfall of Arthurian society, in which Chrétien
was not interested), and morally condemned in the *Queste,*[19]
the instrument by which the Arthurian world comes to a genu-
inely tragic conclusion.

Chrétien never finished his *Lancelot,* and, as I have suggested
in chapter 6, he exploited the adulterous relationship between a
great knight of Arthur's court and the wife of his sovereign for
its ironic rather than its tragic potential, as an image of a passion that first liberates, then imprisons the seeker for personal
fulfillment. But the potential was there, nonetheless, and was
actualized when the relationship was given a pseudo-historical
context in the Vulgate cycle, thanks to the insight of a great,
anonymous author who was probably also responsible for com-

bining the separate parts of the cycle into their final shape.[20] In the *Mort le roi Artu,* the downfall of Arthurian society results from the working out of a relentless logic: the chivalric vision of complementary love and prowess, as developed, tested, and criticized in twelfth-century chivalric romance, offered a private relationship as the key to personal—and in some cases, social—fulfilment and *joie.* The love relationship, because it was private and, in its origins, arbitrary, could well lead to a knight's loving another man's wife—as happened to Lancelot and, of course, to Tristan. Now if and when Arthurian society becomes an entity with its own life (history), instead of simply a metaphor for public obligations or repressive custom that hinder the individual in quest of happiness, its welfare will become an issue, and the claims of that welfare on its constituent members—and on the reader—may well become an appropriate, indeed an inevitable, theme of the story. And now comes the conflict: the ideal chivalric society (the Round Table), as part of its mission of service, attracts the best chivalric knight(s). The chivalry topos suggests that the best knight will love, serve, and finally win the best lady, but the canonic impulse suggests with equal force that the great king who presides over the ideal society should have the best lady for a wife. Lancelot, Arthur's best knight and the pillar of his society, falls in love with Guinevere on the day she dubs him knight;[21] he is stimulated by love of her to perform the great deeds of prowess that uphold the greatness and security of the Round Table. For a certain period, an adulterous love paradoxically contributes to the joy of the cuckold-king and his world.

But this situation cannot last. The Arthurian vision, insofar as it is both social- and individual-centered, contains an inner contradiction which must sooner or later destroy it. Once Arthur's almost willful blindness to his wife's infidelity is cured by the revelations of Lancelot's enemies at court, the irreversible sequence of tragic events must run its course. (It is a mark of our involvement in the unstable vision that we don't want the truth to come out, and the *Mort* author exploits our weakness by making the bringers of truth hateful to us.) Arthur and

Lancelot fall out, the inhabitants of the Arthurian world divide into two warring camps, and the way is finally open for the kingdom to fall prey to Modred's baser treachery, with which we do not sympathize, but which, we realize with chagrin, is only a gross parody of Lancelot's, an attempt to do more openly what Lancelot has done in secret.

The effect of this denouement is to make the reader aware of how he, like the Round Table, is torn between the claims of two visions, social and personal. We wish success to Lancelot, the knight-lover who represents our own desire to achieve individual fulfillment,[22] yet we also want to enjoy, and be part of, a harmonious, triumphant, just society which, however, depends upon law and on the subordination of personal desire to the good of the king and the *res publica,* on justice and honesty in the dealings of all the members with each other. By impaling us on the horns of this dilemma of equally attractive, opposed choices, the *Mort le roi Artu* teaches us that the asocial, ahistorical vision of the individual's quest for fulfillment propagated by the twelfth-century romances has told only part of the story. The full story, and its lesson, testify by their existence and popularity that the thirteenth century's chivalric vision, in at least one of its most moving manifestations, has abandoned that faith in the primacy and autonomy of individual experience which moved Chrétien de Troyes and his contemporaries to create some of the greatest poetic narratives of the Middle Ages.

Introduction

1 This is not to suggest that economic and social stability was equally distributed in twelfth-century society. On the dislocation of many peasants,
who moved to the towns and became a rootless urban proletariat, and
whose situation provided the stimulus for millennial fervor and violence, see N. Cohn, *The Pursuit of the Millennium*, 2d ed. (London,
1970), especially pp. 52–60.

2 See, for example, with regard to political theory, W. Ullman, *Individual
and Society in the Middle Ages* (Baltimore, 1966); Latin poetry, P.
Dronke, *Poetic Individuality in the Middle Ages* (Oxford, 1970); hagiography, R.W. Southern, *Saint Anselm and His Biographer* (Cambridge,
1963); social history, M. Bloch, *Feudal Society*, trans. L.A. Manyon
(Chicago, 1961, repr. 1964), especially pp. 103–08: "The Intellectual
Renaissance in the Second Feudal Age. I: Some Characteristics of the
New Culture"; penitential doctrine, J.-C. Payen, *Le motif du repentir
dans la littérature française médiévale* (Geneva, 1968), especially pp.
54–75.

3 (Boston, 1973), p. 203.

4 (New Haven, 1953), pp. 253–55.

5 *The Discovery of the Individual* (London, 1972), pp. 121–38.

6 *The Meaning of The Middle Ages*, pp. 217–29.

7 There is a sizable body of criticism directed at refuting the patristic
critics; two particularly effective exemplars are Donald R. Howard,
The Three Temptations (Princeton, 1966), chap. 1, "Medieval Litera-
ture and the History of Ideas"; and E. Talbot Donaldson, "Patristic
Exegesis in the Criticism of Medieval Literature: The Opposition," in
*Critical Approaches to Medieval Literature: Selected Papers from the
English Institute, 1958-1959*, ed. Dorothy Bethurum (New York,

1960), reprinted in *Speaking of Chaucer* (London, 1970), pp. 134-53. To my knowledge, there are no analogous critiques of the aesthetic critics, as yet.

8 A.E. Mahler, "The Representation of Visual Reality in *Perceval* and *Parzival,*" *PMLA* 89 (1974): 537-50, is interested in an interdisciplinary approach to some of the aspects of what I call narrow mimesis, using French and German romances and visual media including painting and sculpture. Her emphases are, however, different from mine, and the fact that she reaches some very different conclusions about, e.g., Chrétien's use of time and space results, I believe, from her exclusive use in the article of the *Perceval,* Chrétien's last work and one in which he seems to turn away in part from the secular, humanistic, individual-centered world of the earlier romances. See further the afterword on this change of emphasis.

9 See *Peter Abelard's Ethics,* ed. and trans. D.E. Luscombe (Oxford, 1971), p. 13: "But what, you will say, do we gain before God out of what we do whether willingly or unwillingly? I reply: nothing, certainly, since he considers the mind rather than the action when it comes to a reward, and an action adds nothing to merit whether it proceeds from a good or a bad will"; p. 29: "For God thinks not of what is done but in what mind it may be done, and the merit or glory of the doer lies in the intention, not in the deed. . . . Through the diversity of their intention, the same theory is done by diverse men, by one badly, by the other well." Cf. Dronke, *Poetic Individuality,* p. 30, on Abelard's six *Planctūs,* poems of lamentation uttered by beleaguered Old Testament figures: "The poet both uncovers his characters' extremes of emotion with a dialectician's accuracy, and allows them to reveal nuances of thought, impulse, and motive in a way that perhaps only a poet who was also a major innovator in the realm of ethical analysis could have achieved." See also *Ethics,* pp. 45, 55, and Luscombe's commentary, and R. Blomme, *La doctrine du péché dans les écoles théologiques de la première moitié du XIIᵉ siècle* (Louvain, 1958).

10 See *Ethics,* pp. 85ff., especially p. 89: "And this indeed is truly fruitful repentance for sin, [when] sorrow and contrition of mind proceeds from love of God, whom we consider to be so kind, rather than from fear of punishments. Moreover, with this sigh and contrition of heart which we call true repentance sin does not remain. . . . In this sigh we are instantly reconciled to God and we gain pardon for the preceding sin." But see chapter 1, note 3, below, for inconsistencies in Abelard's argument.

Chapter 1

1 A combination of factors, including political instability and a Christian world view dominated by a corporate, as opposed to a personal, vision of the role of Divine Providence in human life, determined the lack of a developed concept of the individual in early medieval society. The subject has not been sufficiently studied and cannot adequately be dealt with here. On Christian communalism in the primitive and later Church see Colin Morris, *The Discovery of the Individual, 1050-1200* (London, 1972), pp. 144-52 (the vision of Jerusalem in Revelation and its interpretation); R.L.P. Milburn, *Early Christian Interpretations of History* (London, 1954), chap. 2. On the typological system of interpretation underlying the presentation of history and its heroes from a Christian point of view, see J. Daniélou, *Les figures du Christ dans l'ancient testament: "sacramentum futuri"* (Paris, 1950). On the anti-individualistic norms of hagiography in the early medieval period see R.W. Southern, *Saint Anselm and His Biographer* (Cambridge, 1963), pp. 320-21, and C.W. Jones, *Saints' Lives and Chronicles in Early England* (Ithaca, 1947), chap. 4. The studies by Morris, Southern, and Cantor cited on p. 2, above, are informative on the anti-individual climate of early medieval Europe, though they are not presented as self-contained discussions of the subject.

2 See D.W. Robertson, *Abelard and Heloise* (New York, 1972), pp. 119-35; R.W. Southern, "The Letters of Abelard and Heloise," in *Medieval Humanism* (New York, 1970), pp. 86-104. For the most recent denial of the authenticity of the correspondence of Abelard and Heloise, and of the *Historia calamitatum,* see J. Benton, "Fraud, Fiction, and Borrowing in the Correspondence of Abelard and Heloise," in *Pierre Abélard-Pierre le Vénérable, Les courants philosophiques, littéraires et artistiques en Occident au milieu du XIIe siècle* (Paris, 1975), pp. 469-512. For defense of the letters against earlier charges of inauthenticity, see E. Gilson, *Héloise et Abélard* (3rd ed. rev., Paris, 1964), pp. 169-91; J.T. Muckle, "Abelard's Letter of Consolation to a Friend (*Historia Calamitatum*)," *Medieval Studies* 12 (1950): 172-74. See also the balanced presentation of J. Monfrin, "Le problème de l'authenticité de la correspondance d'Abélard et d'Héloïse," in *Pierre Abélard - Pierre Le Vénérable,* pp. 409-24.

3 "Abelard and Individuality," in *Die Metaphysik im Mittelalter,* ed. P. Wilpert (Berlin, 1963), pp. 165-71.

4 See *Peter Abelard's Ethics,* ed and trans. D.E. Luscombe (Oxford,

1971), 39–45. Abelard argues that "common utility" requires acts redounding to "common ruin or public detriment [to] be punished with greater correction"; but he also says that such punishments may be unjust, "for men do not judge the hidden but the apparent, nor do they consider the guilt of a fault so much as the performance of a deed." Only God is in a position to judge the former accurately, i.e., to make judgments on *individual* sinners.

5 *Discovery of the Individual,* p. 156. On Bernard's two views, see pp. 153–57; in the sermons and elsewhere "he spoke of the individual as fulfilled, not lost, in the encounter with the eternal Word" (p. 155), whereas in *On the Love of God* "Bernard was putting his emphasis on the unity of the Soul and God, and was relatively little concerned to make a distinction between them" (p. 154). See the quote from *On the Love of God* in chap. 6, pp. 205–06, below.

6 *The Steps of Humility,* trans. G. Burch (Cambridge, Mass., 1940; repr. South Bend, Ind., 1963), pp. 149, 233. Bernard offers instead a series of steps away from humility into its opposite vice, pride; these steps, as he describes them, become less introspective and more satirically descriptive of the behavior of a proud monk whose vice finally drives him from the convent. Bernard then tells the reader to examine this descent, so that "you will find [in it], perhaps, the steps leading up, and ascending will read them *in your own heart better than in my book*" (p. 233, italics mine).

7 For a statement of this opposition of impulses as it operated within one central part of medieval society, see J.B. Russell, *A History of Medieval Christianity* (New York, 1968). Russell sets out "to investigate the tension within the [medieval] Church between the spirit of prophecy and the spirit of order. . . . The spirit of order has attempted to reform men and their institutions to correspond with the will of God, while the spirit of prophecy has sought to *transform* them, to lift them out of this world into the world and life of God" via an inner experience of this higher reality (p. v). Of the eleventh and twelfth centuries Russell says, "Enthusiasm for reform . . . encouraged the prophetic spirit as well as the spirit of order. Indeed, the more the forces of order transformed the Church into a formalized and corporate organization, the more did religiously enthusiastic people seek elsewhere for fulfillment. The powerful thrust of the prophetic spirit is thus the result not only of popular movement for reform in general but of rebellion against the advance of the spirit of order" (p. 134). I am less willing than Russell to award absolute causal priority to either impulse.

8 On Abelard's innovations in the field of ethical analysis, see Luscombe's edition of the *Ethics*, pp. xiii–xxxvii. On Bernard, see Leif Grane, *Peter Abelard*, trans. F. and C. Crowley (London, 1970), chap. 6; on inner spirituality, Southern, *The Making of the Middle Ages* (New Haven, 1953), chap. 5, Morris, *Discovery of the Individual*, chaps. 4 and 5, Southern, *Saint Anselm and His Biographer*, pp. 27–47, 67–76. On the related issue of self-knowledge as a Christian norm replacing obedience to divine and ecclesiastical law, see Morris, *Discovery of the Individual*, pp. 65–70, and (in connection with repentance) J.-C. Payen, *Le motif de repentir dans la littérature francaise médiévale* (Geneva, 1968), with further bibliography as cited in Payen's notes. Finally, see the excellent summarizing remarks on inwardness and self-knowledge as the bases of twelfth-century spirituality in G. Constable, "Twelfth-Century Spirituality and the Later Middle Ages," in O.B. Hardison, Jr., ed., *Medieval and Renaissance Studies* 5 (Chapel Hill, 1971), especially pp. 32–36.

9 I have borrowed the idea of victimization as a stimulus to pathos from M.W. Bloomfield, "The Man of Law's Tale: A Tragedy of Victimization and a Christian Comedy," *PMLA* 87 (1972): 384–89. See Southern, *Making of the Middle Ages*, pp. 240–47, on the evolution of a pathetic image of the Crucifixion in the twelfth century, and G. Shepherd, ed. *Ancrene Wisse, Parts Six and Seven* (London and Edinburgh, 1959), pp. li–lii, on "passionate attachment to the person of Christ" and "memories of Christ . . . devised to appeal to the senses and sensibilities, often, it would seem, to stimulate an emotional, almost physical, response. . . . Out of this vivid imagining was to spring a consciousness of the presence of Christ." Two recent Columbia University dissertations shed much light on medieval pathos: Hope Weissman, "Chaucer's Bad Tales" (1973), and James Marrow, "From Sacred Allegory to Descriptive Narrative: Transformations of Passion Iconography in the Late Middle Ages" (1974). See below, pp. 45–48, on pathetic elements in the *Life of Christina of Markyate*.

10 On the systematizing genius of the early scholastics, see the chapter "The Masters of the Theological 'Science'," in M.D. Chenu, *Nature, Man and Society in the Twelfth Century*, trans. J. Taylor and L.K. Little (Chicago, 1968), pp. 270–309, and Grane, *Peter Abelard*, chap. 1; on the need for, and process of, articulation of the "orders of the world" in eleventh- and twelfth-century monasticism, see J. Leclerq, "The Monastic Crisis of the Eleventh and Twelfth Centuries," in N. Hunt, ed., *Cluniac Monasticism in the Central Middle Ages* (Hamden, Conn., 1971), p. 221f. On the theoretical literature of the Investiture

Controversy in England, see N. Cantor, *Church, Kingship and Lay Investiture in England, 1089–1135* (Princeton, 1958), pp. 168–74. On the systematization of ecclesiastical structures generally, see R.W. Southern, *Western Society and the Church in the Middle Ages* (Harmondsworth, 1970), pp. 100–33, and *Medieval Humanism*, pp. 29–60, esp. 50–58; as Southern puts it (p. 51), in the twelfth century, "government by ritual came to an end and government by administration began."

11 Southern, *Western Society and the Church*, pp.105–25, outlines the perseverance and cunning with which the nascent system of ecclesiastical law was manipulated throughout the twelfth century—the "heroic days for litigants," as he calls them. See especially the example of the monks of Canterbury acting in defense of their prerogatives in a dispute with the archbishop spanning the years 1185–1201 (pp. 117–19).

12 On the Abelard-Bernard controversy, see A.V. Murray, *Abelard and St. Bernard* (Manchester, 1967); Grane, *Peter Abelard*, chaps. 7 and 8; D.E. Luscombe, *The School of Peter Abelard* (Cambridge, 1970), chap. 4. Bernard's anti-Abelardian writings are collected in Albino Babolin, ed., *Bernardo di Chiaravalle, Le Lettere contro Pietro Abelardo* (Padua, 1969).

13 *The Owl and the Nightingale* (ca. 1189), provides a humorously trenchant representation of this view. (ed. E.G. Stanley [London and Edinburgh, 1960]). See especially lines 665–90, in which the nightingale, forced into a tight corner by the arguments of her opponent in the course of a brilliant but completely unprincipled debate, must rely on *ginne* (the Middle English form of *ingenium*) in order to combat and overcome the truth. Throughout the poem, the clever poet (probably a Paris-trained cleric who had become a civil servant within the system of English royal justice) shows himself equally well versed in techniques of legal pleading and the tricks of dialectic. Using his amoral, irascible birds as a transparent cover, he takes a jaundiced look at the ways in which intellectual abilities can be used to subvert truth, dignify prejudices, and gain unfair personal advantage. For a perceptive recent comment on this aspect of the poem, see J. Schleusener, "*The Owl and the Nightingale*: A Matter of Judgment," *Modern Philology* 70 (1972–73): 185–89.

14 Even Benton, in "Fraud, Fiction and Borrowing," grants that the letter is a twelfth-century work using many of Abelard's favorite classical quotations. See below, pp. 31–32, on the parallels in outlook between the *Historia* and the later letter attacking Bernard.

15 Guibert's "memoirs" (usually referred to by an earlier editor's title, *De*

vita sua) have been translated with an introduction on Guibert's psychological profile (as it is revealed in the memoirs) in John Benton's *Self and Society in Medieval France: The Memoirs of Guibert of Nogent* (New York, 1970). Perhaps the most interesting insights of the memoirs concern Guibert's mother, whose tumultuous inner spiritual life, especially her tearful sieges of contrition, mark her as very much a person of her time. M. McLaughlin, "Abelard as Autobiographer: The Motives and Meaning of His 'Story of Calamities'," *Speculum* 42 (1967): 486-87, points out, briefly and perceptively, the contrast between Abelard's self-presentation and Guibert's; her conclusion is that Guibert "was perhaps too much at home in his world to separate himself clearly from it, or to experience himself fully apart from it"–statements that could never be made about the Abelard of the *Historia!* McLaughlin's article offers the most stimulating and acute reading I know of the *Historia*: I am much indebted to it.

16 Southern, *Medieval Humanism* (see n. 2, above), pp. 88-90.

17 Ibid., p. 91. The topics quoted by Southern were widely used as organizing principles and exegetical keys of human action in early medieval and late classical Christian historiography; the histories of Eusebius and Orosius were particularly influential in this respect. See Milburn, *Early Christian Interpretations of History*, chaps. 4 and 5; and R.W. Hanning, *The Vision of History in Early Britain* (New York, 1966), especially chaps. 1-3.

18 See McLaughlin, "Abelard as Autobiographer," p. 469; Southern, *Medieval Humanism*, pp. 91-92; and D.F. Frank, "Abelard as Imitator of Christ," *Viator* 1 (1970): 107-13.

19 There is a modern English translation: Athanasius, *The Life of St. Anthony*, trans. M.E. Keenan, S.C.N., in R.J. Deferrari, ed., *Early Christian Biographies* (New York, 1952), pp. 133-216. On the popularity of the *Life*, see, e.g., P. Hunter Blair, *The World of Bede* (London, 1970), pp. 272-74. See also the commentary on the *Life* and its relationship to the life of the desert ascetics of the fourth century in J. Lacarrière, *Men Possessed by God*, trans. Roy Monkcom (New York, 1964), pp. 51-67.

20 See *Historia*, p. 12, where Abelard describes with a military metaphor his decision to study dialectic. (All quotations and page references in the text and notes are from J.T. Muckle, trans. *The Story of Abelard's Adversities* (Toronto, 1964). I have also used J. Monfrin's Latin edition (Paris, 1959, repr. 1967). On the ascetic saints as athletes of God, see Lacarrière, *Men Possessed by God*, p. 87 f.

21 In the *Life of St. Anthony*, the saint's successive moves further and
   further away from civilization (chapters 3, 8, 11, 49) seem to stand for
   stages of spiritual growth and inward orientation, so that at his furthest
   reach, he locates himself on an "inner mountain" to instruct the monks
   whom his example has drawn into the wilderness (chaps. 54, 84). In the
   ninth-century *Voyage of St. Brendan*, the entire spatial world comprises a series of symbolic loci representing the stable monastic life by
   which the Christian hero "voyages" to his salvation.

22 For Anselm, see below, n. 28.

23 "I could then feel but cannot now express the grief which welled up
   within me, the shame that confounded me, the despair that upset me"
   (p. 52).

24 On the importance of despair and shame in Abelard's career and in the
   process of attaining self-awareness, see McLaughlin, "Abelard as Autobiographer," 474–75. See also G. Ladner, *"Homo Viator:* Medieval
   Ideas on Alienation and Order," *Speculum* 42 (1967): 233–59, on the
   ambivalent medieval response to the concept of the alienated person.

25 Cf. p. 29, where Abelard says he "was filled with shame and remorse"
   when Heloise's uncle discovers the love affair. In this case, however,
   where the shame can be shared, and subordinated to sympathy for
   another person, shame is overcome by desire: "Neither one of us com-
   plained of our own trials or bewailed our own misfortune but those of
   the other. . . . But shame gradually disappeared and made us more
   shameless . . ." (p. 30). How different from the self-bewailing attitude
   of much of the *Historia*, which, if McLaughlin is correct ("Abelard as
   Autobiographer," p. 469), Abelard in fact was writing to console himself, not the hypothetical friend to whom the letter is ostensibly
   addressed. Cf. Abelard's depiction of the intense emotional and personal life of Old Testament figures in some of his verse *planctūs*, discussed by P. Dronke, *Poetic Individuality in the Middle Ages* (Oxford,
   1970), pp. 114–20. Dronke relates the "individual portrayal and analysis of emotions" in three *planctūs* to "the reverberations that their
   themes had for Abelard himself" (p. 116), though rejecting a downright
   allegorical reading.

26 See above, pp. 27–28.

27 R. Klibansky, "Peter Abailard and Bernard of Clairvaux: A Letter by
   Abailard," *Medieval and Renaissance Studies* 1 (1961): 21. Cf. D.E.
   Luscombe's comment that, among contemporaries, "the sharpness of
   Abelard's intellect, his *ingenium*, was repeatedly recorded" (*The School
   of Peter Abelard*, p. 8 and n. 1).

28 On Anselm, see J.W. Baldwin, *Masters, Princes and Merchants: The Ethical Ideas of Peter the Chanter and his Circle* (Princeton, 1970), vol. 1, pp. 151–53; B. Smalley, *The Study of the Bible in the Middle Ages,* 2d ed. (Oxford, 1952; repr. 1964), pp. 49–51; J. De Ghellinck, *Le mouvement théologique du XIIᵉ siècle,* 2nd ed. (Bruges, 1948), p. 133 f. As Grane puts it, "his attitude was distinctly conservative, strongly bound up with the Fathers, and in his treatment of dogma not very systematic, in that he discussed the various problems within the biblical, historical framework. Dialectic [and hence, for Abelard, *ingenium*] played a very limited role in his theology" (*Peter Abelard,* p. 42).

29 The language Abelard uses to describe the lovers' progress in passion is splendidly Ovidian in tone and serves as an example of literary *ingenium* parallel to the clever strategy of the *magister* in finding his way into such a delightful situation: "Under the pretext of work we made ourselves entirely free from love and the pursuit of her studies provided the secret privacy which love desired. We opened our books but more words of love than of the lesson asserted themselves. There was more kissing than teaching; my hands found themselves at her breasts more often than on the book. Love brought us to gaze into each other's eyes more than reading kept them on the text" (p. 28). Note the artful parallels and contrasts of the prose, and the neat opposition of real passion to pretended learning.

30 McLaughlin, "Abelard as Autobiographer," p. 482, aptly notes the parallel between Abelard's prolonged "time of wandering and testing" as a young intellectual and the *jeunesse* of aristocratic warriors, a parallel first made by G. Duby. On Duby's portrait of the *juvenes,* see below, pp. 60–61.

31 See Klibansky, "Peter Abailard and Bernard of Clairvaux," pp. 21–24. This view that Abelard's consistent understanding of his career is intimately related to his sense of identity differs from McLaughlin's analysis of the *Historia* as a turning point in Abelard's career, "a study in pride and shame and the struggle to transcend them," and the product of a "crisis that impelled him to tell the story of his calamities and thus to begin the task of mastering and comprehending them, to initiate the therapeutic process whose outcome is more fully recorded in his correspondence with Heloise and in the achievements of his later years" ("Abelard as Autobiographer," pp. 475, 484). McLaughlin's position, convincing in so many ways, seems not to account for the similarity of viewpoint between the *Historia* and the later letter. But see her comment on Klibansky's essay (p. 471 and n. 32).

32 The quotation from Ovid's *Remedia amoris* (i. 369) that closes this passage in the *Historia* is repeated in the later letter (see "Peter Abailard and Bernard of Clairvaux," p. 7), underscoring the continuity of outlook between the two documents.

33 Cf. pp. 63–64, where the attacks of two "new apostles," stirred up by Abelard's old enemies because of envy, lead Abelard to the state in which "whenever I learned of a meeting of ecclesiastics, I supposed it was to condemn me. Like one who expected to be struck by lightning, I was straightaway overcome with fear that like a heretic or one irreligious I would be dragged before a council or synagogue." The reference to lightning may reflect Abelard's sense of himself as the "tallest tree in the forest," the one most liekly to be hit by the lightning of envy. The submerged metaphor, if it is there, is perfectly consistent with the Ovidian quotation identified in the preceding note.

34 See also the comment of Leclercq, "Modern Psychology and the Interpretation of Medieval Texts," *Speculum* 48 (1973): 476: "In writing, as in sculpture and painting, the resistance of a medium, the dictates of the laws proper to each genre, set up obstacles which must be taken into account. Between the produced work and the sincerity of the author, there is nearly always, in the middle ages, a screen of rhetoric; literary techniques tend to become defence mechanisms." On the interaction of genius and literary convention, two instructive studies are C. Muscatine, *Chaucer and the French Tradition* (Berkeley and Los Angeles, 1957), and J. Burrow, *Ricardian Poetry* (London, 1971).

35 Cf. Klibansky's remarks about Abelard's encounter with Bernard at the Council of Sens: "Up to the last moment Abailard thought of the dispute in terms of a personal contest, an *agon*, in a spirit entirely foreign to Bernard . . . [who] regarded himself as the representative of the unassailable impersonal power of the Church" ("Peter Abailard and Bernard of Clairvaux," pp. 24–25).

36 All references and quotations are from *The Life of Christina of Markyate*, ed. and trans. C.H. Talbot (Oxford, 1959).

37 See Talbot's introduction, p. 6: "The whole tone of the story is autobiographical rather than historical."

38 See, for example, *The Life of St. Ambrose* in *The Western Fathers*, trans. F.R. Hoare (New York, 1954, repr. 1965) pp. 150–51, for similar natal miracles, or Cuthbert's childhood miracles in Bede's *Life of St. Cuthbert*, chaps. 1–3 (*Lives of the Saints*, trans. J.F. Webb [Harmondsworth, 1965], pp. 72–76).

39 Examples of the two basic versions of *The Life of St. Cecilia* are

offered by G.H. Gerould, "The Second Nun's Tale," in W. F. Bryan and G. Dempster, eds., *Sources and Analogues of Chaucer's Canterbury Tales* (New York, 1941; repr. 1959), pp. 671–84. Several other similar female saints are included in the calendar of the Saint Alban's Psalter, which probably belonged to Christina, and which also contains the Old French *Vie de St. Alexis,* the legend of a msculine version of the Cecilia-Christina paradigm. See Talbot's introduction to the *Life of Christina,* pp. 22–27.

40 The nearest parallel I have been able to discover to this type of analysis in early medieval hagiography appears in *The Life of St. Honoratis,* in *Western Fathers,* pp. 251–52; the saint's "sweet disposition," athletic skills, and other virtues so entrance his family that "all feared to have snatched from them a kind of ornament owned by the whole family. . . . For they could not believe that all these gifts would be changed and remoulded into something better." Thanks to the clearer rendering of her family's social situation, Christina emerges much more clearly as a person from her biographer's analysis than does Honoratis from his.

41 The rendering of Autti's sense of shame in this passage reveals the author's interest in "secular" human feelings, an interest that connects him to Abelard, in the latter's presentation of his crippling shame (on which see above), and separates the *Life of Christina* in yet another way from early medieval hagiography. Autti's contention that Christina's attitude will shame the entire nobility should be evaluated in light of the fact that Christina "came of a family of ancient and influential English nobles and the whole of that district about Huntingdon for miles around was full of her relatives" (p. 83).

42 Evidently "all [Christina's] friends and relatives" shared the misgivings of Autti and Beatrix about her decision to avoid her social responsibilities by becoming a nun, for they "united force together" to attempt to convince her to accept Burthred, and thus all her parents' plans for her (p. 47). Yet, as Talbot points out (introduction to *The Life of Christina,* pp. 12–13), "the spiritual movement of which we have a conspicuous example in the biography [of Christina] was particularly strong among the natives of the country," that is, among precisely the Anglo-Saxon stock from which she was descended. The attitude of Autti and Beatrix and the response of Christina, then, both proceed from the same socio-political situation—what Talbot calls "an undercurrent of national feeling" animating native Englishmen who find themselves ruled by Norman foreigners.

43 The author emphasizes Christina's sense of separateness from the world

early in the *Life* in an important passage (p. 37): "Christina used to talk to [Christ] on her bed at night just as if she were speaking to a man she could see; and this she did with a loud, clear voice, so that all who were resting in the same house could hear and understand her. She thought that if she were speaking to God, she could not be heard by men." Note that this is presented not as a miraculous fact but as a psychological, characterizing observation, intended to establish the protagonist's embrace of a purely private dimension of experience, and the assumption that she is isolated within her private world. By contrast, Christina's family "could not bring themselves to consider anything but the joys of the present world, thinking that anyone lacking them and seeking only invisible things would end in ruin" (p. 61).

44 For a convenient summary and assessment of Flambard's career, see Southern, *Medieval Humanism*, pp. 183–205.

45 Cf. the remarks of J. Leclercq on another twelfth-century saint's life: "Comme beaucoup d'autres pièces de la littérature réformatrice des XIᵉ et XIIᵉ siècles . . . cette vie [of S. Étienne d'Obazine] comporte une critique des gens d'Église installés, évêques et chanoines." (From a review of *La vie de S. Étienne d'Obazine*, ed. M. Aubrun [Clermont Ferrand, 1970], in *Medium Aevum* 46 [1972]: 144.) The critical impulse Leclercq finds in the French saint's life undoubtedly underlies in part the English author's portrayal of the Norman-dominated ecclesiastical establishment.

46 Fredebert is here playing a role analogous to that of the Roman judge in a narrative of the *passio* of an early martyr—yet he is a cleric!

47 My emphasis. The Gospel reference is to Matthew 19:29. Christina's reference to God's witness of her conscience recalls Abelard's emphasis on God's judgment of private intentions rather than public deeds in *Ethics*, pp. 29, 45.

48 See above, n. 7, on the reaction of the "spirit of prophecy" against the "spirit of order."

49 Roland Barthes makes an apposite comment on the symbolic role of clothing: "garments—which as we know extend the body in an equivocal way, both masking and flaunting it—are responsible for dramatizing the state of the body: they *weigh down* in transgression, they *come undone* in agitation" (*On Racine*, trans. R. Howard [New York, 1964], p. 15.).

50 See *Ancrene Wisse*, especially the introduction, p. xxx f., "The Eremitical Life." Part two of the *Ancrene Wisse*, on guarding the heart through control of the senses, is especially useful for the point I am making; see

the edition of J. R. R. Tolkien (Oxford, 1962), pp. 29–63. The emphasis on constraint as an instrument of freedom in twelfth-century spirituality should also be considered in the light of some memorable portraits of contemporaneous women struggling with the potentially destructive force of inner feelings—feelings newly recognized in this age—and profiting from structures of control; see, e.g., the contritional spasms of the mother of Guibert of Nogent (reported in his *Memoirs,* pp. 75–76), that "begat in her soul indescribable anguish until she reached the familiar waters of penitence or confession."

51 For other images of constraint, see: the wild bulls confined in mud in Christina's dream (p. 99); the enclosure in which God pens up Abbot Geoffrey of St. Albans (pp. 161, 165); and Christina's subsequent depiction of herself as a protective enclosure for Geoffrey (p. 169). The ambivalence of the image testifies to God's power to reveal definitively the significance of experience as he sees fit. We see an example of this when Autti, in a fury, strips Christina and decides to drive her naked from the house (p. 73). For Autti this is a gesture of humiliation, denying Christina her status in, and the protective enclosure of, the household. But Christina, we are told, "prepared to be sent away both naked and at night, for the sake of getting her freedom to serve Christ." The difference between her own and Autti's interpretation of the act is her inspired, *personal* desire which replaced and negates the normal *social* reponse to her situation.

52 Note also the mimetic touch stressing Christina's purely human feelings and responses when the moment of escape arrives. She is with her accomplices and the horses that will carry them away. "She paused, covered with embarrassment," but only for a moment; then "she put aside her fears and, jumping on the horse as if she were a youth [*viriliter*], and setting spurs to his flanks, she said to the servant, 'follow me at a distance: for I fear that if you ride with me and you are caught they will kill you'" (p. 93). The author's attention to Christina's hesitation, her conquest of it through courage, and her concern for her accomplice, as well as his precise depiction of a characterizing gesture (her spurring of the horse), show how much he is interested in her as a particular human being whom he has closely observed.

53 It was in the course of the twelfth century that the Bride of Christ, traditionally the Church, began to be interpreted as the individual soul. (The source of the image is, of course, the Church's allegorical exegesis of the Song of Songs.) See *Ancrene Wisse,* p. xlix, and note to p. 15, l. 38; and M.-M. Davy, "La thème de l'âme-épouse selon Bernard de

Clairvaux et Guillaume de Saint-Thierry," in M. de Gandillac and E. Jeauneau, eds., *Entretiens sur la renaissance du 12e siècle* (Paris and The Hague, 1968), pp. 247-61.

54 Cf. Christina's tender feelings for the mysterious pilgrim who visits her chapel in the last extant section of the *Life*—feelings that may seem more like erotic sentimentality than religious devotion to a Christ-like figure. See pp. 185-89.

55 See D. Grivot and G. Zarnecki, *Giselbertus, Sculptor of Autun* (New York, 1961), pp. 149f. and plate 1 following p. 152 (Eve); and plate 2 following p. 82 (the angel and the magi).

56 On Geoffrey's historiography and its relationship to the Anglo-Norman historians, see Hanning, *The Vision of History*. chap. 5; on the conventional rhetoric of the medieval historian see B. Lacroix, *L'historien au moyen âge* (Paris and Montreal, 1971), and the review of it by R.W. Hanning in *History and Theory* 12 (1973): 421-34.

57 The most extensive survey of European courtly literature is R.R. Bezzola, *Les origines et la formation de la littérature courtoise en occident (500-1200),* 5 vols. (Paris, 1944-63); volumes 3, 4, and 5 deal with the twelfth century. Some of Bezzola's literary judgments are open to question. The excellent chapters on early courtly literature in M.D. Legge, *Anglo-Norman Literature and Its Background* (Oxford, 1963) stress the double purpose—to entertain and instruct—of the literature. E. Auerbach characterizes the courtly audience in "The Knight Sets Forth," *Mimesis,* trans. W. Trask (New York, 1957), pp. 107-24, and in *Literary Language and its Public,* trans. R. Manheim (New York, 1965), pp. 203-19, working backward from the content and style of the courtly texts. The romances and other courtly narratives define their audience as one of *clercs* and *chevaliers;* see, e.g., *Le roman de Thèbes,* ed G.R. de Lage (Paris, 1966), ll. 13-16.

58 See Legge, *Anglo-Norman Literature,* pp. 7-43 passim.

Chapter 2

1 In addition to the work of Bezzola and Legge mentioned at the end of the last chapter, see also Legge, "La précocité de la litterature anglo-normande," *Cahiers de civilisation médiévale* 8 (1965): 327-49; A. Fourrier, *Le courant réaliste dans le roman courtois en France au moyen-age,* vol 1. (Paris, 1960), pp. 160-74, 179-210; J. Benton, "The Court of Champagne as Literary Center," *Speculum* 36 (1961): 551-91 (a revisionist approach); W.F. Schirmer, "Die kulturelle Rolle des

englischen Hofes im 12. Jahrhundert," *Studien zum literarischen Patronat in England des 12. Jahrhunderts* (Cologne and Opladen, 1962), pp. 9-23.

2 For a brief, somewhat wry history of the term "courtly love" and its limitations, see E.T. Donaldson, "The Myth of Courtly Love," *Ventures: Magazine of the Yale Graduate School* 5 (1965): reprinted in his *Speaking of Chaucer,* (London, 1970), pp. 154-63. There is a good consideration of some theories of courtly love in Howard, *The Three Temptations* (Princeton, N.J., 1966) pp. 77-109. By far the best overall discussion of medieval love literature is J. Ferrante and G. Economou, eds., *In Pursuit of Perfection: Courtly Love in Medieval Literature* (Port Washington, N.Y., and London, 1975), a collaborative study.

3 See the speech of Phaedrus in Plato's *Symposium,* 178d on the benefits of a fighting force made up of lovers, who will fight better from a desire not to be shamed in the eyes of the beloved.

4 References are to the *Historia regum Britanniae* ix.13. The edition is by A. Griscom (London, New York, Toronto, 1929).

5 In the crown-wearing episode, for instance, Wace both multiplies rich refined details and inserts a realistic, rueful description of men gambling amidst the festivities (10557-96). References are to the edition of I.D.O. Arnold, 2 vols. (Paris, 1938-40).

6 Wace is specific about the knights' activities during the joust (*behorder,* 10521-38), and also about the correspondingly appropriate behavior of the ladies: "Qui avoit ami an la place/Tost li tornoit l'uel et la face" (10541-42). For a good general survey and evaluation of courtliness as revealed in twelfth-century literature, see J. Frappier, "Vues sur les conceptions courtoises dans les littératures d'oc et d'oil au XIIe siècle," *Cahiers de civilisation médiéval* 2 (1959): 135-56.

7 Verbal references occur at lines 1153f., 1765-66, and 4379-84. For a perceptive discussion of how the topos begins to become a vessel for real human emotions and actions, see R.R. Bezzola, *Les origines et la formation de la littérature courtoise en occident (500-1200),* part three (Paris, 1963), 1 [vol, 4], 275-78.

8 Bezzola, *Les origines,* p. 276, aptly calls this encounter a "pastourelle courtoise." It has about it none of the element of self-recognition which appears in the Ovidian *contes* and subsequent chivalric romances.

9 Lines 4685-88. She goes on to say that she will sleep with her lover, "ou face bien ou ge foloi" (4691-92), thereby underlining the sensual reality of the passion which Geoffrey presents more formally in his description of the ladies on the walls of Caerleon. Athes is wearing

Ysmaine's "manche de syglaton" (4679-82), which looks back to, and vivifies, Geoffrey's remark that knights and ladies wore clothes of matching colors (*HRB* ix. 13).

10 Athes' death precedes the sisters' conversation in the text, so that the conversation is observed by the audience from an ironic perspective.

11 See E. Faral, *Recherches sur les sources latines des contes et romans courtois du moyen âge* (Paris, 1913), 410-15; H.C.R. Laurie, "*Enéas* and the *Lancelot* of Chrétien de Troyes," *Medium Aevum* 37 (1968): 142-56; E. Auerbach, *Literary Language and Its Public in Late Latin Antiquity and in the Middle Ages,* trans R. Manheim (New York, 1965), chap 3 passim; A. Dressler, *Der Einfluss des altfranzösischen Eneas-Roman auf die afrz. Litteratur* (Göttingen, 1907); J.J. Salverda de Grave, ed., *Enéas,* 2 vols. (Paris, 1925, 1929), pp. xxxv-xxxvi. All references to the text of the *Roman d'Enéas* are to this edition.

12 See H.C.R. Laurie, "Narcissus," *Medium Aevum* 36 (1966): 111-16; Laurie, "Piramus et Tisbé," *Modern Language Review* 55 (1960): 24-32; C. Muscatine, "The Emergence of Psychological Allegory in Old French Romance," *PMLA* 68 (1953): 1160-82.

13 See, for example, *Narcisus,* ed M.M. Pelan and N.C.W. Spence (Paris, 1964), lines 225-96, 332-96, 541-626; *Piramus et Tisbé,* ed. C. de Boer (Paris, 1921), lines 150-203, 221-306.

14 *Enéas,* 8445-662, 8708-719. On the Ovidian source for the girl in the tower, see E. Faral, *Sources latines* p. 130, and Auerbach, *Literary Language,* pp. 210-15.

15 On the implications of this example of *engin,* see chap. 3, pp. 110-11, below.

16 During the battle leading up to Enéas's final encounter with Turnus, and during the duel, no mention is made of Lavine. The twelfth-century poet retains Vergil's reason why Enéas kills Turnus (vengeance for the latter's slaughter of Pallas), although it conflicts, at least by implication, with Enéas's ostensibly chivalric motivation (see 9343-838, especially 9792-814).

17 See the study of G. Duby, "Au XIIe siècle: Les 'Jeunes' dans la société aristocratique," *Annales* 19 (1964): 835-46.

18 For a good example of their disruptiveness, see the incident recounted by Jocelyn of Brakelond in his *Chronicle,* ed. H.E. Butler (London and Edinburgh, 1949), pp. 55-56: eighty *iuuenes* come to Bury St. Edmund, accept the abbot's hospitality, then begin carousing and mocking him. After they break through the town gates the abbot excommunicates them.

19 I follow the datings argued for in Fourrier, *Le courant réaliste,* pp. 384-85, and in his "Encore la chronologie des oeuvies de Chrétien de Troyes," *Bulletin bibliographique de la Société Internationale Arthurienne* 2 (1950): 69-88.

20 Note Guivret's immediate preparations for departure and arming, 3668-75. (All line references and quotations from *Erec* use the edition by M. Roques [Paris, 1959].)

21 Cf. a deed such as Roland's sounding his horn to summon Charlemagne from far away, and fatally wounding himself in the process (*Chanson de Roland,* 1753-87; cf. 2099-102). The fact that only Roland could sound a horn blast thirty leagues, and that he thus kills himself, whereas none of his Saracen adversaries can do so, makes his feat self-defining as well as self-destroying. The act, irrespective of its consequences (Charlemagne's arrival with the Franks to avenge Roland on the Saracens), stands as an absolute emblem of the hero, his powers, and his destruction by them.

22 Later in the romance, Erec will appear to die, only to be revived by a danger to Enide analogous to the danger to him which here "kills" and then galvanizes her. Cf. the very different, conscious use of a false state of death by the protagonists in Chrétien's *Cligès* in order to obtain their desires. The common denominator in these situations—and many other uses of unreal death by Chrétien—is the poet's exploration of the violently disruptive effect of external experience on private identity, as defined by intention, will, or awareness.

23 Cf. the episode of vain, selfish Count Galoain, of whose evil intentions Enide must warn Erec because she "sees" them first; Galoain has threatened to kill Erec to get Enide for his *amie,* and she must warn Erec of their host's treachery, but without alerting Galoain to their plan to escape.

24 Chrétien underlines the parallel by referring to Erec's self-forgetting, 3749; this was of course his state when, overcome by his love for Enide, he "forgot" his identity as a prowess-seeking knight after his wedding. Cf. 2430-33.

25 Chrétien teases his audience about the meaning of the protagonists' adventure quest once it has been happily completed. Erec tells Arthur's court about his and Enide's trials, and Chrétien adds: "Mes cuidiez vos que je vos die/quex acoisons le fist movoir?/Naie; que bien savez le voir/et de ice, et d'autre chose,/si con ge la vos ai esclose . . ." (6420-24).

26 See P. Haidu's perceptive discussion of Chrétien's verbal irony, *Aesthet-*

ic Distance in Chrétien de Troyes: Irony and Comedy in "Cligès" and "Perceval" (Geneva, 1968), pp. 25–63; the techniques illustrated by Haidu from Cligès charactertize Chrétien's style throughout his works.

27 See above, pp. 55–58, where examples are given of the lady (or ladies) watching a battle from a raised, secure, and slightly distant place.

28 On the importance of identity in the romance world, see chap. 6; on prowess and its subversion of identity as a major theme of Hue de Roteland's *Ipomedon,* see chap. 3.

29 See chap. 4 for a comparison between early medieval ideas of exile and intrusion and those of romance.

30 There is, however, a further irony, for when Erec and Guivret next meet, Erec is disguised by his armor and weakened by his exertions in battle and Guivret, not recognizing Erec, whom he has set out to aid, nearly kills his friend. Enide is again able to save Erec from Guivret's prowess, this time by identifying her husband to the little warrior. In this restatement of the themes of the first meeting, love again saves the knight by rendering him an individual (exposing his personal identity), while impersonal prowess nearly kills him. See 4915–5024, 5046–54.

31 The extant manuscripts of *Partonopeu* actually offer three different conclusions of greatly differing lengths. I follow the reconstruction of the earliest version suggested by L. Smith in his introduction to in *Partonopeu de Blois,* ed J. Gildea (Villanova, 1967–70), vol. 2 part 2, pp. 3, 15–27.

32 On romance characters' multiple identities see chap. 6, and R.W. Hanning, "The Social Significance of Twelfth-Century Chivalric Romance," *Medievalia et Humanistica* n.s., 3 (1972): 10–12.

33 See, e.g., 3401–08, when Partonopeu, having been allowed by Mélior to return to France from Chef d'Oire to win glory and aid the French king, is engaged in deadly combat with the enemy of France, Sornegur: "Parthonopeus hauce l'espee,/Que Melior li ot donee;/Et quant le voit clere et forbie,/Dont li ramembre de s'amie./Li cuers li lieve molt et saut,/Molt en amende et devient baut,/Molt en devint fors et legiers,/S'en fiert miex et plus volentiers." This is the chivalry topos working classically, in a situation where prowess is a social force—a *chanson de geste*-style heroism—transformed by *courtoisie* and love. Cf. Chrétien's divergent picture of basic, amoral (and asocial) prowess in the Guivret episode.

34 The figure of the naive huntsman schooled (and often wounded) by love is at least as old as Euripides' Hippolytus; more nearly contempo-

rary with Partonopeu is Guigemar, hero of a *lai* of Marie de France, who wounds a marvellous hind, but his arrow rebounds to wound him. A mysterious boat takes him across the sea to a lady who heals the physical wound but replaces it with a far deadlier emotional one; after various adventures, Guigemar and the lady are united in love forever.

35 On the "prelapsarian" idyllic but immature love of Partonopeu and Mélior before the romance's crisis, see chap. 6, and Hanning, "Social significance," pp. 21–22.

36 Anselot's speech of plangent recrimination against Partonopeu after the latter's desertion (5715–44) echoes the situation in which Mélior finds herself, betrayed by her lover's disobedience (4554–698). Anselot specifically calls his master's action betrayal: "Sire . . . traï m'avés/ Quant sens moi vos estes livrés/A mort et a destruction" (5717–19).

37 Urraque's tolerant understanding of Partonopeu's disobedient act is made clear in her first speech, 4929–50; after complimenting her sister on her choice of *ami* ("Car a plus bel ne a mellor/Ne peüssiés avoir amor," 4939–40), Urraque reminds Mélior that Partonopeu's fault, while serious, was not malicious, nor his own devising ("N'est ses engiens, ains est autrui," 4943). Knowingly, even cynically, she urges forgiveness: "Mais ço est la fins de la fable:/Quanc'amis fait est pardonable," (4949–50). Mélior, of course, is too distraught to accept this advice, coming as it does only a few moments after her lover's betrayal.

38 Already in Homer's *Odyssey*, the oar is a symbol of man's attempt to overcome Fortune (the sea) by calculated effort; the fallen hero is buried in a grave marked by his oar, placed upright on it. See the burial of Elpenor, book 11, lines 51–80.

39 Cf. the famous comment in Boethius's *Consolation of Philosophy,* that the memory of past happiness exacerbates present grief, book ii. prose 4.

40 There are other intrusions by the narrator, describing his feelings and his lovesickness (for example, 1861–86, 3423–48, 4039–52, 4537–48, 7519–52, and the "epilogue" to the original version, 10607 f.) in which he promises to tell the further adventures of his hero, if his *amie* wishes him to.

41 On the effect of combining a lovesick, "lyric" narrator's voice and a narrative of chivalry, see Hanning, "Social Significance," p. 24, and P. Haidu, "Realism, Convention, Fictionality, and the Theory of Genres in *Le bel inconnu," L'Esprit Créatur,* 12 (1972): 37–60, esp. 47–51.

Chapter 3

1 This trick, referred to but not described in *Aeneid* i. 367–68, also appears in Geoffrey of Monmouth's *Historia regum Britanniae* vi. 11, where Hengist perpetrates it on Vortigern.

2 The relationship between the *Enéas* and the *Aeneid* has been studied by many scholars including E. Faral, *Recherches sur les sources latines des contes et romans courtois du moyen âge* (Paris, 1913), pp. 73–157, passim; J. Crosland, *"Enéas* and the *Aeneid," Modern Language Review* 29 (1934): 282–90; and H.C.R. Laurie, *"Enéas* and the *Lancelot* of Chrétien de Troyes," *Medium Aevum* 37 (1968): 142–43.

3 Vergil condemns all artful, tricky behavior in the *Aeneid*, especially his hero's trick of disguising himself and his followers as Greeks during the final battle with Troy (book 2). The epic view of life is generally inhospitable to *engin* although Odysseus, in many ways an atypical epic hero, introduces and represents it in the infinitely varied Homeric universe. Cf. the one, unambiguously negative use of *engin* in the *Chanson de Roland,* line 95, where the Saracens set out to trick Charles: "Nes poet [Charles] guarder que alques ne l'engignent." *Enéas,* line 398, quoted in the text, echoes this line, but the different context elicits a completely different response from us.

4 Cf. 503–04, where *engin* carries this meaning: "ne engin ne li [i.e., Dido's keep] forsfeist,/se devers lo ciel ne venist."

5 For example, the obsequies for Pallas involve long speeches of grief, much kissing of and fainting over the dead body, and orgies of extreme mourning behavior "Quant la novelle oi li rois,/les crins, qu'il ot blans et chenuz,/O ses dous mains a deronpuz,/sa barbe arache o ses doiz,/il s'est pasmez plus de vint foiz,/hurte son chief, debat sa chiere,/plorant an vet contre la biere" (6252–58). Grief dominates 6143–374, at which point follows the description of the preparations for burial, immediately preceding the ecphrasis of the tomb.

6 As she puts it (8756–68), ". . . ainz que la bataile soit,/li voil primes faire savoir [of her love],/s'an ert plus fiers al mien espoir;/se de m'amor est a seur,/molt l'an trovera cil plus dur,/molt an prendra grant hardement . . ./Savoir m'estuet si com ge cui,/qu'il m'amera se ge aing lui."

7 *Enéas,* 8775–840. A tower or other elevated observation place, first introduced in Geoffrey of Monmouth's *Historia regum Britanniae* ix. 13, was the standard vantage point from which a lady could watch her beloved in action. Cf. Ovid, *Metamorphoses* viii. 17f. where Scylla sees

and loves Minos from her tower. (The parallel with Ovid is mentioned by Faral, *Recherches sur les sources latines des contes et romans courtois du moyen age* (Paris, 1913), p. 130, and E. Auerbach, *Literary Language and Its Public in Late Latin Antiquity and in the Middle Ages,* trans. R. Manheim (New York, 1965), p. 210 f.

8 The "pictorialism" or ecphrastic quality of poetry is the subject of J.H. Hagstrum, *The Sister Arts* (Chicago and London, 1958); while Hagstrum's specific focus is on Neoclassic English poetry, the first part of his study ("The Tradition," pp. 3–170) contains much general discussion and useful medieval examples of ecphrases of sculptures and other works of art or artifacts (see esp. pp. 37–56).

9 For example, the definition supplied by Castiglione for the courtier's *sprezzatura*—the art that hides art—reappears in critical works by Lodovico Dolce (*Aretino,* or *Dialogo della pittura,* 1557) and Philip Sidney (*An Apology for Poetry,* ca 1581, publ. 1595), applied respectively to pictoral and verbal art. See further D. Javitch, "Poetry and Court Conduct: Puttenham's *Arte of English Poesie* in the Light of Castiglione's *Cortegiano,*" *Modern Language Notes* 87 (1972): 865–82, on the parallel between poetic theory and courtly behavior in sixteenth-century England.

10 *Partonopeu de Blois* likewise brings its lovers out of their private, isolated world into the danger- and opportunity-filled world of external experience about halfway through the romance. In *Yvain* and *Ipomedon,* on the other hand, the poet emphasizes the essentially private nature and vision of the love relationship and never takes it out into the adventure world, which poses special dangers to the hero's love-quest.

11 The scene is full of verbal references to, and formulae of, loyalty and treason; see 3333, 3354, 3365, 3398, 3402–03, 3407, 3416–17, 3459, 3467, 3481, 3486.

12 The parallel between the two scenes is developed in chap. 6, n. 19.

13 See J.C. Payen, *Le motif de repentir dans la littérature française médiévale* (Geneva, 1968) for a consideration of how the chivalric poets use the theme of repentance and a consideration of the theological and ethical background in twelfth-century society. Cf. notes 2, 5, and 6 to his introduction and chap. 1, p. 20. The repentance of Galoain parallels the twelfth-century "contritionist" theory of penance, in which the sinner's tears of repentance are the sign that man realizes he has sinned and therefore repents, receiving God's loving forgiveness at once, quite apart from the institutional absolution and penance the

priest may assign him in confession. (Payen, pp. 54–75; cf. *Peter Abelard's Ethics,* ed. and trans. D.E. Luscombe [Oxford, 1971] , p. 77f., for a contritionist analysis of repentance.) Galoain's reformation has no outer, sacramental confirmation; no penance is administered nor works of repentance undertaken in accord with a social rule. Enide's role is not that of a priest-confessor, but of an agent of moral consciousness raising; in this she parallels the function of the fourth and fifth parts of the *Ancrene Wisse;* see L. Georgianna, *"Ancrene Wisse: Tradition and Design,"* (Ph.D. diss., Columbia University, 1976), chap. 3.

14 On the epic of revolt, see W.C. Calin, *The Old French Epic of Revolt* (Paris and Geneva, 1962). The downright betrayal of Arthur by Count Angrés of Windsor also looks forward, like a simple type anticipating its complex fulfillment, to the network of Byzantine treachery—Alis betrays Alixandre, Cligès betrays Alis—which will complicate our judgment of the protagonists' actions later in the romance.

15 See her intervention, 2231f. She says to Alixandre and Soredamors, "D'Amors andoctriner vos vuel,/Car bien voi qu'Amors vos afole:/Por ce vos vuel metre a escole . . ." (2252-54). She warns them of the dangers of concealing their love from each other (2260-63)—another comment with ironic resonances for the next generation in the romance, where revelation and secrecy in love become inextricably tangled in a moral knot tied by Fénice, Cligès, and Alis.

16 Alixandre disguises himself at 1815f.; the Greeks who do not join him in the ruse to get inside the stronghold of Count Angrés discover the arms Alixandre has forsaken to perpetrate his *engin* and are crushed with grief, 2036f. Soredamors is also deceived, but conceals her grief (2092f.), thus duplicating her beloved's strategem even as she feels the pain it can cause; see n. 15 on the queen's warning to the lovers about secrecy. Cligès disguises himself in Saxon armor (3473f.), in order to attack the Saxons; he lets his own horse go in order to terrify the Greeks ("por les Grezois feire esmaier," 3480), who, thinking him dead, grieve for him (3514-16). Chrétien suggests that, whereas the sorrow that accompanies Alixandre's *engin* was an unintended and unavoidable by-product of the trick, Cligès enjoys the confusion caused by his disguising, which thereby becomes more an artful performance, designed to trick its audience, than an exigency of combat. But in the process he is in fact working against his own welfare by winning the woman he loves for the man who, in marrying her, will break his promise to

Cligès's father that he would not marry so that Cligès could succeed him as emperor.

17 See *Cligès,* 4543-5004. On the trick of fighting in a tournament in a different suit of armor, see below, p. 133, on *Ipomedon.* While Cligès is performing "mainte chevalerie" (5012) for Arthur after he has revealed his identity, he is oppressed by his love and finally resolves to return to Fénice, disappointing Gawain and Arthur in the process (5027-29).

18 see P. Haidu, *Aesthetic Distance in Chrétien de Troyes: Irony and Comedy in "Cligès" and "Perceval"* (Geneva, 1968), pp. 91-97; D.D.R. Owen, Profanity and its Purpose in Chrétien's *Cligès* and *Lancelot,"* in D.D.R. Owen, ed., *Arthurian Romance: Seven Essays* (Edinburgh and London, 1970), pp. 39-42, 47-48.

19 See *Cligès,* 3105-09, in which Fénice declares, "'Mialz voldroie estre desmambree/Que de nos deus fust remanbree/L'amors d'Ysolt et de Tristan,/Don mainte folie dit an,/Et honte en est a reconter." Cf. 5249f., where Fénice refuses to run away with Cligès for the same reason. Many critics have discussed in detail the relationship between *Cligès* and the *Tristan* story and have offered hypotheses about Chrétien's intent in creating his own, ironic version of Tristan and Isolde. See J. Frappier, *Le roman breton. Chrétien de Troyes: Cligès* (Paris, 1951), and other studies cited in Haidu, *Aesthetic Distance,* p. 25, n. 2.

20 Fénice, planning her false death in order to be with Cligès, refers to Thessala, whose aid she will enlist, as "ma mestre an cui je molt me croi" (5303)—a line suggesting that the servant is both the instructress and the deity of her lady. Cligès replies, speaking of Jehan, "Un mestre ai que j'en veul proier" (5314)—again suggesting that the lovers are treating *engin* (and its creators) as their god.

21 Haidu, *Aesthetic Distance,* pp. 102-04. Note that Bertrand's entirely accidental discovery of the lovers is Chrétien's parodistic version of the elaborate spying of which the lovers are the victims in other versions of the Tristan story.

22 See Fourrier, *Le courant réaliste dans le roman courtois en France au moyen-age,* vol. 1 (Paris, 1960), pp. 117-78.

23 Mélior, heroine of *Partonopeu de Blois,* is also an empress of Byzantium (1341).

24 On the ironies of the situation see W.T.H. Jackson, "Problems of Communication in the Romances of Chrétien de Troyes," in J. Mandel and B.A. Rosenberg, eds. *Medieval Literature and Folklore Studies:*

Essays in honor of Francis Lee Utley (New Brunswick, N.J. 1970), pp. 45–48. Laudine's grief in 1415–19, where she grabs herself by the throat while reading from an illuminated psalter, has elements of comic hyperbole and anticlimax. On Yvain's double imprisonment, see chap. 6, p. 226, below.

25 Though Chrétien does suggest that Laudine is also motivated by love when she acquiesces to her councillors' wish that she should marry Yvain: "Tant li [i.e., Laudine] prïent que ele otroie/ce qu'ele feïst tote voie,/qu'Amors a feire li comande/ce don los et consoil demande;/mes a plus grant enor le prant/quant congié en a de sa gent" (2139–44).

26 C. Muscatine, *Chaucer and the French Tradition* (Berkeley and Los Angeles, 1957), pp. 47–54, finds it a puzzling and rare case of Chrétien parodying by means of style a courtly love situation; Jackson (see n. 24) see Chrétien undercutting Yvain, while F. Whitehead, "Yvain's Wooing," in F. Whitehead, A.H. Diverres, and F.E. Sutcliffe, eds., *Medieval Miscellany Presented to Eugéne Vinaver* (Manchester and New York, 1965), pp. 231–36, focuses blame on Laudine, interpreting the scene as a version of the story of Oedipus and Jocasta that Chrétien borrowed from the *Roman de Thèbes*.

27 On Lunete's gratitude, see chap. 6, p. 212, and n. 26. Her concern that Yvain act moderately is made clear in 1322–35, which sound the theme of control discussed in chap. 6. She makes the same plea to Laudine, 1670f.

28 While Laudine does not share Yvain's transports of love, the text twice suggests that love exists within her, too. See the passage quoted in n. 25, and cf. 1775–82, in which Chrétien says that "par li meïsmes s'alume/ensi come li feus qui fume/tant que la flame s'i est mise,/que nus ne la soufle n'atise" (1779–82). The image of the flame within is a traditional love metaphor. The possibility that Yvain would be killed by Laudine as her husband's slayer is raised by Laudine when Lunete presents Yvain to her, 1977f.

29 See Whitehead, "Yvain's Wooing," p. 333.

30 Whitehead puts this last point well, though in applying it to the entire romance he misses what I take to be Chrétien's balancing of metaphoric analysis of the individual's quest and self-conscious play with convention: "The main attraction of the work lies perhaps in the *expertise* and impudent self-consciousness with which the author handles the asperities of a plot which the romanticization of the story has done nothing to mitigate. It is the virtuosity with which Chrétien manages an almost

unmanageable story . . . that produces most of the pleasure and satisfaction that can be extracted from the work" ("Yvain's Wooing," pp. 326–27).

31 Arthur's trick consists of announcing that he will settle the quarrel and then asking where is the damsel who has defrauded her sister of her land (6378–81). The older sister, caught unawares, answers, "Sire, fet ele, je sui ci" (6382). The king's reply, when his entrapment works is, in effect, "Aha! I knew it all along!": "La estes vos? Venez donc ça./ Je le savoie bien pieça/que vos la deseriteiez" (6383–85). The sister tries to argue that she has merely said a silly thing (6390–91), but the king insists, "coneü m'avez le voir" (6387), i.e., that the criminal stands convicted out of her own mouth.

32 For a fuller discussion of these two incidents, see R.W. Hanning, The Social Significance of Twelfth-Century Chivalric Romance," *Medievalia et Humanistica* n.s. 3 (1972): 18–19.

33 For Arthur's extortion of a confession from the guilty sister, see n. 31; for his threat to declare Gawain defeated, see 6408–13 (and Chrétien's comment that he was bluffing, 6414–22). Laudine complains that she has been tricked in 6749f. She claims that Yvain does not love her and that she would rather endure the fountain's storms than take him back (6756f.) were it not evil to break her word. I find this passage ambiguous: is Laudine simply twitting Yvain for *his* previous inability to keep his word, and thus establishing her moral superiority, or does she really mean what she says? I suspect that Chrétien built the ambiguity into the lines.

34 The clearest acknowledgment that the world of *Yvain* is fallen comes from Arthur, who, in tricking the wicked sister, recognizes that she will never give back the property she has taken from her younger sister if she is not impelled by "force ou crieme" (6422). When Yvain rescues the lion from the poisonous serpent, but must cut off a piece of the beast's tail in the process, he creates a striking emblem of the romance's insistence that its characters can only discover imperfect solutions to the problems of existence (3378–83). For a different, but highly intelligent, reading of this episode in the context of *Yvain* as a whole, see E. Schweitzer, "Pattern and Theme in Chrétien's *Yvain*," *Traditio* 30 (1974): 144–89.

35 See, e.g., La Fière's entry into a beautiful *verger* to greet the king of Sicily (2201f.), where the heavily sensual elegance of the moment culminates in Hue's remark about the size of the heroine's *cunet;* also the splendidly obscene allegory with which the poet takes leave of his

readers (10557f.). All references are to the edition of *Ipomedon* by E. Kölbing and E. Koschwitz (Breslau, 1889).

36 Such is the judgment, by and large, of M.D. Legge, *Anglo-Norman Literature and its Background* (Oxford, 1963), pp. 85–96; cf., however, P. Ménard, *Le rire et le sourire dans le roman courtois en France au moyen age* (Geneva, 1969), pp. 342–43, 348–49, 352–53, 360, 366–75, on Hue and his romance. Ménard seems to understand the thematic function of Hue's comedy and *engin*, but the nature of his study prevents a connected discussion of the romance.

37 See W.T.H. Jackson, *Anatomy of Love* (New York, 1971), pp. 164–80, 188–93, for parallel juxtapositions of *engin* and chivalry in Gottfried von Strassburg's *Tristan*.

38 Ipomedon's first adventures, before the tournament, simply involve seeking out *tribuil* and *guerre*, and winning *pris* (769–80). After the tournament he intervenes in a war between two brothers, and his aid to the wronged sibling (cf. Yvain and the wronged younger sister at the end of *Yvain*) brings about peace and a just reconciliation (7265–602). Finally, in fighting Léonin, he is moved by *pité* for all the ladies of Calabria, as well as by love for La Fière (9613–23; cf. the social implication of the battle suggested at 9322f., 9413f.) As to La Fière, her refined understanding of where her happiness lies—in personal desire, not in conformity to her oath—issues in her resolve after Léonin seems to have defeated Ipomedon: "Meulz veut guerpir tut le pais,/Ses chasteaus e tute s'hunur,/Ke prendre celui a seignur" (9960–62).

39 See, for example, 4263–68: "De tuz les chevalers del munt,/Ki unkes furent ne ki sunt,/Dunc unke poussez oir,/Ne ne sout nuls issi cuvrir;/ S'il fut pruz, ne s'en vanta mie:/Co fu duble chevalrie." Cf. 5455–68, etc.

40 On Hue's sources, see Kölbing's introduction to his and Koschwitz's edition, p. vi; L. Gay, "Hue de Rotelande's *Ipomedon* and Chrétien de Troyes," *PMLA* 32 (1917): 468–91, denies that Hue was influenced by Chrétien, but Legge disagrees, *Anglo-Norman Literature*, pp. 85–96. Fourrier, *Le courant réaliste*, pp. 447–48, stresses Hue's debt to *Partonopeu*.

41 On this gap see P. Haidu, *Lion-queue-coupée: L'écart symbolique chez Chrétien de Troyes* (Geneva, 1972), chap. 3, esp. pp. 49–78.

42 The procession, inspired I believe by the simpler one with which Erec leaves his father's court in search of adventure (*Erec,* 2762f.), is in fact a pageant combining a proleptic description of Ipomedon's behavior at the tournament (there are four horses of different color, each accom-

panied by a squire bearing a suit of armor of color to match the horse) with the paraphernalia of his other disguise as hunter (dogs, hunting weapons, etc.). Ipomedon brings up the rear of the procession.

43 For the nuisance effect of Ipomedon's noisy early-morning departures, see, e.g., 4477–518; everyone in the castle, no matter how deaf, is awakened by the horns and joyfully barking dogs.

44 See, e.g., 3206, 3207, 3262, 4510 (the queen), 5297, 6284, (the king of Sicily), 6528, 6711, etc.

45 See Haidu, *Lion-queue-coupée*, pp. 60–61 and n. 59.

46 Hue sums up this difference in worth via a rhyming pair of moral opposites, when he says that Ipomedon "se cumbat pur sa franchise,/ Pur eus [i.e., La Fière's subjects] oster de cuvertise" (9417–18).

47 See the reference to these passages on p. 131, above.

48 See 6645f., where Ipomedon says that when young men marry too soon, "s'un en amende, mil empirent" in terms of wining *pris*.

49 See *Erec*, 6002–88, esp. 6083–88; see R.R. Bezzola, *Le sens de l'aventure et de l'amour* (Paris, 1947), p. 198f.

50 The abruptness of the ending after its feint toward potentially infinite repetition also creates a special kind of surprise, release, and awareness of the artist's control; cf. the similar effect at the end of the scherzo of Beethoven's seventh symphony, where an apparent third playing of the trio is interrupted by the five loud chords that bring the movement to a close.

51 This is the response proposed or analyzed in D.H. Green, "Irony and Medieval Romance," in *Arthurian Romance*, pp. 49–64; N. Susskind, "Lore and Laughter in the *romans courtois,*" *French Review* 37 (1963–64): 651–57; and P. Ménard, *Le rire et le sourire*, passim.

52 The description of the trio reading occupies 5354–65; at 5366 Chrétien unobtrusively shifts attention from the social group centered around the *romans* to the beautiful damsel. The next several lines are given over to an extended conceit about the god of loving falling in love with such a beautiful creature by wounding himself with his dart (5370–78). Finally, Chrétien says he could say much about the wounds of love, except that people don't love they way they used to, or even want to hear about love any more (5383–90). The whole passage is a studied, virtuosic, and ironic sidestepping of the moment—an elaborate joke calling attention to the fact that the poet can turn his narrative into a parade of conventional topoi (such as "love wounded by his arrows," and "the good old days") at any moment, if he desires to avoid serious themes.

53 In the opening lines of his earliest romance, *Erec,* Chrétien distinguishes between his ability to derive a "bel conjointure" from a "conte" and the treatment of such a story by his competitors: ". . . d'Erec, le fil Lac, est li contes,/que devant rois et devant contes/depecier et corronpre suelent/cil qui de conter vivre vuelent" (19–22). *His* version, by contrast, "toz jorz mes iert an mimoire/tant con durra crestiäntez;/de ce s'est Crestiens vantez" (24–26).

54 Weaving has been a metaphor of both art and life or fate from classical antiquity onward. See, e.g., the weaving contest between Minerva and Arachne in Ovid, *Metamorphoses* vi, and the woven tapestry containing the account of the Trojan War that Helen, the cause of the war, is weaving in *Iliad* iii. The three Fates of mythology wove together the threads of every human life.

55 See the complaint of the damsels about their miserable economic situation, in which their efforts makes the evil duke rich while they receive only four *deniers* for every *livre* they earn (5298–318).

Chapter 4

1 The early medieval centuries thought about time and its passage almost entirely in terms of objective systems such as the Seven Ages of the World or the movement of salvation history from the Creation and Fall of Man through the events of biblical history and the life of Christ to (leaping over everything in between) the objective culmination of time at the Last Judgment. For a brilliant example of the subjective apprehension of time see Augustine's *Confessions,* book xi; Augustine's other masterwork, *The City of God,* is organized entirely around objective time schemes controlled by Providence.

2 J. Burrow, *A Reading of "Sir Gawain and the Green Knight"* (London, 1966), pp. 1–3.

3 A. Bonjour, *The Digressions in Beowulf* (Oxford, 1950), offers a good example of this literature and provides references to various stages of the controversy.

4 On this point see R.W. Hanning, *"Beowulf* and Heroic History," *Medievalia et Humanistica* n.s. 5 (1974): 98–99, where comparison is made between *Beowulf* and the *Dream of the Rood* with respect to views of progress in Christian and heroic history.

5 Ibid., p. 96.

6 See 702b, 710, 720; the psychological force of this "progress report" on Grendel's approach is discussed by A.G. Brodeur, *The Art of Beo-*

wulf (Berkeley and Los Angeles, 1959), chap. 4, "Design for Terror," pp. 88–91, and by R.M. Lumiansky, "The Dramatic Audience in *Beowulf,*" *Journal of English and Germanic Philology* 51 (1952): 545–50.

7 See E. Vinaver's comments in *The Rise of Romance* (Oxford, 1971), pp. 23–27; he believes that the courtly poets were guided in this psychological analysis by "the feeling that certain ways of presenting even the most straightforward issues are part of the kind of artistry that the reader expects and enjoys" (p. 26). Cf. C. Muscatine's distinction between the purely *descriptive* psychological analysis of chivalric romance and *prescriptive* analysis of moral allegories, "The Emergence of Psychological Allegory in Old French Romance," *PMLA* 68 (1953): 1160–82.

8 "Roland and Ganelon," in E. Auerbach, *Mimesis,* trans. W. Trask (Princeton, N.J., 1953; repr. New York, 1957), pp. 83–107.

9 Cf. laisses 273–79, in which the various consequences of Charlemagne's return to Aix—Alda's death on learning of Roland's, the beginning of Ganelon's trial and his consecutive, seemingly contradictory statements defending himself against the charge of treason—rather than the responses of a single character are juxtaposed but not reconciled.

10 God's angel appears to warn Charlemagne of new crises he must attend to in various parts of Christendom; the old king weeps and complains of his hard life (3993–4001) but clearly cannot refuse the divine summons. It is an interesting comment on the *Roland* poet's rejection of "biographical" time that his epic begins with an ending (laisse 1 describes the state of Spain at the end of Charlemagne's seven-year campaign) and ends with a beginning.

11 "Carles li reis, nostre emperere magnes/Set anz tuz pleins *ad estet* en Espaigne"; *La Chanson de Roland,* ed. F. Whitehead (Oxford, 1942), lines 1–2 (italics mine). The famous quasi-symbolic setting of the battle at the pass of Roncesvals is also set in a timeless present: "Halt sunt li pui, e li val tenebrus,/Les roches bises, les destreiz merveillus" (814–15).

12 The fact that Ganelon's trial takes place on St. Sylvester's day (December 31; see 3745–46) suggests, as does the description of Charlemagne's new champion, Thierry, that the Franks have reached the end of their heroic era. (Although there were several possible ways of reckoning the beginning of the year in the Middle Ages, the Roman New Year's date, January 1, remained popular; cf. the annual cycle of *Sir Gawain and The Green Knight.*) See further J. Halvorsen, "Ganelon's Trial," *Speculum* 42 (1967): 661–69, on the animus of the poet toward

heroic but antisocial relationships among the Franks. In a forthcoming essay in *Zeitschrift für romanische philologie,* Frederick Goldin argues that Ganelon in effect represents the destructive forces at work at any given moment within the poem's feudal-heroic vision.

13 C.W. Jones, *Saints' Lives and Chronicles,* (Ithaca, 1947) chaps. 1 and 2.

14 In the *Life of St. Anthony,* Athanasius rejects the connected flow of moments that comprise the personal experience of time for a series of short, self-contained episodes, each making an exemplary point; it is impossible to judge how much time has elapsed between these chapters, nor is there any indication we are to think of them as temporally in sequence with each other. They begin with vague temporal references like "once" (chaps. 15, 40, 54), "one day," (chap. 16), "on another occasion" (chap. 3), or "after" (chaps. 46, 48). The saint's life, fragmented in this way, becomes a kind of mosaic given its unity and meaning by the light of God's grace, rather than by a personal consciousness within, shaping a unique response to life's challenges. Anthony specifically warns against the dangers of an individual-centered view of time as a continuum of personal experience when he tells the monks, "Let us all make this resolution especially: not to give up once we have begun, not to become faint-hearted in our labors, and not to say, 'We have spent a long time in the practice of asceticism.' Rather, let us increase our zeal each day as if we were beginning anew, for, if measured by the ages to come, the whole of human life is very short, and all our time is nothing as compared with eternal life." The subjective measurement of time can lead to discouragement, so we must compare each day only to the entire, divinely ordained system of time and eternity (chap. 16, p. 150). References are to the translation of the *Life* by M.E. Keenan, S.C.N., in R.J. Deferrari, ed., *Early Christian Biographies* (New York, 1952).

15 The voyage made by Brendan and his monks on their way to the earthly Paradise involves an annual cycle of visits to specific, marvellous places, repeated seven times, the visits are made at Christmas, Easter, and Pentecost, the central feasts of the liturgical year. The whole process clearly stands for the life of monastic observance, imagined as a pilgrimage through the week of life, to the Sabbath-reward of perfection. See *The Voyage of St. Brendan,* in *Lives of the Saints,* trans. J.F. Webb (Harmondsworth, 1965), pp. 33–68.

16 There is an interesting echo of Chrétien's narrative irony in *Purgatorio,* xviii. Dante encounters those whose expiation for lukewarmness (and thus slowness) in doing well during their lifetime is accomplished by

racing around their circle. Commenting on their haste, Vergil says, "O gente in cui fervore aguto adesso/ricompie forse negligenza e indugio/ da voi per tepidezza in ben far messo . . ." (106–08).

17 Yvain first raises the problem of timing in 3937–45; he will be happy to rescue the damsel from the giant "se li jaianz et vostre fil/venoient demain a tele ore/que n'i face trop grant demore" (3938–42). See further 3986–92, and 4024–85, in which the family pleads with Yvain not to leave, and only at the last moment does he agree to wait a little longer. See also 4292–97, and Lunete's comment when Yvain arrives in the nick of time to rescue her: "S'un po eüssiez plu esté/par tans fusse charbons et cendres" (4399–400).

18 See 3692f., 3906f., 4734f., There is a parallel between Arthur's foolishness in letting Kay persuade him to take Guinevere away and Yvain's in letting himself be talked, by Gawain, into leaving his wife; there is also a contrast between Gawain's disinterested quest to find the queen and Yvain's personal quest to be reconciled with his wife.

19 See M. Bloch *Feudal Society* trans L. A. Manyon, 2 vols. (Chicago, 1964), pp. 73–74: "These men [of the early medieval centuries] lived in a world in which the passage of time escaped their grasp all the more because they were so ill-equipped to measure it. . . . Reckoning ordinarily—after the example of antiquity—twelve hours of day and twelve of night, whatever the season, people of the highest education became used to seeing each of these fractions, taken one by one, grow and diminish incessantly according to the annual revolution of the sun."

20 See Asser's *Life of Alfred*, chap. 104, as reported in *Feudal Society*, p. 73. Bloch adds, "such concern for uniformity in the division of the day was exceptional in that age"; the invention of clocks in the fourteenth century accomplished the "mechanization . . . so to speak, of time itself" (p. 74)—but this technological advance ratified the change in *perception* of time that I am here documenting in twelfth-century romances.

21 Cf. Vinaver's different use of the analogy between polyphony and romance narrative, *The Rise of Romance*, pp. 23, 28. On questions of polyphonic rhythm and its notation in the twelfth-century "Notre Dame School" of Leonin and Perrotin, see W. Waite, *The Rhythm of Twelfth-Century Polyphony* (New Haven, 1954). I am grateful for the assistance of Professors Ernest Sanders and Barbara R. Hanning in my attempt to articulate the implications of polyphony for an understanding of twelfth-century attempts to organize time intellectually and analytically.

22 See 7560–80; Partonopeu is confident of victory in the coming tournament: "Certes je vaintrai le tornoi;/Ne s'en porroit nus faire a moi,/Car
   il ne porroit estre pas/Que g'i fusse vencus ne las,/Por coi je pensasse
   de li [Mélior] /Ne m'eüst sempres refreschi" (7567–72).

23 In the midst of Beowulf's description of his fight with sea monsters
   during his swimming match with Breca, he inserts, by means of a negative construction, a contrary-to-fact image of the monsters feasting on
   him at the bottom of the sea (562–64); the effect of this evocation of
   disappointed anticipation is to blur our sense of the precise spatial
   reality of the scene.

24 See R.W. Hanning, "Sharing, Dividing, Depriving: The verbal Ironies of
   Grendel's Last Visit to Heorot," *Texas Studies in Literature and Language* 15 (1973): 203–13.

25 From *The Exeter·Book*, ed. G.P. Krapp and E.V. Dobbie, Anglo Saxon
   Poetic Records, vol. 3 (New York, 1936), p. 134: "he must stir the icy-
   cold sea with his hands [i.e., row] , travel the paths of exile."

26 See *The Seafarer*, ed. I.L. Gordon (London, 1960), introduction, pp.
   4–8, for a summary of various interpretations of the exile-journey, and
   D. Whitelock, "The Interpretation of *The Seafarer*," in C. Fox and B.
   Dickens, eds., *The Early Cultures of North-west Europe: H.M. Chad-
   wick Memorial Studies* (London, 1950), pp. 261–72, on the phenomenon of voluntary exile as a religious practice during the early Middle
   Ages. There is a paradox here, or rather a contradiction between the
   theological view of the *civitas Dei* on pilgrimage, shunning earthly
   abode in order to find God, and the psychology of the period, clearly
   rendered in *Beowulf*, of the high value placed on centers of security,
   such as Heorot, in a time of political instability. Note, however, that
   this paradox is in a sense resolved by the monastery—a place of exile
   from the "world" for the sake of salvation, but also a tightly knit
   community whose life was regulated and made secure by its dependence on ritual observance and daily schedules ordering all other activities of the monks.

27 There is also Bede's description of the island of Britain at the beginning
   of his *Ecclesiastical History* which, as its most recent editors point out,
   may have been suggested to him by the histories of Orosius and Gregory
   of Tours. See Bede, *Ecclesiastical History of the English People*, eds. B.
   Colgrave and R.A.B. Mynors (Oxford, 1969), p. 14, n. 1. It is, in any
   case, a cumulative, "objective" inventory of the total resources of a
   place, quite separate from the perceptions of the place held by any
   particular person or people.

28 See chap. 3, pp. 109-10.

29 Cf. 764-72 (where the castle shimmers indistinctly among the thick trees that surround it), 781-90 (where the knight notes the castle's closed gates and walls of "harde hewen ston" in its lower parts), and 791-802 (where his eye, traveling upward, discovers the decorated pinnacles ahd chimneys that make the castle seem less a fortress, more a paper cut-out). The result of these juxtaposed descriptions is to make the reader experience the castle entirely through the eyes of the isolated protagonist, that is, subjectively.

30 For an interesting discussion of the evolution of landscape representations in the Christian art of the early Middle Ages, see F. Bucher, "Medieval Landscape Painting: An Introduction," in *Medieval and Renaissance Studies*, ed. J.M. Headley, vol. 3 (Chapel Hill, 1969) pp. 119-69, esp p. 143 f. What Bucher calls the "two-dimensional world view" of the age is the visual equivalent of what I am here describing: space perceived symbolically and systematically, not perceptually and from an individual perspective.

31 I refer to the "beginning" described by Spenser in his explanatory letter to Walter Raleigh, but never actually written (See *The Poetical Works of Edmund Spenser*, eds. J.C. Smith and E. de Selincourt [Oxford, 1909], vol. 3, pp. 486-87.). On each of twelve consecutive days, strange damsels or knights enter Gloriana's court to describe an adventure that a knight of the court must undertake by leaving the court.

32 Cf. chap. 1, pp. 48-50, above, where I cite episodes in *The Life of Christina of Markyate,* and the *Eve* of Giselbertus, as evidence for similar concerns with the spatial configurations of individual experience in other twelfth-century media.

33 The contrast between this next phase of *Yvain* and the section just described is striking: the precisely described passageway is suddenly "transformed" by the poet into a richly decorated room (963-66, "la sale . . . /qui tot estoit cielee a clos/dorez, et pointes les meisieres/de boene oevre et de colors chieres"). This deliberate blurring of spatial specificity after establishing it is a self-consciously ironic manipulation by Chrétien, suggesting that the prowess-imprisonment into which Yvain has gotten himself is about to be transformed into the more refined but equally secure "prison" of love. Cf. the establishment in *Lancelot* of a precise, ostensibly impassible boundary between the two kingdoms of Logres and Gorre: Lancelot must attempt to pass into the latter by means of the extremely perilous sword bridge—yet well before he

arrives at it, he seems to have entered Gorre (see, e.g., 2051f.). Here Chrétien seems to suggest that Logres and Gorre are to some extent coterminous: that the Arthurian world, until freed by the quest of the inspired individual knight, is as much dead as alive. (On this aspect of the romance, see the fine discussion by Joan Ferrante, "The Conflict of Lyric Conventions and Romance Form," in *In Pursuit of Perfection*, eds. Joan M. Ferrante and George D. Economou [Port Washington, N.Y., and London, 1975], pp. 150–56.)

34 See his comment on hearing the name of the adventure: "Rien ne me porroit retenir/que je n'aille querre la Joie" (5424–25).

35 My analysis of this episode owes much to R.R. Bezzola, *Le sens de l'aventure et de l'amour* (Paris, 1947), pp. 198–226.

36 It is no accident that the description of the monsters' lake seems to stem from the same source as a description of hell in a later Anglo-Saxon homily. See *Beowulf*, ed. F. Klaeber, 3rd ed. with first and second supplement (Boston, 1950), pp. 182–83.

Chapter 5

1 Ovid, *Metamorphoses*, ed. and trans. F.J. Miller (London and Cambridge, Mass., 1916, repr. 1971), iii. 138–252. The theme of art's power and limits runs through the *Metamorphoses* and constitutes a major part of the Ovidian legacy to the Middle Ages and Renaissance, as I hope to show in a later study. The chivalric poets' interest in *engin* is a version of the same concern. On the use of Actaeon as an archetype in medieval lyric and narrative see S.G. Nichols, Jr., "Rhetorical Metamorphosis in the Troubour Lyric," in J. Dufournet and D. Poirion, eds., *Mélanges de langue et de littérature médiévales offerts à Pierre Le Gentil* (Paris, 1973), pp. 569–85.

2 The parallels—and contrasts—between book 3 of the *Iliad* and twelfth-century texts in which ladies and other spectators watch jousts or battles from castle walls or towers are instructive. See above, chap. 2, pp. 55–58, on this use of spectator-perspective in Geoffrey of Monmouth's *Historia regum Brittanniae* and later texts.

3 At the beginning of this sequence in the *Iliad*, the various perspectives of the actors in the coming scene are proleptically undermined by the fact that Helen is presiding over the making of a tapestry incorporating scenes from the Trojan War when she is called away to the city walls to see the duel of Paris and Menelaos. The tapestry is a palpable image of fate—an objective and fixed record of men caught up in a great action over which they have no control.

4 Cf. 1008–16, in which Roland's heroic self-centeredness is inextricably intertwined with his self-definition as Charles's vassa!: "Ben devuns ci estre pur nostre rei:/Pur sun seignor deit hom susfrir destreiz/. . . Malvaise essample n'en serat ja de mei"; and 2389–90, where Roland, dying, offers his glove in fealty to God, and Gabriel accepts it.

5 On the social meanings of these words, see. G. F. Jones, *The Ethos of the Song of Roland* (Baltimore, 1963), pp. 21–25.

6 On the mimetic and ethical implications of the paratactic style of the *Roland*'s verse, see E. Auerbach, "Roland Against Ganelon," in *Mimesis*, trans. W. Trask (Princeton, N.J., 1953; repr. New York, 1957), pp. 83–107; on the clash of legal systems, see J. Halvorsen, "Ganelon's Trial," *Speculum* 42 (1967): 661–69.

7 See J.R.R. Tolkien, "*Beowulf*: The Monsters, and the Critics," *Proceedings of the British Academy* 22 (1936): 245–95; H.L. Rogers, "Beowulf's Three Great Fights," *Review of English Studies* n.s. 6 (1955): 339–55; D.R. Barnes, "Folktale Morphology and the Structure of *Beowulf*," *Speculum* 45 (1970): 416–34.

8 On other forms of the "outdoing" topos, see E.R. Curtius, *European Literature and the Latin Middle Ages*, trans. W. Trask (New York, 1953), pp. 162–65.

9 See F. Goldin, *The Mirror of Narcisus* (Ithaca, 1967) on this image in medieval lyric and narrative.

10 A notable descendant of this moment in a great work of later narrative is the first meeting of Lydgate and Rosamond in book 1, chap. 12 of George Eliot's *Middlemarch*, at the end of which Lydgate picks up Rosamond's riding whip to give to her: "She bowed and looked at him; he of course was looking at her, and their eyes met with that peculiar meeting which is never arrived at by effort, but seems like a sudden divine clearance of haze. I think Lydgate turned a little paler than usual, but Rosamond blushed deeply and felt a certain astonishment." The meaning of this moment is the sum total of the individual perspectives and responses that constitute it; once again (though George Eliot emphasizes it less than does Chrétien) the presence of others—Mr. Featherstone, Fred Vincy—who do not perceive what has happened individuates the protagonists' response and emphasizes its subjectivity.

11 He also passes the best golden cups to her and engages in joking, flirtatious conversation. See Geoffrey of Monmouth, *Historia regum Britanniae*, ed. A. Griscom (London, New York, Toronto, 1929), viii. 19 (p. 423).

12 King Lac reluctantly grants leave to his son to go off unaccompanied save for Enide, at which point (2738f.) he begins to cry and is joined in

this reaction by all the *dames et chevaliers*; Chrétien adds, "ne cuit que greignor duel feïssent,/se a mort navré le veïssent" (2747-48). Later, when Erec, though wounded, refuses to stay at Arthur's court to be healed, the courtiers respond analogously: "Lors les veïssiez toz plorer/ et demener un duel si fort/con s'il le veïssent ja mort" (4262-64).

13 On the dating and social milieu of Gautier's romances, see Fourrier, *Le courant réaliste dans le roman courtois en France au moyen-age,* vol. 1 (Paris, 1960), pp. 179-207, and on *Eracle,* pp. 207-75. See also P. Nykrog, "Two Creators of Narrative Form in Twelfth-Century France: Gautier d'Arras—Chrétien de Troyes," *Speculum* 48 (1973): 258-76.

14 E.H. Gombrich, *Art and Illusion* (Princeton, 1960, repr. 1972), p. 137. Gombrich is interested here in how an artist individuates human figures in a painting by means of gestures and actions, so that our response will include "imaginative sympathy" (p. 136) to each figure's personal involvement in, or perspective on, the event depicted. *The Battle of Alexander and Darius,* Gombrich's main example, interprets Alexander's victory not simply as a celebration of power but as the sum total of responses in a moment of war, so that "it is not only the triumph of victory we are made to share but also the tragedy of defeat"—each depicted individual response contributes to the overall, complex impact of the image.

15 C. Muscatine, *Chaucer and the French Tradition* (Berkeley and Los Angeles, 1957), p. 61, p. 59.

16 Athanais complains, "Confaite chose/Qu'om m'a pour noient ci enclose!/. . . Mais li moie [consciënce] ne me dit rien/Que ainc desservi el que bien/. . . Mieuz ameroie, en ma chemise,/Estre a honeur et a delivre/Qu'empereriz a honte vivre" (3240-41, 3250-51, 3327-29).

17 "Envie, espoir, m'a encusee,/Et si me porte pour çou faide/Que je ne sui pas li plus laide,/Et que j'ai maintenu en moi/Honeur et loiauté et foi;/Envie het touz jours biauté,/Honeur et foi et loiauté,/Et pour çou m'est ele anemie/Que je lour ai esté amie" (3265-73).

18 "S'ele savoit çou que je pens,/Jel comperroie, al mien pourpens;/car feme est orguilleuse et fiere/Nès vers le chose qu'ele a chiere;/Feme enrichie, ensourquetout,/A mout le cuer fier et estout . . ." (3798-803).

19 See Muscatịne, *Chaucer and the French Tradition,* p. 140.

20 In support of her assertion that women pay no heed to men who are taken with them, but only to men who mistreat them, and by whom they are smitten (4170-73), the old lady testifies, "Jel di pour moi, qui feme sui:/Jou ai fait a maint hone anui/Quant jou estoie juene touse;/

Je n'amasse home pour Toulouse,/Pour qu'il m'amast, ainz l'amu-
soie, . . . A ceus le donoie a droiture/Qui de m'amour n'avoient cure"
(4174–81).

21 Gautier extends this to his putative audience by suggesting on two
occasions that only someone who has experienced love can understand
how the lovers feel. Implicit in this formulation is the idea that we
respond to literature (or don't) in terms of our own *personal*, that is,
individual, experience. See 3838–54, 4613–17.

22 This plan results from a *parlement* among the ladies held while Guinevere is "fors del pais" (5359–60); Chrétien thus suggests that this
social and conventional application of the chivalry topos, ending in
marriage, is an alternative mode of sexual relationship that functions
in the absence of a more private, passionate relationship in which love
prompts prowess instead of vice versa.

23 There is a play on words between the name of the tournament place
(*Noauz*) and the idiom "to do poorly" (*faire noauz*)—a quibble that
calls attention to the disruptive effect of the personal love quest, with
its quintessentially individual goal, on social chivalry.

24 Cf. Chrétien's use of religious resonances to bolster his point: Lancelot's trip to Gorre to liberate the men and women of Logres imprisoned
there is a "harrowing of hell" in which the Christ figure is himself
imprisoned!

25 The herald's cry when Lancelot appears—"or est venuz qui l'aunera!"
(5563)—marks him as a secularized, parodic John the Baptist announcing Lancelot-Christ; all the more ironic is his dismay at seeing
Lancelot disgraced and "defeated."

26 In chap. 3, above, I discuss how the hero of Hue de Roteland's *Ipomedon* quite intentionally uses chivalry as an instrument to educate
courtly observers in the shortcomings of prowess as a way of life. Here,
the lesson is inadvertent—or rather, it is taught by Chrétien, not by his
protagonist.

27 A typical excerpt: "'Cil escuz fu féz a Lymoges,/si l'an aporta Piladés/
qui an estor vialt estre adés/et molt le desirre et golose. . . ./Cil vint de
Lÿon sor le Rosne:/n'a nul si boen desoz le trosne,/si fu por une grant
desserte/donez Taulas de la Deserte/qui bel le porte et bien s'an
cuevre. . . .'/Ensi devisent et deboissent/les armes de ces qu'il
conoissent. . . ." (ll. 5804–5824).

28 See *Erec*, 285–98 (on the threat of chaos); 335–41 (the queen's suggestion to await Erec's return before awarding the kiss).

29 R. Guiette, "Symbole et 'senefiance' au Moyen Age," "Lecteur de

roman, lecteur de symbole," "Le symbole et les réalitiés," in *Questions de littérature* (Gand, 1960), pp. 33–60. Cf. P. Haidu's discussion of this approach in contrast to the symbolizing analyses of Robertson and Bezzola, in *Lion-queue-coupée* (Geneva, 1972), pp. 11–15.

30 Such a statement of artistic freedom from the restraints of reality does appear to inhere in works of "mannerist" painters like Rosso Fiorentino, Parmigianino, or, closer to the twelfth century, Rogier van der Weyden.

31 *Art and Illusion,* p. 138.

32 See ibid., pp. 138–39, where Gombrich offers evidence that aboriginal tribesmen do not like art that represents "incomplete" images in an attempt to render perceived reality (e.g., a bird seen from such an angle that one of its wings is hidden from sight and therefore is "missing"). One thinks also of the "timeless" frontality and objectivity of early medieval mosaics in which saints are presented in standard, static postures, and clearly not from a perspective of individual visual perception.

Chapter 6

1 As Fourrier points out, *Le courant réaliste dans le roman courtois en France au moyen-age,* vol. 1 (Paris, 1960), pp. 448–49.

2 On the concept of participating in a literary mode, see T.M. Greene, *The Descent from Heaven* (New Haven, 1963), p. 9.

3 See, for example, the analysis and discussion of Babylonian new year's rituals, in which the king "dies" and is reborn for and with his people, in G. R. Levy, *The Sword from the Rock* (London, 1953), chap.1.

4 On the concept of literary displacement, see N. Frye, *Anatomy of Criticism* (Princeton, 1957), pp. 136–40. Frye defines romance in this section as the fictional category illustrating "the tendency . . . to displace myth in a human direction and yet, in contrast to 'realism' to conventionalize content in an idealized direction" (pp. 136–37).

5 See Levy, *The Sword from the Rock,* pp. 14–15, 48f., 120–21, and her *The Gate of Horn* (London, 1948), chap. 2.

6 This persistent myth receives attentive scrutiny in H. Levin, *The Myth of the Golden Age in the Renaissance* (Bloomington and London, 1969).

7 Ibid., pp. 21–22.

8 See ibid., p. 8, and the chart on p. 9, which illustrates the relationship

between the temporal version of the myth (golden age → now → golden age regained) and its spatial version (arcadia → here → utopia).

9 On the large cyclical implications of both Old and New Testament views of history see J. Daniélou, *Les figures du Christ dans l'ancien testament: "Sacramentum futuri"* (Paris, 1950), chap. 1, "Adam et le paradis."

10 Even in an ironic romance like Chrétien's *Cligès*, where the consummation of the love relationship between hero and heroine is undercut by their being confined to a tomblike tower—a work of art cut off from nature's light and freedom—the ironies operate as effectively as they do because they are set in a framework of assumptions like the one just outlined concerning the progressive, inner self-realization of the protagonist through the quest for fulfillment. See above, chap. 3, on this romance and its ironies.

11 On the courtly additions to the Latin *vita* in the Anglo-Norman St. Brendan, see M.D. Legge, *Anglo-Norman Literature and its Background* (Oxford, 1963), pp. 8–18, and *The Anglo-Norman Voyage of St. Brendan*, ed, E.G.R Waters (Oxford, 1928), pp. lxxxi–cv, passim. Cf. also the legend of Amicus and Amilius which existed in two basic forms in the Middle Ages, characterized by the most recent editor of one redaction as "les versions à caractère 'romanesque' . . . et les versions à caractère nettement hagiographique."*Ami et Amile*, ed. P.F. Dembowski (Paris, 1969), p. ix.

12 *The Cloud of Unknowing*, ed P. Hodgson, Early English Text Society, no. 218 (Oxford, 1944, repr. 1958), p. 40. Cf. the passage on the origin of personal love for God from chap. 2 of Bernard's *On the Love of God*, quoted in chap. 1, above.

13 This paradigm of a religious quest based on awareness of distance from God can be partially applied to a patristic-age work like Athanasius's *Life of St. Anthony* (or to Augustine's quasi-hagiographical *Confessions*), but early medieval saints' lives lost this dimension and became exemplary tales of God's power working through man in the form of public miracles that reveal nothing of the saint's inner life or awareness. The twelfth century reincorporated such awareness—and individuality— in hagiographical works like the *Life of Christina of Markyate*. See chap. 1, n. 1.

14 *The Book of St. Bernard on the love of God*, ed. and trans. E.G. Gardner (London, [1915]), pp. 99–103.

15 *The Discovery of the Individual*, pp. 152–57.

16 N. Cohn, *The Pursuit of the Millennium* (London. 1957; rev. ed. 1970), p. 176.

17 In *Deonise Hid Diuinitie and other Treatises on Contemplative Prayer related to the Cloud of Unknowing,* ed. P. Hodgson, Early English Text Society, no. 231 (London, 1955), p. 64.

18 The nature and effect of this plot structure in Chrétien's *Erec* and *Yvain,* and also in Gautier's *Ille et Galeron,* are discussed provocatively by J.P. Collas, "The Romantic Hero of the Twelfth Century," in F. Whitehead, A.H. Diverres, and F.E. Sutcliffe eds., *Medieval Miscellany presented to Eugène Vinaver* (Manchester and New York, 1965), pp. 80–96.

19 Erec's literal and metaphorical awakening by Enide's complaint as he lies asleep in their bed (2503f.), and his subsequent setting out on adventure accompanied by his wife, who must ride before him in silence, has provoked much critical debate as to its significance and Erec's motivation in leaving the court with Enide. No summary can be attempted here, but see Z.P. Zaddy, "The Romance of Erec and Enide: An Essay in Interpretation," in her *Chrétien Studies* (Glasgow, 1973), pp. 1–14, for a statement and rebuttal of various earlier views and a new reading. I have alluded to my own understanding of the turning point in *Erec* in chap. 2 and will return to the matter in a subsequent essay. The image of awakening is central to the romance; cf. Erec's later awakening from supposed death at the court of Oringle of Limors (4815f.), and the moral awakening of Count Galoain to his "malveise oevre" (3622) in trying to steal Enide from Erec; this latter onset of moral awareness is linked to Erec's awakenings by Chrétien's description of the wounded count's actions immediately prior to his confession: "contre mont s'est un po dreciez/*et les ialz un petitet oevre* . . ." (3620–21; italics mine; and cf. 2503–09).

20 On the problematic tone of the episode, see chap. 3, pp. 118–20, and cf. below, p. 226.

21 Collas, "The Romantic Hero," p. 88, argues that Chrétien's audience, knowing the structural model of *Erec,* "would foresee the breach of Yvain's promise the moment it was made, [and] would be eager for Yvain to break it expeditiously. . . . By normal criteria Yvain's forgetfulness is as unpardonable as Laudine makes it; it may also be inexplicable. By the criteria of romance it is an obligation, and there is not time to account for it." In other words, the reader sees the lapse of memory as simply a necessary device to get through the brief middle part of the

romance and liberate the hero for the adventures of the expansive last
section. My own interpretation differs, of course: Yvain's forgetfulness
is a metaphoric expression of his unawareness of the primacy of his
private world and desires in his long-range quest for happiness and
fulfillment.

22 On the related images of the storm, madness, and other instances of
control lost in *Yvain*, see below, p. 225 and n. 51.

23 I have discussed the role of memory in creating the apparently insurmountable gap between present and future selves in chap. 2, pp.
81, 97–98, in connection with the analogous personal crisis of the hero
in *Partonopeu de Blois*.

24 That Chrétien was thinking of the analogy I have drawn between a
religious awakening and the self-alienation of the newly aware chivalric
hero is made likely by his having Yvain describe himself at line 6771 as
a *pecheor* on whom Laudine should have mercy; she is the "God" who
can give him saving grace.

25 Yvain's progress from eating uncooked, unseasoned meat at the height
of his madness (2827–28, 2875–76) to cooking the meat killed for him
by his newfound companion, the lion (3452–54), and feeling the
absence of salt, wine, a tablecloth, and a knife (3462–64), is Chrétien's
way of underscoring the hero's movement back towards civilized standards, though this time incorporating personal loyalty.

26 When Lunete first enters the romance to aid Yvain, who is trapped in
Laudine's castle, she brings this theme of reciprocal service with her:
she will help Yvain because earlier, when she came to Arthur's court,
he alone of all the knights aided her. See the important statement in
1001–15.

27 As P. Haidu fully indicates, *Lion-queue-coupée: L'écart symbolique
chez Chrétien de Troyes* (Geneva, 1972), p. 57f.

28 See 1363–84, on how she fell in love with him, and her praise of his
lineage and *noblesce*, 1501–14; also 921f., which describe how a
pensers de noblece leads him to seek out the most beautiful palace in
Chef d'Oire in which to eat and sleep—Mélior's palace.

29 See 3401–30, where love motivates Partonopeu to win a climactic
battle, thereby illustrating for the first time in the poem the chivalry
topos. Cf. the fuller statement of the topos, 7560–76.

30 Fourrier, *Le courant réaliste*, p. 390, attempts to rationalize the potion as probably the intoxicating effect of wine on a fifteen-year-old
boy. He misses the point that in this scene Partonopeu is being

tempted, by all that society can offer, to follow its plans for him and forsake his private destiny. The potion stands for the lure of self-forgetfulness, implicit in accepting the good life lived at court.

31 See 4061-64, "Quant cil ot s'amie [Mélior] nomer,/Tantost se prent a porpenser,/Et en la guise del porpens/Li est tos revenus li sens."

32 The lantern has been given to Partonopeu as a stimulus to, and symbol of, spiritual perception to ward off the snares of the devil. When Partonopeu realizes "qu'il a ovré moult folement" (4532), he throws the lantern against the wall and it goes out (4536), indicating graphically that his treason has in fact brought a new moral darkness to his love vision. See 4531-32.

33 The long speech by Partonopeu (4783-20) not only admits his awareness of his *traison* (4790), *felonie* (4793), and *folie* (4798), but repeatedly expresses' his wish to die and his conviction that awareness will make life a living death for him (4805-16). Cf. the analogously self-condemning soliloquy, 5203-58, discussed above, chap. 2, pp. 81-83.

34 Mélior tells Partonopeu (4667-70) that his treason has caused the destruction of that part of her formidable education in arts which enabled her to perform the illusions that hid Partonopeu from her vassals. But if magic is no longer there to serve desire, her *engiens, ars,* and *livres* are still hers (4664-65); it is precisely such aids that Urraque, her sister, will use to save Partonopeu and to bring the lovers together again, as we have seen.

35 See F.-E. Godefroi, *Dictionnaire de l'ancien langue francaise,* 10 vols. (Paris, 1881-1902), s. v. *deviser*; meanings include, "établir une séparation," "ranger, mettre en ordre," "ordonner la construction de"; also (in an artistic sense) "racconter." (In this latter sense, the protagonists can be seen as their own storytellers.) Cf. 111-12 of *Partonopeu,* where the poet, speaking of the portrayal of both good and evil in literature, says, "Mal et bien i doit on trover/Par conoistre et par deviser"; here *deviser* carries clear implications of understanding and learning as a result of perceiving clearly.

36 Cf. the brief but brilliant discussion of this motif in *Lanval* and *Yonec* (where it is sexually reversed, with a prince appearing to a captured wife in the form of a bird) in J.M. Ferrante, *Woman as Image in Medieval Literature* (New York, 1975), pp. 95-97; Ferrante has a useful section on *Partonopeu* which in several respects parallels my own views about the romance, pp. 84-87.

37 See H. Newstead, "The Traditional Background of *Partonopeus de*

Blois," *PMLA* 61 (1946): 916-46, on the poet's use of this myth and other folkloric material in the romance. Also see Fourrier, *Le courant réaliste,* p. 384f.

38 Mabonograin unwittingly promises his secret mistress that he will remain with her in a beautiful garden with invisible walls until he is beaten by a knight who enters the garden to challenge him. His size and strength give him victory after victory, and his honor will not let him lose deliberately, so he remains trapped in the garden, a prisoner of self-defeating prowess "inspired" by love and by fear of losing his beloved. See *Erec,* 5998-6064.

39 On Lunete's gratitude to Yvain, see n. 26, above. Yvain's role as Lunete's benefactor isolates him for her from all other Arthurian knights; his courtesy *is* his individuality, from her unique perspective.

40 The adventures begin with a joust at the *gué perilleus,* a rite of initiation, in which Guinglain rejects *couardie* and passes bravely into the life of adventure (321-486), overcoming the attempts of Arthur's court and the damsel Elie to discourage him from so doing. Subsequent adventures show him to be prudent, patient, and faithful to his promise to rescue the damsel of the *fier baiser,* even at the cost of leaving the "Pucele as blanches mains," whose hand he wins by defeating the knight who defends her castle against all challengers (1870-2492). Many of these adventures are clearly influenced by or borrowed from Chrétien's romances. See the summary and comments in D.D.R. Owen, *The Evolution of the Grail Legend* (Edinburgh and London, 1968), pp. 83-89, and the analysis of P. Haidu, "Realism, Convention, Fictionality and the Theory of Genres in *Le Bel Inconnu,*" *L'Esprit createur* 12 (1972): 37-60.

41 See 2773-3252, and esp. Esmaree's explanation of the marvels and recent history of Sinaudon, 3304-3400. This reading of the *fier baiser* episode is tentative; I hope to expand on it in a future essay.

42 As the text puts it, "Amors li cange son pensser" (3677). See the description of his change of heart and resultant love monologue, 3675-736.

43 After she accepts Guinglain's apology for leaving her, the Pucele gives him a rich bed to sleep in that night and tells him that she will be sleeping nearby in her chamber with the door open, but forbids him to try to come to her (4489-504). Confused by the contradiction between the Pucele's words and deeds ("Ma dame le [i.e., going to her bed] m'a desfendu,/Et par sanblant ai je veü"/Qu'ele veut bien que je i aille," 4531-33), Guinglain twice tries to enter her bedroom and twice seems

to fall into mortal traps—once he hangs by his hands from a board suspended over a cauldron of boiling water (representing the self-destructive "boiling up" of the passions?), once the entire weight of the palace
seems to collapse on his neck—only to discover, when the Pucele's re-
tainers answer his frantic cries for help, that these are illusions, punishments inflicted on him by the Pucele for his reliance on his own *penssers*
(4678) in interpreting her command with something other than complete obedience.

44 See 5010-16, where the Pucele, extending her love and magic hospitality to Guinglain, says "Des or mais serrons a repos/Entre moi et
vos sans grant plait,/E saciés bien tot entresait/Que, tant que croire
me vaurois,/Ne vaurés rien que vos n'aios;/Et quant mon consel ne
croirés/Ce saciés bien, lors me perdrés."

45 On the narrator's framing *persona* as a "lyric lover"—the suitor of a
distant lady for whom he is writing the romance—see R.W. Hanning,
"The Social Significance of Twelfth-Century Chivalric Romance,"
Medievalia et Humanistica n.s. 3 (1972): 24; J.L. Grigsby, "The
Narrator in *Partonopeu de Blois, Le Bel Inconnu,* and *Joufroi de
Poitiers,*" *Romance Philology* 21 (1967-68): 536-43, and Haidu,
"Realism, Convention, Fictionality."

46 Although the Pucele tells Guinglain that she loves him for his prowess
and allowed him to leave her the first time he came to her castle in
order that he might fulfill the adventure of the *fier baiser* and win
honor (4948-60), she also tells him, "Li miens amis,/Molt mar i fu
vostre proece,/vostre sens et vostre largece,/Qu'en vos n'a rien a
amender/Fors tant que ne savés amer" (4426-30). Guinglain, when he
returns to the Pucele and first pleads for her mercy, says "Doce dame,
je ne menc pas:/Lors me promistes vostre honnor,/Mais je m'en parti
par folor/Par le secors que je vauc faire" (4034-37; italics mine).

47 On the *Life of Christina,* see chap. 1, above; the second part of the
Life shows Christina forced to live a life of secrecy (and extreme
physical discomfort) in a tiny hermitage in order to avoid being sur-
rendered to her parents; she easily puts up with the difficulties of this
"imprisonment" in order to be free to love and serve God. The author
of *Ancrene Wisse* exploits the paradoxical notion of enclosed freedom
not only in his imagery (a dammed-up mouth raises the anchoress's
thoughts to heaven as a blocked stream rises behind its dam; see the
translation by M.B. Salu [London, 1955], pp. 31-32), but in his complex exploration of the inner world of temptation and contrition as the
world within which the anchoress is radically free to damn or save her

soul. See further L.M. Georgianna's "*Ancrene Wisse*: Tradition and Design" (Ph.D. diss., Columbia University, 1976).

48 See the perceptive discussion in C.H. Taylor, Jr., "The Obstacles to Odysseus' Return," in *Essays on the Odyssey*, ed C.H. Taylor, Jr. (Bloomington, 1963), pp. 87-99.

49 It may be significant that in the romances of Chrétien custom usually operates as a negative force, hindering the individual protagonist from reaching fulfillment, or perpetuating an injustice (as in the evil custom of Pesme Avanture in *Yvain*) or a socially disruptive impulse (such as the custom of the white stag in *Erec*). The past and its legacy are thus presented metaphorically as an obstacle to be overcome, a prison from which the hero must liberate society, its victims, and its leaders. (Arthur justifies the near-calamity of the custom of the white stag by saying, "L'usage Pandragon, mon pere . . ./voel je garder et maintenir,/que qu'il m'an doie avenir" [1767-70].)

50 In Guillaume IX's comic *canso*, "Farai un vers, pos mi somelh," the "imprisoned lover" topos is parodied in the experience of the narrator pent up with two nymphomaniacal women for more than eight days; he compares this captivity to an oven. For a more conventional use of the theme of love's imprisonment, see Cercamon, "Quant l'aura doussa s'amarzis," lines 4-6, 45-48; Bernart de Ventadorn, "Non es meravelha s'eu chan," lines 21-24, etc. All references are to poems in *Lyrics of the Troubadours and Trouveres*, ed. F. Goldin (New York, 1973).

51 *Yvain*, 42f.: Arthur leaves the feast to go to bed with his queen, abdicating his place as monarch which is, in effect, taken by the quarrelsome Kay, who sows discord where Arthur should be promoting unity; 800-72: after the violence of the storm, the defender of the fountain appears to challenge Yvain, and the two strangers hack away at each other until their shields hang in scraps (824-30) and their riddled hauberks are useless to them (843-47); 1150f.: the description of Laudine's grief, which begins, "mes de duel feire estoit si fole . . . "; and 2783f.: the terrifying account of Yvain going mad, which Chrétien characterizes as a storm breaking in his head (2806-07: "Lors se li monte uns torbeillons/el chief. . . ."), an image directly linking this inner loss of control to the storm-causing fountain and thus underscoring the symbolic nature of the latter.

52 See 1535-44: ". . . Amors et Honte le retienent/qui de deus parz devant li vienent:/il est honiz, se il s'en va/que ce ne recresroit en ja/qu'il eüst ensi esploitié;/d'autre part, ra tel covoitié/de la bele dame veoir/au moins, se plus n'en puet avoir,/que de la prison ne li chaut:/

mialz vialt morir que il s'en aut." Cf. 1942-44: ". . . sanz prison n'est nus amis,/por ç'a droit se prison le clainme/que sanz prison n'est nus qui ainme."

53 Cf. 2242-45, 2260-62; Yvain wishes only to offer Kay "un po de honte," and, once he has unhorsed him, "plus d'enui feire ne li quiert"—a use of prowess markedly different in its control from the mortal battle relentlessly fought by Esclados and Yvain at the fountain, as described in n. 51, above.

54 See 3500-56, and Haidu, *Lion-queue-coupee,* pp. 65-66, on the indisputable comedy of the lion's suicide attempt.

55 The issue of proper control, as opposed to its excess or deficiency, in one's chosen sphere of personal activity is raised early in the romance when Calogrenant recounts his meeting, seven years before, with a bestial, giant herdsman in the forest (276-407). The herdsman represents in appearance and manners the very opposite of courtly and chivalric ideals; it is no casual touch by Chrétien that in reply to Calogrenant's request to be pointed toward an *aventure* appropriate to a knight errant such as he (362-66), the herdsman replies, ". . . d'aventure ne sai je rien,/n'onques mes n'en oï parler" (368-69). Still, for all his lack of refinement or vision, the herdsman does his job, which is to control his wild bulls so that they do not leave the pasture (339-40). He controls the bulls by using just enough force to scare them into submission: "Einsi sui de mes bestes sire" (355). Calogrenant's supposition that a savage beast can only be controlled by imprisonment (335-38) is incorrect; the herdsman has found the middle ground between anarchy and enclosure, and thus represents the possibility of control at even the least cultured level of humanity. His solution to his problem proleptically states that of the romance's protagonist much later.

56 See D.D.R. Owen, "Profanity and its Purpose in Chrétien's *Cligès* and *Lancelot,*" in *Arthurian Romance: Seven Essays,* ed. D.D.R. Owen (Edinburgh and London, 1970), pp. 42-44, 47-48, on the harrowing of hell adaptation, and, for a more profound understanding of its significance in the romance, J.M Ferrante, "The Conflict of Lyric Conventions and Romance Form," in *In Pursuit of Perfection,* eds. J.M. Ferrante and G.P. Economou (Port Washington, N.Y., and London, 1975), pp. 150-56.

57 See 43-195. The ironic texture of this passage is remarkable: Kay announces his intention to leave the court; Arthur then asks Guinevere to plead with the seneschal since, he says, Kay will heed her prayer. Guinevere seeks to constrain Kay by falling at his feet and refusing to

rise until he grants her wish that he stay; Kay then says he will leave unless Arthur grants *his* wish, which turns out to be his undertaking to fight Meleagranz with the queen as the prize of combat. In this pattern of constraints, the queen is in fact (at Arthur's request) pleading for— and determining—her own physical imprisonment in Gorre; forcing Kay to stay *means* forcing Guinevere to go. All are victims and prisoners of each other's shortcomings of action or perception.

58 Her forcing him into a bed he does not wish to enter (946–60) constitutes a comic reversal of the last episode in which Lancelot enters a beautiful bed which a damsel has forbidden him to sleep in (he is, she says, unworthy of it); cf. 467–534. Both beds comment metaphorically on the role of sexual desire and its control in the private love-quest— desire represented in the earlier scene by the flaming lance aimed to strike Lancelot "par mi les flans" (517).

59 As elsewhere love constrains and frees Lancelot simultaneously, here it is responsible for his wounds (received on love-quest) and concurrently the agent of his "healing": "mains et genolz et piez se blece,/mes tot le rasoage et sainne/Amors qui le conduist et mainne,/si li estoit a sofrir dolz" (3112–15).

60 The gap between aspiration and reality in love is cleverly underscored by the language with which Chrétien frames Lancelot's and Guinevere's lovemaking; beforehand, the rhetoric of Christian adoration (". . . et puis vint [Lancelot] au lit la reïne,/si l'aore et se li ancline,/car an nul cors saint ne croit tant," 4651–53)—itself a reversal, since until now Lancelot has been the Christ figure, the "cors saint"—and afterward, Meleagranz's recapitulation of a standard moral (quoted in the text above) from the *fabliau* genre, with its delineation of love as a purely appetitive impulse.

61 See the different but complementary analysis of the problem of *Lancelot* in Ferrante, "The Conflict of Lyric Conventions."

62 On the first part of *Partonopeu*, see above, pp. 213–18; the literal imprisonment of Partonopeu by Armans de Tenedon occurs at 7651f.

Afterword

1 On Jean Renart, see C. Cremonesi, *Jean Renart: Romanziere del XIII secolo* (Milan, n.d.); R. Lejeune-Dehousse, *L'oeuvre de Jean Renart, contribution à l'étude du genre romanesque au moyen age* (Paris and Liège, 1935).

2 This is the attitude toward the thirteenth century taken by F. Heer,

The Medieval World, trans J. Sondheimer (Cleveland, 1962), and N. F. Cantor, *The Meaning of the Middle Ages* (Boston, 1973). R.W. Southern, *Western Society and the Church in the Middle Ages* (Harmondsworth, 1970) offers documentary evidence to support it, but interprets the increasing firmness of ecclesiastical structures in at least the first half of the thirteenth century in a much more favorable light than do the other two historians. See also Southern, *Medieval Humanism* (New York, 1970), pp. 29-60.

3 See K. Hoffman, *The Year 1200: I. The Exhibition* (New York, 1970), commenting on the exhibition of the same title at the Metropolitan Museum of Art, New York, 12 February–10 May 1970. Also, on the evolution of Gothic style toward "Gothic for art's sake," see G. Henderson, *Gothic,* chap. 3, pp. 81-141.

4 See J.A. Jungmann, *The Mass of the Roman Rite: Its Origins and Development,* trans. F.A. Brunner, 2 vols. (New York, 1951-1955), pp. 113-22, and cf. chap. 8, n. 10.

5 In 1215 the Lateran Council had proclaimed the doctrine of transubstantiation—the belief that the body and blood of Christ become truly present, under the appearance of bread and wine, when the priest consecrates the Host during the Mass. Thomas Aquinas's eucharistic hymn *Pange Lingua* indicates how faith allows the Christian to transcend the limits of his senses to perceive the reality of Christ's presence in the Host: "praestet fides supplementum / sensuum defectui."

6 An interesting example of this impulse operating at a more mechanical level is Bibl. Nat. MS fr. 1450, a thirteenth-century manuscript of Wace's *Roman de Brut* into which all five of Chrétien's romances have been inserted at the point where Wace says Arthur remained in France for nine years after conquering it and experienced "mainte mervoille" during this time. The compiler's logic was clearly that, since the romances are full of marvels, but never show Arthur at war in the tradition of Geoffrey and Wace, they must stem from this particular interlude. See *Brut,* 10,133-46.

7 On the importance of the concept of apocalypse, and of the Book of Revelation as the ending of the Bible, see F. Kermode, *The Sense of an Ending* (Oxford, 1967), p. 6f.

8 Where history does figure in chivalric romance, as in the opening of *Partonopeu* or in *Cligès,* it tends to be used as sheer background, as in the former, or ironically, as in the latter.

9 See his comments on fiction, which become more open to interpretation and reinterpretation as we place them in a larger scheme of meaning that encompasses a historical world view, pp. 5-7.

10 On these two Arthurs, the Arthur of history and the Arthur of legend, see K.H. Jackson, "The Arthur of History," and "Arthur in Early Welsh Verse," in *Arthurian Literature in the Middle Ages, A Collaborative History*, ed. R.S. Loomis (Oxford, 1959), pp. 1–19. Cf. T. Jones, trans. G. Morgan, "The Early Evolution of the Legend of Arthur," *Nottingham Medieval Studies* 8 (1964): 3–21.

11 See R.W. Hanning, *The Vision of History in Early Britain* (New York, 1966), p. 237, n. 142. On Merlin's career before Geoffrey adopted him, see A.O.H. Jarmon, "The Welsh Myrddin Poems," in *Arthurian Literature in the Middle Ages*, pp. 20–30.

12 We see what we may call a transitional phase between the two kinds of marvellous in *Le Bel inconnu*, in the episode of the *fier baiser* at Sinaudon, where a mysterious voice informs Guinglain of his natal identity after he has kissed the serpent. We later discover that this was the voice of the Pucele as blanches mains, who has guided Guinglain through this episode out of a very personal love for him which she wishes him to reciprocate; she is a twelfth-century heroine disguised for the moment as a thirteenth-century heavenly exhortation. See *Le Bel inconnu*, 3212–44. In *Partonopeu de Blois*, by contrast, the atmosphere of "gothick" mystery that enshrouds the city of Chef d'Oire and the heroine Mélior is exploded by the hero when he betrays his beloved—but in the process forces their love to face the real world. See chap. 6, above, on the poet's ambivalence about the "magic" of secret, young love.

13 See Robert de Boron, *Le roman de l'estoire dou Graal*, ed. W. Nitze (Paris, 1927), which also includes the fragment of Robert's *Merlin* continuation. On Robert, see further P. Le Gentil, "The work of Robert de Boron and the *Didot Perceval*," in *Arthurian Literature in the Middle Ages*, pp. 251–57, and the bibliography in Le Gentil's notes. Two complete prose versions of the *Merlin* circulated in the early thirteenth century.

14 The literature on Chrétien's *Perceval, ou le conte del Graal* is enormous and of multiple intent. On the possible evolution of the Grail story, see D.D.R. Owen, *The Evolution of the Grail Legend* (Edinburgh and London, 1968); for literary analysis, P. Haidu, *Aesthetic Distance in Chrétien de Troyes: Irony and Comedy in "Cligès" and "Perceval"* (Geneva, 1968), pp. 113–259.

15 This atmosphere of sadness and nostalgia marks the *Queste*, and also the *Mort le roi Artu* which concludes the Vulgate cycle, as what Frye calls "sixth phase" romances. See N. Frye, *Anatomy of Criticism* (Princeton, 1957), pp. 202–03.

16 See *La Queste del saint Graal,* ed. A. Pauphilet (Paris, 1923, repr. 1965), p. 16, where Gawain, after experiencing the momentary presence of the Grail at Camelot on Pentecost, vows to enter on a quest to see the Grail "plus apertenant," and is immediately joined in his vow by all those of the Round Table. "Et quant li rois vit qu'il avoient fet tel veu, si en fu molt a malese: car bien set qu'il nes porra retorner de ceste emprise." The king pleads with Gawain nonetheless, because, by his vow, "vos m'avez mort . . . car vos m'avez ci tolue la plus bele compaignie et la plus loial que je onques trovasse, et ce est la compaignie de la Table Reonde" (p. 17).

17 The availability of the highest experience to a few chosen knights who are, moreover, annihilated by it, strikes at twelfth-century conceptions of individual experience, in which everyone can open himself to experience so that its *kairoi* are subjective and reflective of individual choices. The Grail experience is an objective *kairos,* existing in precise relationship with past events or objects of a providential nature (e.g., the typological relationship between the table of the Last Supper, Joseph of Arimathea's Grail Table, and the Round Table, *Queste,* pp. 74-79), but available only to an elite, as an experience that destroys, rather than perfects, the self. See N. Cohn, *Pursuit of the Millennium* (London, 1957; rev. ed. 1970), pp. 172-76, on the heresy of the Free Spirit, a movement containing interesting parallels to the Grail experience.

18 On the *Queste's* use of allegorical symbols, see Pauphilet, *Étude sur la Queste del saint Graal* (Paris, 1921; repr. 1968), p. 106f, "symboles et allégories"; and F.W. Locke, *The Quest of the Holy Grail* (Stanford, 1960), esp. chap. 2, on the writer's use of scriptural typology.

19 In fact, Lancelot's moral failure because of his love for Guinevere (a love that makes him the best of all knights) is stressed in the *Lancelot,* the work preceding the *Queste,* and the largest segment of the Vulgate cycle. Lancelot's baptismal name is Galahad but, unlike his illegitimate (yet morally perfect) son, Lancelot cannot use the name of the Grail Knight (see *Lancelot del Lac,* ed. H.O. Sommer [3 vols., Washington, D.C., 1910-1912), vols. 3, 4, and 5 of *The Vulgate Version of the Arthurian Romances;* vol. 3, chap. 1), a sign of his imperfection and incompleteness as a Christian knight. (I owe this observation to David Raybin.) Cf. *Queste,* pp. 61-71, where Lancelot has a vision of the Grail but does not respond to its presence, is reproved for his sin by a divine voice, and confesses to a hermit who explains that his love for the queen will cost him the Grail, unless he abandons his adulterous passion.

20 See J. Frappier, *Étude sur La mort le roi Artu* (Paris, 1936; repr. 1961), pp. 27–148, 440–54, on the structure and unity of the *Lancelot, Queste,* and *Mort* sections of the cycle. There were still later versions of the cycle as a whole, so that the term "final shape" cannot be used absolutely. See F. Bogdonow, "The *Suite de Merlin* and the Post-Vulgate *Roman du Graal,*" in *Arthurian Literature in the Middle Ages,* pp. 325–35, and *The Romance of the Grail* (Manchester and New York, 1966).

21 *Lancelot del Lac,* chap. 20; the two lovers do not confess their love for each other until chap. 36, in a moving scene immortalized by Dante's Francesca (*Inferno* 5).

22 Lancelot is also the noblest and most beloved of all the characters in the *Mort*; the author involves us with Lancelot in many ways, none more attractive than the moment at the very midpoint of the romance where Lancelot defeats Mador de la Porte to clear Guinevere of the charge of murdering Gaheris, and, instead of killing him, offers to intercede with the king and queen to have him fully pardoned. The text continues, "Quant Mador entent la debonereté et la franchise que cil li offre, il connoist maintenant que ce est Lancelos; si s'agenoille devant li, et prent s'espee, si li tent et dit, 'Sie, tenez m'espee, ge me met del tout en vostre merci. . . .'" *La mort le roi Artu,* ed. J. Frappier (Paris, 1936; repr. 1954), p. 106. Mador's recognition of the disguised Lancelot by his inherent virtues and his spontaneous adoption of a posture of reverence and servitude toward the great man recapitulate and objectify our own response to Lancelot's uniqueness.

INDEX